CALIFORNIA STATE UNIVERSITY, SACRAMENT

This book is due on the last date stamped below
Failure to return books on the date due will
of overdue fees.

Interests, Ideas, and Deregulation

Interests, Ideas, and Deregulation

The Fate of Hospital Rate Setting

John E. McDonough

Ann Arbor

THE UNIVERSITY OF MICHIGAN PRESS

Copyright © by the University of Michigan 1997
All rights reserved
Published in the United States of America by
The University of Michigan Press
Manufactured in the United States of America
⊗ Printed on acid-free paper

2000   1999   1998   1997   4   3   2   1

A CIP catalog record for this book is available from the British Library.

Library of Congress Cataloging-in-Publication Data

McDonough, John E.
    Interests, ideas, and deregulation : the fate of hospital rate
setting / John E. McDonough.
      p.   cm.
    Includes bibliographical references and index.
    ISBN 0-472-10888-3 (alk. paper)
    1. Hospitals—Rates—Government policy—United States.
    2. Hospital care—United States—Cost control.   3. Hospitals—Rates—
United States.   I. Title.
    RA981.A2M383   1997
    338.4'336211'0973—dc21   97-32100
                                                         CIP

To my parents,
Helen and Joseph McDonough,
with love.

Preface

Professor Leon Wyszewianski told me early in my graduate studies at the University of Michigan School of Public Health that much doctoral education consists of "getting things out of your system that have been hanging around there for too long." That caution serves as an appropriate welcome to this book, the end result of four years of doctoral studies and a dozen years of state legislative policy work. At least to Leon's point, there should be little disappointment.

Between 1985 and 1997, I served as a state representative in Massachusetts, representing inner city Boston neighborhoods. By a series of coincidences—including support for the winning side in a speaker's fight—I became a member of the Joint Committee on Health Care in 1985 as the sole Boston representative. As I said at the time, I barely knew the difference then between Medicare and Medicaid.

In Massachusetts health policy circles in that period, key interest was focused on battles related to the all-payer hospital rate regulation system. Hospital officials wanted maximum flexibility to increase charges to sustain and enhance their institutions. Insurers, labor, and business wanted to keep on maximum pressure to lower costs in the most expensive hospital system in the world. Consumers, progressive legislators, and a few others wanted to keep costs down to expand access and to lay the groundwork for future battles for universal coverage.

For six years, I engrossed myself in learning this impossibly complex regulatory model, trying to rationalize it and make it work, trying to hold on to a road map of the promise made in 1988 for universal health care for all Massachusetts residents. In 1991, it fell apart. First, a newly elected governor set a different direction for market-oriented health economics. Then, key interest groups that had sustained the regulatory system moved away from their prior support. Finally, legislators rejected my arguments for either an alternative regulatory model (Maryland's) or a single-payer alternative and embraced instead the logic of deregulation and the market. At that time, we were the only one of the four major rate setting states that moved in this direction, though New Jersey followed in the next year.

Before, during, and after that legislative conflict, the interplay between interest group agendas and policy ideas had fascinated and perplexed me. I recall reading Feldstein's *The Politics of Health Legislation* in 1990 or 1991 and becoming convinced of his argument that the self-interest model explained nearly everything while the pristine public interest model—in which I had naively believed—was useless. In the context of the Massachusetts State House, interest groups and their lobbyists were everywhere and their influence seemed boundless. By contrast, the health services researchers, whom I had begun to meet in 1985 through the National Center for Health Services Research, were nowhere. Their research seem to be noticed and embraced only when it concurred with beliefs already held, and ignored and scorned the rest of the time.

In the course of doctoral studies at the University of Michigan, I had the opportunity to explore many ideas and opportunities for research before finding my way back to the issues and themes that have been with me throughout my legislative career. The process led me to findings and conclusions that are different from those that I held at the time of my first appearance at the School of Public Health in Ann Arbor in 1992.

Briefly, some of the worst predictions about deregulation never occurred, and some—though not all—of the positive predictions have come to pass. We have seen considerable reshaping of the hospital sector, but without the massive closings that were predicted. Costs are still relatively high, but not as high as they were at the end of regulation. Hospitals mostly have shifted their focus from gaming government to determining their own fates based on their ability to survive in a merciless market. Surely, not all the results have been favorable or positive. Access to insurance worsened considerably, but not simply because of the move to deregulation. Confidence in the quality and fairness of the health system has diminished considerably for many consumers. Overall, what I fought so hard against in 1991 has been mixed, but on balance, a benefit.

Meanwhile, interests do not appear quite as fearsome as they did in prior days. To be sure, they are not to be ignored, provoked, or messed with unnecessarily—when strong groups are strongly united, they can still kill almost anything in their paths, as they recently did to my recent proposal for a minimal health care employer mandate. But they can also be understood, worked with, and helped in ways that make real progress possible. Most importantly, when policy ideas are on the table in compelling and immediate ways, it is often the interests who must learn to accommodate. It is not just ideas that matter in health policy, but it is not just interests either.

This study is the result of my pilgrim's progress in grappling with the meaning of state rate regulation's demise, and with the larger interplay between interests and ideas in policy-making, centered on the dynamic field of health care policy. I hope that the results can assist other health policymakers in both the public and private spheres to be effective and thoughtful in our efforts to shape a system that better meets the needs of the American people.

Jamaica Plain, February 1997

Acknowledgments

I had extraordinary help with this study, which in its initial form was my doctoral dissertation in public health. Major thanks go to my Dissertation Committee cochairs, Catherine McLaughlin and Barry Rabe of the University of Michigan School of Public Health, who were most patient and supportive. Special thanks goes to William Weissert who introduced me to the punctuated equilibrium model and helped me to shape the structure of this study. Thanks also to John Tierney of Boston College, who introduced me to great political models and ideas and won the strong allegiance of my classmates for his intelligent and thoughtful approach to politics.

Special thanks go to the 60-plus interview subjects in Maryland, Massachusetts, New Jersey, and New York. Whether they knew me beforehand or not, they opened up their thoughts to me in ways that I never could have predicted: their candid quotes that I have used throughout this study are the proof of their openness. They are listed in the appendix.

Thanks also to funders who gave me resources to complete this study in a relatively rapid period of time. These include the Health Care Financing Administration of the U.S. Department of Health and Human Services, and the Michigan Blue Cross and Blue Shield Foundation. Their support was invaluable in enabling me to complete the interviews quickly, all of which were done in person in the subject's home state. Thanks also to the Pew Charitable Trust for its vital support of the doctoral program at the University of Michigan's School of Public Health.

Finally, thanks to my children, Devlin and Amy, who put up with intolerable absences and distractions during more than two years of course work, and during another 18 months of dissertation distress.

Contents

Tables

Figures

Abbreviations

AFL-CIO	American Federation of Labor-Congress of Industrial Organizations
AHA	American Hospital Association
DRG	diagnosis-related group
GNYHA	Greater New York Healthcare Association
HANYS	Healthcare Association of New York State
HCFA	Health Care Financing Administration (US)
HHS	Department of Health and Human Services (US)
HIAA	Health Insurance Association of America
HMO	health maintenance organization
HRET	Hospital Research and Educational Trust (NJ)
HSCRC	Health Services Cost Review Commission (MD)
MHA	Maryland Hospital Association
MHA	Massachusetts Hospital Association
NJHA	New Jersey Hospital Association
RBRVS	Resource Based Relative Value Scale
SHARE	Standard Hospital Accounting and Rate Evaluation System (NJ)

CHAPTER 1

Interests and Ideas in Health Policy: An Introduction

In 1972 and 1973, Congress passed two distinctly different laws to attempt largely untried methods at controlling rapidly growing public and private health care expenditures. First, in section 222 of the 1972 amendments to the Social Security Act (PL 92-603), Congress gave states the authority to establish prospective rate setting programs with federal participation to control hospital costs. Second, in the 1973 Health Maintenance Organization Act (PL 93-222), Congress provided incentives and guidelines to encourage development of prepaid group practices to control overall health care expenditures.

Though the long-term impact of these two statutes was unknowable at the time of their enactment, by the early 1980s it seemed clear that experiments with the prospective reimbursement law had made the greater mark. By 1981, more than 30 states had established some form of prospective hospital rate setting or budget review, and a subset were experimenting with mandatory controls on all public and private payers.[1] President Jimmy Carter attempted to impose a federal form of prospective rate setting on all acute care hospitals across the nation in his ill-fated 1979 hospital cost containment proposal. Despite the Reagan administration's coolness to rate setting, Congress passed further amendments to the Social Security Act in 1983 (PL 98-21) directing the Health Care Financing Administration to grant Medicare waivers to states seeking to establish more expansive all-payer rate setting systems. In that same act, Congress also mandated the development of the Prospective Payment System, incorporating diagnosis-related groups (DRGs) as the national reimbursement mechanism for Medicare inpatient hospital fees—a system modeled after New Jersey's pioneering hospital rate setting program. The Medicare Resource Based Relative Value Scale, a physician payment system established later that decade, represents yet another national form of prospective rate setting that has expanded throughout the health system. Beginning in 1980, empirical studies showed for the first time that states with mandatory rate setting programs had a pattern of lower hospital cost increases than states without such regulation.[2]

By contrast, HMOs had grown to cover only about four percent of the U.S. population in 1980, far less than expectations at the time of the HMO Act's adoption.[3] In 1981, the Reagan administration eliminated all further federal development grants to HMOs, leaving their future prospects very much in doubt. One major 1983 study of the 1973 HMO Act and subsequent federal statutes concluded that no significant surge in HMO growth could be expected for the foreseeable future.[4]

By the mid-1990s, the landscape has changed considerably. Most states have dismantled their rate setting structures, and of the four states that had established mandatory statewide controls in the 1970s on all public and private payers, only one left them in place. HMOs, by contrast, had grown from 236 in number in 1980 to 672 in 1992, and from 9.1 million covered lives in 1980 to 58.2 million in 1995, or more than 19.5 percent of all covered lives.[5] While some interest in rate setting persisted as a policy option through the early 1990s, it was the HMO and managed care that formed the organizational core of President Bill Clinton's proposed Health Security Act in 1993 as well as 1995 Republican proposals to revamp Medicare.

What accounts for the demise of rate setting as a central policy option in state health cost containment? What lessons can be learned for future health policy making from rate setting's rise and fall? How and why did the disposition of rate setting vary from state to state? What role did the rise of managed care play in the fate of rate setting? What political and economic theories can help to explain rate setting's fall from grace? What role did interest groups and policy ideas play in the transformation? What can rate setting's demise tell us about the interplay between interests and ideas in health policy? These are the central questions posed by this book.

Using the case-study approach, this book examines economic and political factors leading to the demise of hospital rate setting in Massachusetts in 1991, in New Jersey in 1992, and in New York in 1996, as well as the factors accounting for the continuation of rate regulation in Maryland as of 1997.

This study further explores what two rival theories—the *theory of economic regulation* and the *punctuated equilibrium model of policy change*—can explain about the disposition of rate setting in these four states. In the terms of economic theory, we ask whether the treatment of rate setting in these states is consistent with assumptions about the rational behavior of interest groups and public officials as outlined in the theory of economic regulation, and especially as that theory relates to cases of deregulation. In terms of political theory, we ask whether a longitudinal model of policy change that emphasizes the role of ideas in shaping policy development can help to explain the evolution and outcome of this regulatory tool. What can the experience of these states explain to us in understanding the future of rate setting as a regulatory tool in health care cost containment? What can the work of these states offer as we examine the continuing dynamic between regulatory and competitive approaches to health care cost control? What can the rate setting case histories from the states tell us about the broader interplay between interests and ideas in health policy making? Finally, what can these theoretical models tell us about the future of health policy in the states that have deregulated?

Specific Aims/Theoretical Models

This book poses three central research questions: (1) What factors help to explain the demise of hospital rate setting in Massachusetts in 1991, in New Jersey in 1992, and in New York in 1996, as well as the continuation of rate setting in Maryland? (2) To what extent can these outcomes be explained by the theory of economic regulation and the punctuated equilibrium model of policy change? (3) What does this experience tell us about the interplay between interest groups and policy ideas in health policy making?

State hospital rate setting is defined as the prospective establishment of rates of payment by major payers for hospital services, regulation performed by the state or some other approved entity or group of entities, and having either voluntary or mandatory compliance. Rate setting for hospitals can be traced back to the 1950s in two states, though the practice did not proliferate widely until the 1970s when it spread in a variety of forms to more than 30 states. Four states (Maryland, Massachusetts, New Jersey, and New York) adopted mandatory, state administered rate setting on all public and private payers for periods of time from as early as the 1970s through the 1990s.

In numerous empirical studies, mandatory rate setting has been found to lower the rate of inpatient hospital expenditure growth relative to non–rate setting states on a per diem, per admission, and per capita basis. Substantial differences from state to state and time period to time period have also been observed.[6] Chapter 2 will review the financial performance of rate setting systems in greater detail. Chapter 3 will review the financial performance of rate setting in the four states.

All state rate setting systems vary markedly from one to another in structural details, including the mandatory programs in the four states. Four items characterize the states included in this study: (1) the rate setting system was operated by a state government agency; (2) compliance with the system was mandatory; (3) all major public and private payers (Medicare, Medicaid, Blue Cross, commercial payers) were at one time subject to the same set of rules; and (4) the system had been actively in operation since at least 1976.[7] These characteristics provide the rationale for the selection of the four study states.

One particular regulatory feature is explored in detail: the extent to which health maintenance organizations were permitted to operate outside of the regulatory framework by negotiating discounts for hospital services below charges permitted to other insurers. Only one of the four states, Massachusetts, permitted unlimited discounting, thus creating a disequilibrium between HMOs and other payers in those states. However, New Jersey and New York permitted forms of discounting that, as we will see, undermined the stability of their systems. The extent to which this feature played a major role in undermining the larger regulatory structure will be an important aspect of this investigation. Beyond the particular example of discounting, special attention will be paid to the growth and development of HMOs in the four states. The prospective rate setting systems in these states all began well before HMOs and managed care gained a significant market foothold. The subsequent and rapid development of managed care in the states played a significant role in rate setting's demise. The nature of that interaction is explored in detail.

In accounting for differences among the four states, attention is paid to two rival theories: first, the theory of economic regulation, and second, the punctuated equilibrium model of policy change. Alternative theories are utilized in this study not to create an either/or competition, but in recognition that the use of different "conceptual lenses" is particularly helpful in case-study analysis.[8] In this case, the rival theories present a sharp and dynamic contrast between the roles of interests and ideas in determining policy outcomes.

The Theory of Economic Regulation. While the rival theory—the punctuated equilibrium model of policy change—is quite recent in political science literature, the theory of economic regulation has a long history generally and in health policy specifically.[9] According to this model, regulatory policies and structures are created for the principal purpose of monopolizing the regulated sector: "regulation enables what is or would be a competitive industry to act as though it were in fact a monopoly. The impetus for regulation, or for the capture of the regulatory agency by the industry it is meant to regulate, comes from the industry's desire to use the regulatory process as a vehicle for charging higher prices, restricting its output, raising its profits, and protecting itself from possible competitors." The driving force behind regulation is the set of interests the system is meant to control.[10] The model has also been used to explain cases of deregulation. According to the theory, industries lose their regulatory protection because of changes in relative political support for continued regulation when the benefits offered to legislators by opponents of regulation exceed the benefits offered by the proponents.[11]

Use of this model can be helpful in understanding the array of forces that contributed to the establishment and maintenance of state-based rate setting for more than two decades, and then to its demise. Three sets of interests will be examined in detail. The first group is composed of interests that supported the establishment of rate setting: chiefly hospitals, insurers, businesses, and labor unions; how their positions changed over time is observed. The second group of interest is state government, and in particular the changing nature of its investment in health sector regulation. The third group is composed of those interests who were not players at the time the systems were created, chiefly HMOs. Both the changes in the various interests' positions *and* the changes in their relative political and market strength have relevance to this investigation.

The Punctuated Equilibrium Model of Policy Change. Baumgartner and Jones use longitudinal analysis of policy development to devise a model of change that explains the emergence and recession of policy issues from the public agenda.[12] According to their model, new institutional structures—such as rate setting—are created during brief periods of volatile change when policy ideas are under challenge and previous policy structures and monopolies have become unstable. The new institutional forms, once dominant, may remain in place for decades, structuring participation and creating the illusion of stability. Eventually, the generation of new ideas makes these existing policy monopolies unstable, and thus subject to elimination or alteration during the next period of volatile change. Two key elements distinguish this model from other policy frameworks. First, it emphasizes that policy clashes should be seen as strategic struggles over the definition of issues and the battle of ideas. Both the emergence of new ideas and the strategic redefinition of the "problem" determine the field of conflict in the next period of volatility. Second, the model emphasizes a long-term view of the policy process that increases one's awareness of the long-term fragility of most policy subsystems and regulatory structures.

This long-range perspective is helpful in examining a policy process such as rate setting that survived in some states over a period of more than 20 years. A similar examination of rate setting conducted in 1985 would have led to vastly different conclusions than one conducted in 1995. Thus the longitudinal perspective is important and helpful. The emphasis on the clash of ideas is also important in understanding the interplay between rate setting versus managed care, or regulation versus competition in a broader sense. A major conclusion of this study is that managed care and HMOs are key manifestations of the new policy "idea" that challenged and toppled all but one of the state rate setting policy monopolies.

Another theme of this study is that the *form and structure* of public sector regulation—more than its mere existence—will determine its outcome and impact. While the rate setting systems in the four states, viewed from afar, seem alike, up close they are noteworthy for many important design differences. These subtle differences played important roles in the fate of rate setting in each state. In exploring this theme, it is hoped to advance understanding in the continuing debate between competition and regulation in the health care sector. As Luft notes, "neither strategy has ever been fully implemented. Instead, past and current policies have included combinations of regulatory and competitive efforts as well as components that are difficult to classify."[13] All of the regulatory systems in the four states differed in important ways in their respective creation and development processes. The unique political culture and preexisting market structure in each state had a large impact on each system's progress. This will be especially apparent in examining the interaction of each system with the state's HMO community. By examining the unique aspects of each state, both the differences and similarities are highlighted.

Organization of the Book

The methodology and structure for this investigation are outlined at the end of this chapter. This investigation utilizes the multiple case-study design as outlined by Yin who provides a rigorous model for this type of examination to ensure maximum validity and reliability.[14]

Chapter 2 reviews the relevant literature concerning all aspects of rate setting between 1975 and 1995. Special emphasis is given to the literature describing the development of the theory of economic regulation and the punctuated equilibrium model of policy change. Literature on regulation and competition is examined to understand the interaction between rate setting and other cost containment forms. The specific hypotheses of both theories that are tested in this study are outlined at the end of this chapter.

Analyses of basic descriptive data from the four states, and the background case histories of rate setting in those states, are presented in chapter 3. Data are examined concerning the growth of health and hospital costs in the states, along with HMO membership growth between 1980 and 1993 and other variables. Because the group of rate setting states is so small, and because many interrelated variables account for the shaping of public policy in this area, quantitative analysis of data is only one limited portion of this study.

Chapter 4 explores the role of interests in rate setting in each state and examines evidence to confirm or reject specific hypotheses related to the theory of economic regulation and the behavior of key interest groups and stakeholders. In particular, evidence is examined concerning the behavior and conduct of hospitals, Blue Cross plans, commercial insurers, health maintenance organizations, business groups, labor unions, consumers, regulators, and state health purchasing entities such as Medicaid. Each hypothesis will be examined based on the data and evidence presented.

Chapter 5 explores the role of policy ideas in relation to the fate of rate setting in each state and examines evidence related to the specific hypotheses of the punctuated equilibrium model and the role of ideas in the rate setting stories. Chapter 6 summarizes the findings, draws conclusions from the investigation, and applies these findings to the theory of economic regulation and the punctuated equilibrium model of policy change.

Finally, chapter 7 examines developments in Massachusetts, New Jersey, and New York since the enactment of deregulation. Because of the recent enactment in New York, information on the impact of this change is more limited. Nonetheless, important trends are already apparent that have appeared in all three states. Some tentative conclusions are suggested on the future of health policy in these states and beyond.

Research Methodology

This book utilizes case-study methodology, as opposed to experimental or quasi-experimental research. The case-study option was selected because of the nature of the particular regulatory phenomenon. Yin has done much to provide structure and rigor to the case-study method in his two volumes on the topic. This investigation relies heavily upon his proposed structure. He specifies three criteria necessary to justify use of the case-study technique: (1) when the study "copes with the technically distinctive situation in which there will be many more variables of interest than data points"; (2) when the study "relies on multiple sources of evidence, with data needing to converge in a triangulating fashion"; and (3) when the study "benefits from the prior development of theoretical propositions to guide data collection and analysis."[15]

This investigation satisfies all three of Yin's suggested requirements. First, there are many contextual variables that help to explain the demise of rate setting in three states and its continuation in one other, far more than the data points represented by the four states. These variables fall into numerous domains, including demographic, political, cultural, and economic characteristics; health and hospital market structure; organizational factors; state leadership variables; and much more than can be captured in a purely quantitative study. The case-study method provides the best framework to study these instances of deregulation in a structured and analytical way.

Second, this study required several sources of evidence, including interviews with key participants in the political process, archival records, documentation, journalistic accounts, and other sources. No single data source could provide adequate information to evaluate the reasons for rate setting's fate, and so data and information were sought from a multitude of sources. Triangulation requires that at least three sources converge to provide confidence in any final conclusions relative to the proposed hypotheses.

Third, the case study is designed as a means to test theoretical propositions, not to generalize from a data set to a population. While the results of this study hold lessons for health policy and the political process, we cannot use these results to make any sweeping conclusions about rate setting or regulation in other areas or states. In this investigation, the fate of rate setting in four states was examined to explore the validity of two rival theories—one political and one economic. In the process, we learn not just about the two theories, but also about the phenomenon of state rate setting.

The research design for this study includes the following five key components. Though some of these have already been discussed, they are presented below for summary purposes:

(1) *Study Question.* Why was rate setting discontinued in Massachusetts, New Jersey, and New York in the 1990s, and why has it continued operation in Maryland?

(2) *Study Propositions.* Two rival propositions are examined. Did the demise of rate setting in three states (and its parallel continuation in one other) occur because of self-interest activities on the part of affected institutions, interests, and legislators as explained by the theory of economic regulation? Or did the fate of rate setting happen because of changes in prevailing policy ideas promulgated by leading groups and individuals as explained by the punctuated equilibrium model of policy change?

(3) *Unit of Analysis.* The unit of analysis for the investigation is the state hospital rate setting program within each of the four states. The unit of analysis is *not* the state legislature, the hospital

industry or market, the state itself, nor any other entity. The study is not concerned with the latter effects of deregulation (though these issues will be examined in chapter 7) nor with the merits of either policy option.

(4) *Linkage of Data with Propositions.* The technique used to analyze the data chiefly involves pattern matching. The data from each state's activity are compared to developments in the other states and to the predicted patterns of the two rival theories.

(5) *Criteria for Interpreting Findings.* The key analysis criterion for this study is triangulation, the requirement that all conclusions relative to acceptance or dismissal of the hypotheses must be verified by at least three independent sources. In interpreting the findings, we draw on all relevant evidence, include all major rival interpretations, focus on the critical aspects of the case study, and draw on the author's own prior experience in this subject area.

The principal sources of evidence for the study included: (1) interviews with at least 15 knowledgeable health policy leaders in each of the four states including representatives from hospitals, Blue Cross, commercial insurance, HMOs, business groups, unions, consumer groups, legislative leaders, and executive branch officials; (2) documentation including written reports, analyses and research studies, administrative documents, newspaper accounts, letters, memoranda, lobbying alerts, meeting agendas, minutes, and more; and (3) archival records, including statutes, regulations, legislative proposals, and budget documents. Interviews were mostly conducted between the end of 1994 and the fall of 1995, though additional interviews were conducted in late 1996 to discuss more recent developments.

Personal Involvement. It must be noted that the author comes to this investigation with a lengthy history of prior involvement in this policy matter. Between 1985 and 1997, as a member of the Massachusetts House of Representatives, I have been deeply involved in matters of state health policy, as a supporter of reauthorizations of our hospital rate regulation laws in 1985 and 1988, and as a legislative opponent of deregulation in 1991. I have also been deeply involved in legislative matters relative to managed care in Massachusetts as well as other health policy matters during the same time period. While I do not believe that this personal history creates bias in the findings of this study—indeed, numerous conclusions of this study run counter to my prior policy positions as a legislator—this information is presented for the benefit of readers.

CHAPTER 2

An Overview of the Literature

A substantial body of literature has examined the structure and performance of state-based hospital rate setting. Other large bodies of literature have examined the contrasting approaches of the role of self-interest and rational choice as embodied in the theory of economic regulation and the role of ideas as discussed in the punctuated equilibrium model of policy change. This review will describe the history of rate setting; its performance on cost, quality, productivity, and other indicators; and its place in the broader debate on regulation versus competition. The two rival theories will be discussed in turn. The hypotheses of the respective theories will be presented in the final section.

A Brief History of Rate Setting

The Rise

The earliest examples of rate regulation—albeit voluntary—for hospital cost control date back to 1948 in southwest Ohio and to 1959 in Indiana. The first example of mandatory regulation began in New York in 1970.[1] By 1980 more than 30 states utilized some form of prospective rate setting, termed "the center of the policy paradigm for controlling health care costs during the 1970s."[2] Throughout the first half of the 1980s, some states continued to adopt expanded programs, even as the health policy community held a heated debate over rate regulation's merits.[3]

Some researchers have attempted to identify states more likely to adopt rate setting, though the validity of those studies is weakened by the small number of states. Higher levels of personal per capita income, population density, physician to population ratio, hospital bed to population ratio, and market shares for Blue Cross and Medicaid all have been identified as potential indicators.[4] In addition, high costs per admission and per capita have been found to characterize rate setting states.[5] Another study utilizing regression analysis identified liberal states with budget deficits and large Medicaid hospital expenses as most likely to adopt such programs.[6] (Descriptive data on all of these measures both nationally and in the subject states is detailed in chapter 3.)

As mentioned in chapter 1, the federal government was an active promoter of this trend, beginning with amendments to the Social Security Act of 1972 that encouraged states to experiment with rate setting (PL 92-603, section 222), and culminating in 1983 amendments directing HCFA to grant waivers to states to experiment with all-payer systems. While each national administration pursued its own distinct approach, "throughout the 1970s, the federal government was more or less a friend of the state rate setting concept."[7]

The Fall

In 1980, the first of many empirical studies began to be published that documented the lower rate of hospital expenditure growth in rate setting states as compared to nonregulated states.[8] Prior studies in the 1970s had been unable to detect significant differences. Ironically, it was also at this time that support for rate setting as a cost control tool began to diminish. Specifically, the shift can be observed with the advent of the Reagan presidency that openly rejected rate setting as preferred policy. More generally, it can be observed in the emerging shift of the cost containment paradigm from regulation to competition.[9]

Key interests were active in rate setting policy, in both federal and state venues. Throughout the 1970s, the American Hospital Association (AHA) actively promoted state rate setting as their preferred policy to avert looming federal interference. But in July 1980, "less than one year after Congress rejected President Carter's Hospital Cost Containment Act of 1979, the AHA House of Delegates voted formally to abandon its promotion of state rate setting."[10]

Other interests did not immediately follow suit. The Health Insurance Association of America (HIAA) intensified its activities in support of rate setting during this period to lessen cost shifting to their member companies, and it won legislative battles in some key states. Labor maintained a strong posture in favor of rate setting. And a number of private, state-based business coalitions strongly backed the regulatory approach.[11] Nonetheless, beginning in 1986, a steady stream of states have moved to deregulate their prospective reimbursement systems. Table 2.1 lists states that have deregulated mandatory rate setting systems since 1986, along with those states still maintaining systems as of January 1, 1997.

While some interest in rate setting persisted as recently as 1994 as a regulatory option in states and the federal government, attention from the health services research community, as indicated by publication of literature on the topic, has been far less frequent in recent years. While a few articles have examined factors leading to rate setting's demise in one state or another, none has examined the larger trend of its passage from the center of the policy stage. No article could be identified since 1986 listing which states still maintained such systems. No policy article before 1995 discussed the seeming incongruity of a federal government moving toward broader rate setting for Medicare via DRGs and RBRVS as the state health policy paradigm traveled in the opposite direction. While some national political leaders, such as former U.S. Senate Majority Leader George Mitchell, proposed forms of rate setting in the 1990s, it was managed care and HMOs that formed the organizational core of President Bill Clinton's 1993 Health Security Act and later Republican efforts to reconstruct the Medicare program. With the election of Republican majorities in the U.S. Senate and House of Representatives in 1995, rate setting as a policy option was further marginalized in favor of competitive, market-oriented approaches.

A Review of Rate Setting's Performance

Definitions and Characteristics

Hospital rate setting is defined as the establishment of rates of payment by major payers for hospital services. The American Hospital Association devised a classification system for state-based rate setting that includes four categories: (1) mandatory-regulatory; (2) mandatory-advisory; (3)

TABLE 2.1. Status of State-Based Hospital Rate Setting since 1986

Deregulations since 1986 by Year of Enactment		Continued Mandatory Rate Regulation as of January 1, 1997
Wisconsin	1986	Maryland
Washington	1989	West Virginia
Massachusetts	1991	
New Jersey	1992	
Connecticut	1994	
Maine	1995	
Minnesota[a]	1995	
New York	1996	

Source: Author's survey, January 1995.
[a]Minnesota's rate controls, enacted in 1992, were never implemented.

voluntary-regulatory; and (4) voluntary-advisory.[12] The mandatory/voluntary dichotomy is considered most important because of a consistent finding that voluntary systems did not demonstrate a significant difference in cost control performance from those of non–rate setting states.[13]

One difficulty in comparing studies of state-based rate setting is the range of differences in the set of states examined by each study. This investigation will be limited to four of the six mandatory-regulatory states that have been the subject of most empirical analyses: Maryland, Massachusetts, New Jersey, and New York. (The other two states that fit this description but are not included in this study are Washington, which deregulated its system in 1989, and Connecticut, which deregulated in 1994.) The criteria that distinguish these four states are: (1) the system is/was run by a state agency; (2) compliance by hospitals is/was mandatory; (3) all major public and private payers including Medicare, Medicaid, Blue Cross, and commercial insurers are (or were at one time) subject to regulation; and (4) the system has been in effect since 1976 or before.[14] The fourth criterion reflects the consistent finding that rate setting programs required several years of operation before having any measurable effects upon cost.[15]

A variant in state rate setting that characterizes only the four states in this study is referred to as "all-payer rate setting" in which Medicare is also subject to state rules. This involvement was permitted by the 1972 and 1983 Social Security Amendments, though only Maryland, Massachusetts, New Jersey, and New York took advantage of this option. (Maryland is the only state that maintains a federal waiver permitting Medicare to participate as of 1997.) Some empirical studies have confined their analyses to all-payer systems, though data comparing all-payer and partial-payer mandatory systems did not produce findings of significant differences.[16]

Each state system varies widely from others in structural details; furthermore, most states have modified their systems in substantial ways over each program's life cycle. But all mandatory-regulatory systems needed to face four basic challenges: (1) defining the regulated unit of payment—per day, per admission, or per capita; (2) setting the base level of payment—usually a base year; (3) varying payment rates across different classes of providers and payers; and (4) controlling the rate of expenditure growth from year to year. Also, rate setting systems in the four states never attempted to include outpatient hospital services within their jurisdiction—only inpatient services. With the explosion in outpatient services growth that accelerated with the emergence of prospective payment in Medicare around 1983, this exclusion lessened considerably the amount of total hospital revenue that was subject to state regulation.[17]

Cost Containment

A straightforward evaluation of rate setting's effectiveness in controlling the growth in hospital costs is difficult because different evaluative measures answer different questions. Nonetheless, as this summary demonstrates, mandatory state rate setting programs in general had a positive cost control performance relative to states without such regulation in the period before 1985. Conclusions regarding the post-1985 period are hampered by lack of empirical studies.

Per Admission/Per Discharge. The first and largest set of empirical studies on rate setting evaluated the systems on a per admission or per discharge basis. The first of these, appearing in 1980, found that between 1975 and 1978, the average rate of increase in hospital costs in rate setting states was 11.2 percent as compared with 14.3 percent in states without mandatory regulatory programs. It concluded: "Much of the initial pessimism regarding the effectiveness of hospital rate setting programs . . . may be unwarranted."[18]

The largest study of rate setting, initiated by HCFA, concluded in its 1986 final report that "mandatory programs saved $36 billion dollars from 1969 to 1982 and reduced costs per discharge in states with mandatory programs 12–26 percent."[19] Also in 1986, the authors of the 1980 study extended their initial analysis and found that "between 1976 and 1983, states with rate setting programs have consistently had a significantly lower rate of cost inflation than states without such programs."[20] A 1988 study examining the performance of the four all-payer states compared with California and the rest of the nation found that between 1982 and 1986, the rate setting programs "reduced inflation rates by 16.3% in Massachusetts, 15.4% in Maryland, and 6.3% in New York, compared with the control hospitals in 43 states."[21]

There have been no empirical studies examining the cost performance of state hospital rate setting systems in the period after 1985. As we will see, this represents an important gap in the literature because of evidence that some regulatory systems performed far less well during this latter period.

Per Capita. Critics of the findings mentioned in the previous section suggested that per admission is not the most appropriate measure because it failed to capture other effects such as changing lengths of stay and the shift to outpatient services. They predicted that rate setting states would perform less well in studies that examined per capita hospital costs. However, a 1987 study that used SMSAs instead of states as the unit of analysis found that SMSAs in states with mature mandatory rate setting programs between 1972 and 1982 "had, on average, 4.4 percent lower expenses per capita, 5.6 percent lower expenses per day, and 3.4 percent lower expenses per admission" than regions without such programs.[22]

A 1983 study found that state rate setting programs had lower per capita hospital expenditures of 2.0 percent per year.[23] Schramm et al. reperformed their earlier per admission analysis and found in 1986 that rate setting states had 1.2 percent lower per capita expenditures between 1972 and 1984 than would have been expected in the absence of regulation.[24]

Total Health Costs. Another major criticism of the foregoing studies is that they failed to measure the impact of rate setting on total health (not just hospital) spending, and that the value of the program would be far less if it had just resulted in a shift to other forms of health spending. Finkler observed in 1987 that "the impact of rate regulation on total medical care expenditures reveals a mixed performance."[25]

At least two studies examined this issue empirically. One, in 1983, found that the rate of increase in Medicare Part B expenditures in states with rate setting was lower than in states without such programs, demonstrating that a hypothesized switch to outpatient physician services beyond what was happening on a national basis had not occurred.[26] More recently, a 1991 study used a simultaneous equation model to assess the impact of rate setting on per capita hospital and non-hospital expenditures. "Mature rate setting is associated with lower per capita health care expenditures, including hospital and non-hospital . . . The hypothesis that expenditures for health services in the non-hospital sector will be greater than they would have been if rate setting had not been enacted, due to unbundling, is not supported . . . This is consistent with the view that hospital and non-hospital services are complements rather than substitutes . . . There is an apparent reduction in total expenses for health services associated with rate setting (about 4.3 percent)."[27] Once again, it must be noted that data for these studies were all from the pre-1985 period.

Other Benefits

i. Improvements in Access. An important feature of all mandatory rate setting programs evaluated in this study is inclusion of an explicit mechanism to reimburse hospitals for uncompensated care. No studies have examined that overall use of uncompensated care pools. However, studies from individual states have identified this feature as an important benefit. The New Jersey pool, for example, was identified by one study as its "single most notable success."[28] The New York pool was found to have "resulted in more care provided to uninsured patients" though the program was also referred to as a "leaky bucket" that was not the most efficient mechanism to provide such services.[29]

ii. Reductions in Cost Shifting. An explicit motivation for the establishment of many state programs was to reduce cost shifting among classes of payers, both public and private. It should not be surprising, then, that this goal appears to have been realized and documented in various studies. Rate setting states show a smaller gap between hospital charges and costs than is observable in nonregulated states.[30]

iii. Improvement in Productivity. Evaluations of mandatory rate setting as early as 1982 found evidence of improvements in hospital productivity based on payroll per day and full time equivalent employee (FTE) per day.[31] Examining hospital expenses in 43 SMSAs between 1980 and 1984, Hadley found in 1989 that "almost all of the effect of regulation on costs came from gains in the efficiency in producing hospital care and/or from reductions in the quality of care. It appears that controlling hospital payment rates gave hospitals a strong incentive to provide care at lower cost."[32] However, Anderson was unable to find a difference in the effect of rate setting programs on efficient versus inefficient hospitals.[33]

Negative and Other Effects

i. Impact on Length of Stay and Admissions. Studies have found that rate setting, in some cases, led to longer lengths of stay and higher rates of admission, an observation that will be confirmed in our review of state-specific data in chapter 3. "Rate regulation has brought about, in some states, an increase in hospital occupancy by increasing patients' lengths of stay."[34] Ashby found "some evidence, statistically inconclusive, that rate setting has contributed to relatively higher utilization."[35] And Sloan concluded that "one of the major shortcomings of rate setting is that it provides no incentives to reduce hospital admissions and, under certain circumstances, may even provide an incentive to increase them."[36]

ii. Impact on Quality of Care. Hadley was the first to address the potential negative effects of rate setting on quality of care as an effect related to productivity improvements. While not reaching any conclusions, Morrisey hypothesized a similar effect in 1984 in constructing a theory of rate review on hospital operations and organization: "the hospital product was viewed as a bundle; rate review was looked upon as a ceiling on the value of the bundle. The ceiling creates an incentive to remove elements from the bundle, i.e., to reduce 'quality.'"[37]

Shortell and Hughes provided some evidence of a link between hospital mortality rates and the stringency of rate setting programs,[38] but

Gaumer's results one year later directly contradicted the earlier findings. Gaumer himself found some link between the presence of rate setting and mortality following emergency inpatient admissions; this finding, however, was contradicted by his own later research in 1989.[39] Anderson concluded that there is "some evidence that this [quality] concern may have some validity, although there are serious data concerns with these studies.[40]

iii. Impact on Diffusion of New Technology. Rate setting has also been found to slow the diffusion of services such as open heart surgery, intensive care units, and social work, as well as accelerating the phaseout of redundant services such as premature nurseries. However, these results were statistically significant in only two of 15 states once other factors were incorporated.[41] Given the substantial duplication of services that existed among hospitals since the 1960s, it is difficult to conclude whether this impact is either positive or negative.

Impact on Diffusion of Competitive Health Systems. This topic is controversial and central to the subject of this investigation. Judgments on it are included in the succeeding section in this chapter on regulation and competition.

Overall Assessments and Reviews

Throughout the 1980s, a consistent theme in empirical studies and review articles recognized the success of rate setting in the states that adopted mandatory programs. Coelen found that eight programs "have been successful in reducing expenditures per patient day, per admission, and per capita . . . reducing the rate of increase by two percentage points or more per year and, in some cases, by as much as four to six points."[42] Joskow wrote, "there is substantial evidence that mandatory state reimbursement regulation is associated with a significant reduction in the rate of growth of hospital expenditures."[43] Contrasting rate setting with the managed care approach to cost control, McLaughlin concluded, "prepaid groups practices do not appear to be the systemwide hospital cost reducing tool that HMO supporters have hoped for, apparently taking a back seat to the regulatory approach represented by mandatory rate setting programs."[44] Zuckerman observed that "data confirm that all types of mandatory rate setting systems are effective systems of cost control."[45] Anderson summarized ten years of research noting that "all payer rate setting is able to meet its multiple objectives of cost containment, reduction of the amount of cost shifting, improvement of access to the uninsured, and increased productivity. At the same time, it has not stifled the diffusion of competitive health systems or new technology, and any impact on length of stay, admissions, and quality of care is small, if it exists at all."[46]

Some reviewers, though, have been careful to qualify their overall assessments with important caveats. Noting that "research literature shows conclusively that rate setting has reduced hospital expenditures," Ginsburg notes that the process of setting rates can be a very cumbersome one, and that the "prospects for competitive alternatives are reduced."[47] Concluding that "mandatory rate setting has generally constrained hospital costs where it has been implemented," Eby cautions that "it is not clear that comparable results would be obtained [in additional states]. It is still less clear that rate setting would constrain health care costs more than would increased competition and selective contracting."[48]

Paradigm Shift: From Regulation to Competition

In the voluminous literature on regulation and competition in health care, a significant subset addresses the role of rate setting and its impact upon the development of competitive mechanisms such as HMOs. But a curious pattern emerges as theorists describe how rate setting will harm competition and researchers detail their inability to find evidence of such harm.

Theoretical Predictions

The notion that rate regulation could interfere with market mechanisms is plausible on its face, as observed by Enthoven: "The weight of evidence, based on experience in many other industries, as well as in health care, supports the view that such regulation is likely to raise costs and retard beneficial innovation."[49] Researchers more directly involved with rate setting analyses made similar hypotheses. Sloan notes: "With price competition eliminated by rate setting, who in the private sector will introduce innovative alternatives to the present system which offer the prospect of substantial savings in spending on hospital care?"[50] Ginsburg asserted that under rate setting, "the prospects for competitive alternatives are reduced. These alternatives, such as patient cost sharing, preferred provider organizations, and health maintenance organizations, provide incentives to reduce the volume of services as well as the price."[51]

This line of thought continued throughout the decade with analysts such as Finkler: "Some innovative cost-saving producers will be discouraged from entering medical care markets in which prices are controlled. Also, existing inefficient producers will not be encouraged to exit . . .

thirdly, resource shifting based on regulatory incentives, and not on cost effective service delivery, will become common."[52] And Wholey: "Rate setting might decrease the ability of an HMO to respond to the market place because the regulatory process for rate setting is time consuming, imposes an administrative burden on the HMO, and may limit the HMO's flexibility in bidding for employer contracts."[53]

Evidence on Rate Setting and Managed Care

For about 20 years, researchers tried unsuccessfully to demonstrate a link between various state regulations and HMO growth and development. Goldberg found, "Legal restrictions on HMO development imposed at the state level appear to have had little effect . . . HMOs respond more to impersonal market and demographic conditions than to certain legal restrictions."[54] It is indeed difficult to conclude that rate setting and managed care are antithetical because states with mandatory rate setting generally have witnessed high rates of growth in HMO penetration during the 1980s and 1990s. Over first noticed in 1983 that rate setting was positively related to prepaid group practice and independent practice association (IPA) presence.[55] Anderson made a similar observation in 1991, noting that all mandatory rates setting states except New Jersey had penetration rates substantially above the national average.[56]

This relationship does not suggest that rate setting is responsible for HMO growth, only that the two phenomena are not necessarily incompatible, and that the factors that led a state to adopt rate setting (high per capita health costs) also created a conducive environment for HMO development, a fact noted by McLaughlin: "HMOs should flourish in areas where hospital expenses are higher."[57] Morrissey had demonstrated some years earlier that HMO market share was "determined largely by demand characteristics: search costs, income, demographics" and not by legal restrictions.[58]

Theory Revised

This apparent lack of incompatibility led some theorists to reexamine the role of rate setting in a managed care/competitive paradigm. Schramm suggested it first: "Rate setting programs are not antithetical to competition in the hospital sector . . . They are fundamentally alike . . . The future is one of increased regulation and increased competition for hospitals."[59] Ginsburg and Thorpe attempted to define the relationship: "Rate setting can be highly compatible with the most important aspects of competitive approaches, but only if it is designed to be so. The key is the degree of freedom that competitive health plans have to contract with providers . . . The hospital rate setting experience in the US includes examples of both significant restrictions on competitive plans and lack of restriction. In New York, HMOs must go through rate hearings to obtain permission to pay hospitals rates that differ from those set for other payers. On the other hand, Massachusetts leaves HMOs free to contract with hospitals in any manner. Enrollment in competitive plans in Massachusetts increased dramatically during the 1980s, with 26.5 percent of residents enrolled in a prepaid plan by 1990. While nobody can tell what the HMO market share in Massachusetts would have been in the absence of rate setting, the experience strongly suggests that rate setting was not a major barrier."[60] However, New York and Massachusetts policymakers would later attribute their rate setting systems' collapse to the ability of HMOs to negotiate rates of payment below state-set levels.

In spite of the demise of rate setting in most of the mandatory-regulatory states, interest in the concept persisted through 1994—in various national reform proposals, in state reform initiatives such as Minnesota's, and in academic policy proposals such as Rice's that discussed in 1992 "the feasibility of including an all payer reimbursement system in a universal health insurance program."[61] Anderson's article title in 1991, "Down but Not Out," remained appropriate for rate setting at least through 1994.[62] It remains to be seen whether the concept will reemerge in the wake of growing consumer unrest over the restrictions of many HMOs and the accompanying consolidation in the hospital sector.

Theoretical Frameworks

The theory of economic regulation and the punctuated equilibrium model of policy change serve as the rival conceptual models for this investigation. While the former is substantially older, both have deep roots in economic and political theory from a variety of sources. This section will identify these sources and place them within the context of the overall study.

Theory of Economic Regulation

Through much of world history and political theory, a dual theory of motivation prevailed stressing self- and public interest in the conduct of public affairs. Augustine's *The City of God* divides all humankind into two "cities": "That which animates secular society (*civitas terrena;* the earthly city) is the love of self to the point of contempt for God; that which animates divine society (*civitas caelestis;* the heavenly city) is the love of God to the point of contempt for self."[63] It must be noted that not all thinkers of earlier eras subscribed to this formulation. Machiavelli, for example, in chapter 17 of *The Prince* wrote:

> ... one can generally say this about men: that they are ungrateful, fickle, simulators and deceivers, avoiders of dangers, greedy for gain ... men are less hesitant about harming someone who makes himself loved than one who makes himself feared because love is held together by a chain of obligation which, since men are a sorry lot, is broken on every occasion in which their own self interest is concerned ...

In American writing, the concept of dual motivation had clear support in the writings of Madison in *The Federalist Papers,* number 10 and others, outlining the necessity and means to control factions under the proposed new federal constitution. "Ambition must be made to counteract ambition" to ensure that the greater public purposes of the new federal government are attained.[64]

An important and controversial book, *An Economic Interpretation of the Constitution of the United* States, published in 1913, provided an early challenge to the notion of dual motivation by suggesting that the framers of the federal constitution in 1787 were largely interested in personal and class financial considerations in creating that document. Beard concluded: "The members of the Philadelphia Convention which drafted the Constitution were, with a few exceptions, immediately, directly, and personally interested in, and derived economic advantages from, the establishment of the new system. The Constitution was essentially an economic document based upon the concept that the fundamental private rights of property are anterior to government and morally beyond the reach of popular majorities."[65]

The first major theoretical challenge to dual motivation was made by Schumpeter in the 1930s arguing for a theory based on self-interest alone. "Adversary democracy," in his view, had no place for the common good or public interest—voters followed their self-interests in making demands on the political system to satisfy their needs. Elected officials, in turn, adopted policies to win votes and elections, seeking to satisfy as many and alienate as few as possible. The sum of people's preferences made up the whole without any room for a notion such as "the common good."[66]

Downs went further in creating his economic theory of democracy and laying the foundations for rational/public choice modeling. Democratic governments, he noted, will most often favor producers over consumers to maximize political support because producers are more likely to reward actions favorable to their own interests. Calling his theory "political rationality from an economic point of view," he hypothesized that "parties formulate policies in order to win elections, rather than win elections in order to formulate policy." Though Downs softened his emphasis on self-interest in later years, his earlier work made that concept "the cornerstone of our analysis."[67] Buchanan, Tullock, and others extended this reasoning to the behavior of voters, furthering the growing relationship between microeconomics and political science: "Voters and customers are essentially the same people. Mr. Smith buys and votes; he is the same man in the supermarket and in the voting booth."[68]

The work of Schumpeter, Downs, Buchanan, and others on rational choice theory became influential for many economists and political scientists in the 1950s and 1960s. Their theories were applied in many fields, one of the most fruitful being the theory and practice of government regulation. While Huntington made one of the earliest attempts to analyze regulatory behavior from a self-interest point of view in his investigation of the Interstate Commerce Commission,[69] the essential "theory of economic regulation" was most clearly outlined by Stigler. "The players who count in regulation," he wrote, "are the producers and consumers. Political intermediaries—parties, legislators, administrators—are not believed to be devoid of influence, but in the main, they act as agents for the primary players in the construction and administration of public policy."[70]

This shift in focus from public officials to interest groups as the critical players was first developed by Truman in his noted book that pioneered the development of interest group theory.[71] But Stigler went beyond—and contrary to—some of Truman's central ideas in asserting that "as a rule, regulation is acquired by the industry and is designed and operated primarily for its benefit," with government regulators "captured" by the affected industry. Government has four key means to regulate: direct subsidy, controls over entry, controls over substitutes and complements, and price-fixing. "Even the industry that has achieved entry controls will often want price controls administered by a body with coercive powers."[72]

All of the previously mentioned powers can be found in the health sector generally, and in the hospital sector in particular where hospitals enjoy strong entry controls through state certificate-of-need laws. It has already been noted that the American Hospital Association and many of its state affiliates actively sought and promoted state rate setting in the 1970s. Certainly, the presence of many diverse and powerful interest groups in the health sector lends familiarity to both Truman's and Stigler's themes.

Stigler notes three limitations to industries seeking regulatory protections: first, the power arrangements within the regulated industry change and become nonproportional to industry output; second, substantial costs can be incurred from compliance with public safeguards; and third, the industry councils are opened to potentially powerful outsiders through the public process. All of these impediments must be outweighed by the economic advantages obtained through regulation. In return, the industry "must be prepared to pay with two things a [political] party needs: voters and resources."[73]

Anticipating the growth in research on his theory, Stigler suggests that "economists should quickly establish the license to practice on the rational theory of political behavior." Many did. Hilton concluded that regulators will engage in "minimal squawk" behavior because their individual utility functions discourage them from alienating regulated industries.[74] Peltzman attempted to prove that regulators will choose transfers among favored industries in order to maximize the regulator's personal utility curve.[75]

While economists led the way, political scientists were not far behind in applying this logic to their own models. The objectives were twofold: first, to demonstrate that self-interest was the sole and universal motivater of political behavior by public officials; and second, to characterize public officials as passive agents obedient to interest group desires. Latham identified this pattern, describing legislatures as "referees" who simply "ratify" and "record" the balance of power among the contending interest groups.[76] In the 1970s, researchers found these strains in examining the behavior of the U.S. Congress. Self-interest, namely the pervasive desire for reelection, was identified as the critical factor in explaining members' behavior.[77] Even Wilson, no fan of the rational choice school, observed in 1976 the tendency for interest group needs to dominate legislative deliberations on regulation: "What was created in the name of the common good is sustained in the name of a particular interest. Bureaucratic clientelism becomes self perpetuating, in the absence of some crisis or scandal, because a single interest group to which the program matters greatly is highly motivated and well-situated to ward off the criticism of other groups."[78]

The theory of economic regulation has been applied to the health sector, most notably by Feldstein who used regression analysis to demonstrate that self-interest dominated concerns of congressional members in their votes for or against President Carter's unsuccessful hospital cost containment package in 1979.[79] In other works, Feldstein has applied the theory of economic regulation to numerous political conflicts in the health field, finding self-interest a more reliable and persistent predictor of behavior than public interest. His version regards government as a marketplace where legislative, regulatory, and other public benefits are exchanged for various forms of political support to public executives, legislators, and bureaucrats. Regulatory agencies and their policies are developed for the express purpose of monopolizing an industry, enabling an otherwise competitive set of firms to act as a monopoly—charging higher prices, restricting output, raising profit levels, and protecting itself from competitors.[80]

To Feldstein and others, regulation is demanded by groups because of the benefits it confers, and it is supplied by legislators and government officials at a price. The market price that groups seeking regulation must pay is political support in the form of votes, contributions, and volunteer time. For consumers, high information and transaction costs usually exceed the diffuse benefits of defeating regulation, explaining why industry usually wins. Deregulation is predicted to occur when political support by those regulated declines or when political support from regulatory opponents increases beyond the political benefits offered by those regulated.[81]

Other researchers have also addressed the issue of deregulation—a key aspect of this study—according to the theory of economic regulation. In Becker's view, political support for regulation will wither (and support for deregulation will grow) when the dead weight costs of a regulatory structure become too large to sustain.[82] MacAvoy identified these dead weight losses in the energy and transportation industries, observing that price and entry restrictions had restricted profitability so widely that production and capacity growth were severely restrained, making regulatory change inevitable.[83] Feldstein suggests that deregulation will occur when regulation opponents can offer greater political rewards than supporters of regulation can provide.

Support for self-interest as the sole explainer of political behavior grew rapidly and broadly during the 1960s and 1970s, often going to extremes. To some rational choice theorists, even the most altruistic behavior only made sense when defined in self-interest terms, agreeing with the judgment of Abraham Lincoln:

> . . . having remarked to a companion that "all men were prompted by selfishness in doing good or evil," and having subsequently run to rescue some trapped piglets for their mother, [Lincoln] was asked, "Now, Abe, where does selfishness come in on this little episode?" Lincoln answered, "Why, bless your soul, Ed, that was the very essence of selfishness. I would have had no peace of mind all day had I gone on and left that suffering old sow worrying over those pigs. I did it to get peace of mind, don't you see?"[84]

After a period of theoretical dominance, support for self-interest as the sole motivater of public behavior came under serious assault in the

1980s. The principal reason for the fall from grace of the theory of economic regulation, according to Meier, is simply that the capture theory had been "devastated by the empirical literature."[85] Those attacking the theory of economic regulation and other rational choice modeling did not dismiss the importance of self-interest, just its place as the *sole* or universal motivater of public behavior. "Self interest does a great job explaining the location of a new federal building in Missoula. It fails with regard to the major policy upheavals in the United States of the past decades."[86]

Cone and Dranove tested the theory of economic regulation as an explainer of the adoption of hospital rate setting laws and rejected it for three reasons: first, hospitals in rate setting states had lower prices than they would have had in the absence of rate setting; second, rate setting did not prevent hospitals from charging less than announced rates; and third, "it is impossible to interpret the empirical evidence . . . as supporting the cartel story."[87]

With regard to deregulation, Derthick and Quirk found the theory of economic regulation unhelpful in explaining the elimination of regulations in the airline, trucking, and telecommunications industries: "the success of procompetitive deregulation cannot be attributed to a change in the configuration of economic interests, nor can it be interpreted as the outcome of bargaining among interest groups . . . interest group regimes today derive much of their apparent power merely from the absence of challenges—that is, from the inattentiveness of political leaders and allied forces that might launch an attack."[88] Noll reached similar conclusions in his examination of deregulation dynamics: "Economists have played an important role in the development of explanations of how narrow economic interests influence the political process. The difficulty is that there is ample evidence that there is more to regulatory politics than this. The deregulation movement of the 1970s and the concomitant influence of economists in reforming regulatory policies were certainly not predictable from purely economic models of the political process."[89]

Some pioneers of self-interest/rational choice theory such as Downs and Buchanan in recent years have softened their insistence on self-interest as the sole motivater of political behavior and have embraced a form of dual motivation theory. The same year that he won a Nobel prize in economics for his work in rational choice modeling, Buchanan noted that "both images (self and public interest) are partial. Each image pulls out, isolates, and accentuates a highly particularized element that is universal in all human behavior . . . Each political actor, regardless of his role, combines both of these elements in his behavior pattern, along with many other elements not noted here."[90] In faulting rational choice theory for its failure to survive "systematic empirical scrutiny," Green and Shapiro suggest a more productive role for the theory: "The question would change from 'Whether or not rational choice theory?' to something more fruitful: 'How does rationality interact with other facets of human nature and organization to produce the politics that we seek to understand?'"[91]

This book assumes self-interest and rational choice to be important, though not sole, explainers of public policy behavior. The theory of economic regulation provides one set of "conceptual lenses" that can help us to understand the phenomena of hospital rate setting and its deregulation. Regardless of the ultimate overall validity of any of these theories, using the model allows us to understand rate regulation in a way that would not be possible without its use.

Punctuated Equilibrium Model of Policy Change

While the central dynamic in the theory of economic regulation is *interests,* the central force in the punctuated equilibrium model is *ideas.* While this latter theory is considerably more recent in development than the former, its roots also run deep in intellectual history. The assertion that ideas and "reason" matter more (or at least *should* matter more) than individual interests in the conduct of state affairs has roots that reach to Plato's *Republic.*

The idea of "punctuated equilibrium" can be traced directly to Kuhn's landmark 1962 essay, *The Structure of Scientific Revolutions,* which disrupted the notion of science as a series of linear and cumulative progressions in knowledge and substituted instead a portrait of "scientific development as a succession of tradition-bound periods punctuated by non-cumulative breaks" (208). Copernicus, Newton, Lavoisier, Einstein, and many others triggered scientific revolutions by rejecting "one time-honored scientific theory in favor of another incompatible with it. Each produced a consequent shift in the problems available for scientific scrutiny and in the standards by which the profession determined what should count as an admissible problem or as a legitimate problem-solution" (6). The rejection of a prevailing scientific "paradigm" is not random, but rather "an extravagance to be reserved for the occasion that demands it." But rejection can only occur when a viable substitute has developed: "The decision to reject one paradigm is always simultaneously the decision to accept another" (76–77). While confining his own investigation to the physical sciences, Kuhn recognized that his model could hold lessons for politics as well:

> In the face of vast and essential differences between political and scientific development, what parallelism can justify the metaphor that

finds revolutions in both? . . . Political revolutions are inaugurated by
a growing sense, often restricted to a segment of the political community, that existing institutions have ceased adequately to meet the
problems posed by an environment that they have in part created . . .
In both political and scientific development the sense of malfunction
that can lead to crisis is prerequisite to revolution . . . Political revolutions aim to change political institutions in ways that those institutions themselves prohibit. (92–93)[92]

The use of the term "punctuated equilibrium" seems first to have been
used in the 1970s in paleobiology to describe patterns and spurts in the
evolutionary record over millions of years.[93] Its first known use in the
social sciences was Tushman and Romanelli's adaptation in the 1980s to
organizational theory as a model to predict a firm's progress through
"convergent periods punctuated by reorientations which demark and set
bearings for the next convergent period." Reorientation periods are
"episodes of short, discontinuous change where strategies, power structures, and systems are fundamentally transformed toward a new basis of
alignment."[94]

Baumgartner and Jones in the 1990s introduced the construct to
political science with their "punctuated equilibrium model of policy
change" based on the emergence and recession of issues from the public
agenda. They posit that new institutional structures emerge during distinct
periods when new issues, ideas, or "policy images" emerge into public
view. These new structures can remain in place for decades, structuring
participation and establishing the illusion of equilibrium—until new issues
or images emerge to destroy the institutions, replacing them with others.[95]
The midwives to these changes are called *policy or public entrepreneurs*
who parallel the role played by entrepreneurs in private markets. Schneider and Teske argue that forces for change in government can be either
exogenous or endogenous, or both, but that public entrepreneurs who are
embedded in public systems help trigger the dynamic change periods
within the punctuated equilibrium framework.[96]

Embedded in Baumgartner and Jones's model are important strands
of political theory, among them: (1) the structure and scope of conflict; (2)
the role of ideas in public policy-making; and (3) the nature and pace of
change in political systems. Each of these will be explored in turn.

(1) *The Structure and Scope of Conflict in Policy-Making.* A central
theme in Baumgartner and Jones's model is the potential for upheaval present in all policy subsystems. New policy ideas do not acquire hegemony by
accident or evolution, but through conflict among ideas mediated through
interests espousing them. The idea of conflict as a permanent and key fea-

ture of politics was most forcefully articulated in modern times by Schattschneider: "at the root of all politics is the universal language of conflict . . . politics is the socialization of conflict."[97]

An important facet of political conflict is the inability to limit anyone's involvement: "the distinctive quality of political conflicts is that the relationships between the players and the audience have not been defined and there is usually nothing to keep the audience from getting into the game." The self-interest hypothesis that government acts only as a referee of interest group conflict is absurd to Schattschneider because one can't "predict the outcome of a fight by watching its beginning because we do not even know who else is going to get into the conflict . . . To treat a conflict as a mere test of the strength of private interests is to leave out the most significant factors."[98]

The critical ingredient in conflict, to Olson, is whether apathetic groups and individuals will become involved. Only the presence of "selective incentives," either positive or negative, has the ability to mobilize the apathetic; smaller, more cohesive groups will have a greater likelihood of engaging in collective activity.[99] In this study of rate setting, the size of the stakes and the relative numbers represented by each group help to explain both the strong involvement of hospitals and insurers and the weak involvement of consumers. Of particular interest is the process by which otherwise disinterested groups may become involved in the creation of a new policy monopoly and in the process leading to deregulation. What positive or negative incentives appeared that caused these new parties to become influential players?

Meier presents one framework to predict participation in regulatory politics characterized by whether individuals or groups are winners or losers among both regulated and nonregulated but affected groups. Changes or potential changes in these categorizations can provide a strong rationale for groups and individuals to leave the sidelines and to join the fray.[100] Gormley categorizes the salience of issues based upon the extent of conflict and the degree of technical complexity of the issue; an issue's salience to broad audiences will be low unless both the scope of conflict is broad and the technical complexity is low. His typology helps to explain why some groups will fail to enter a given conflict. In rate setting, where technical complexity is extremely high, the lack of broad public involvement in the conflict is thus more understandable.[101]

While many factors influence groups and individuals to join a conflict, changing or broadening the "scope of conflict" is an essential strategy for those seeking to upset a prevailing policy monopoly.[102] Sometimes, the scope can be broadened by giving a fresh definition to old issues, thus drawing the interest of previously apathetic parties.[103] At other times, the scope can be altered by changing the "venue" in which the conflict occurs. VanHorn et al. describe six distinct venues, each with its own peculiar norms and culture, in which public sector politics occur: boardrooms, bureaucracies, cloakrooms, chief executive offices, courtrooms, and living rooms.[104] We will see in New Jersey, for example, that the shift to the courtroom that occurred from a union court challenge to the state's uncompensated care pool had a fatal impact on that state's rate setting system.

(2) *The Role of Ideas in Policy-Making.* In the punctuated equilibrium model, all existing policy monopolies display two central characteristics: first, a definable institutional structure to shape participation; and second, a powerful supporting *idea* behind the structure. To Baumgartner and Jones, policy monopolies are not toppled by competing interests, but instead by the emergence of powerful new ideas that delegitimize the prevailing concept.[105] With rate setting, I hypothesize that it was toppled largely by the emergence of the idea of marketplace competition in the form of managed care as an alternative means to control costs. Kuhn suggested this as a critical dimension in the success of scientific revolutions: "The decision to reject one paradigm is always simultaneously the decision to accept another."[106]

There is empirical support for the hypothesis that ideas matter in policy-making. Derthick and Quirk's study suggests that the convergence of "elite opinion" among key leaders in Congress and the executive branch was the most significant factor accounting for deregulation in three key economic sectors. Leaders made a significant structural change even though there was no overpowering external force driving them in this direction. As for the regulated groups: "Affected industries had only a limited ability to protect their interests through political action."[107]

Eisner stresses the role of ideas in tracking the evolution of four regulatory regimes from the 1910s through the 1980s: from market regimes in the 1910s, to associational regimes in the 1930s, to societal regimes in the 1960s and 1970s, and finally to efficiency regimes in the 1970s and 1980s. The most recent phase is most properly characterized by the idea that "the justification of all regulatory activity must depend on that activity's economic impact as determined by cost benefit analysis. This single decision rule effectively limited the relevance of political demands."[108] One aspect of this study examines the extent to which cost-benefit analysis—or other economic analyses—played a role in the deregulation decision in the states.

The prevailing idea—or its policy image—is nurtured and supported within specific political subsystems, variously referred to as policy monopolies, iron triangles, or issue networks. Heclo disputes the notion that these subsystems operate as all-powerful iron triangles, noting numerous examples of disagreements among issue networks.[109] Disruption of these subsystems occurs most often through the intervention of larger macropolitical institutions, whether legislative, executive, judicial, or some combination, and not through activities within the system itself.[110]

The "policy idea" behind rate setting has several critical components: one, that state governments have the responsibility and ability to control health costs, and that they can do so better than private entities; two, that health care providers are different from other producers in the economy and require extra-normal market mechanisms to achieve operating efficiency; and three, that "because of health care's intimate nature and critical importance to people's well being, the demand for health services does not obey any of the conventional economic forces that animate markets."[111]

Goldsmith's 1984 article in *Health Affairs* forcefully presented the insurrectionist idea: that because of new market-oriented developments such as managed care, diagnosis-related groups, employer self-funding of health plans, the Blue Cross break with hospitals, and the development of alternative delivery systems, "the economic power of providers nurtured for decades has begun to shift from those who provide care to those who pay for it." Goldsmith observed a change in the prevailing idea, from the notion that health care cannot function as a normal market, to the belief that health care can do so if effectively reorganized.[112] The challenge in this study is to demonstrate that the changed idea—valid or not—translated into policy action in the three deregulated states, and conversely, that its impact did not affect the other study state.

(3) *The Nature and Pace of Change in Political Systems.* One repeated theme in political science literature is the incremental pace of change in political systems. Van Horn et al. observe that "a key feature of the American political system is the slow pace of change. Our political institutions were designed to inhibit change, not to facilitate it."[113] Lindblom, terming the phenomenon "muddling through," observes that "incrementalism can be the result of deliberate steps to make limited reversible changes in status quo because of bounds on the ability of decision makers to predict the impact of their decisions."[114] Wildavsky makes the same essential point in examining the process of public budgeting, noting that new budgets for agencies are most commonly based on the previous year's allocation.[115]

Riker, however, makes the opposite observation that "disequilibrium, or the potential that the status quo be upset is the characteristic feature of politics" and can occur anytime that political actors can introduce new dimensions of conflict, destabilizing a previously stable situation.[116] Through the punctuated equilibrium model, Baumgartner and Jones synthesize the two perspectives into one framework. Policy subsystems can remain in a seemingly stable environment for years or decades, only to be upset when new players upset the stability by introducing new ideas and new policy images.

We can observe that rate setting systems had this characteristic. Most were in effect for about two decades or longer. During that period, the rate setting subsystems were hardly stable and evolved continuously through negative feedback. Through this study, we will examine the nature of that instability and the apparent suddenness with which each system was toppled. We will also seek answers to why the Maryland system remains; under the punctuated equilibrium framework, the Maryland system would seem to be an accident waiting to happen.

In summary, by using these two rival theories, we ask whether changes in interests or ideas were more important in explaining this transformation in state health policy. In the past, the questions posed by Schumpeter, Downs, Stigler, Feldstein, and other rational choice theorists compared self-interest to a pure public interest model. But public interest as a theory is overly simplistic, a straw man easily toppled by any more robust rival theory. The self-interest model deserves a more substantive and compelling rival theory to demonstrate its value as a model of public behavior, a rival more complex and cognizant of the many layers of thought, behavior, and culture that influence political behavior of all interests.

Do legislators and policymakers chiefly follow ideas or interests? Are interests concerned with profit and revenue maximization only, or do they, too, respond to changes in policy ideas? Can we observe the construction and subsequent destruction of policy monopolies as a prelude to significant policy change? Our data and analysis will attempt to answer these questions.

Theoretical Propositions

In designing case study investigation, the research methodology must be organized according to a theoretical relationship to relevant literature, policy issue, or other source. While theory is important in helping to understand and to explain the outcomes of particular cases, the cases also help to test the application of theory in specific situations. If the cases do not conform to the theoretical model, then modification of the theory may be required. This is consistent with the basic definition of case study as inquiry designed to test theory, not to generalize about a data set to a larger population.

Emphasis in case study research has been placed on the use of rival theories to focus data collection on the most important features of a case.

Results of case study analysis are more robust if data from individual cases are demonstrated to support the same theory and do not provide support for an equally plausible rival. Data from each case can be examined to determine which theoretical pattern is more valid. Alison demonstrated the strength of this approach in his use of three "theoretical lenses" to examine the Cuban missile crisis of 1962. While most conventional policy analysis in that period used an implicit rational choice policy approach, Alison also used an organizational process model and a bureaucratic politics model to show that different models can produce vastly different and equally plausible understandings of the same case.[117]

The central questions of this study are: Why was mandatory hospital rate setting discontinued in Massachusetts, New Jersey, and New York in the 1990s, and why is does it continue in Maryland? The rival theories used to interpret the results of this study are, as discussed in the previous sections, the theory of economic regulation and the punctuated equilibrium model of policy change. In the course of the investigation, two sets of hypotheses will be explored. A list of the hypotheses related to the theory of economic regulation *(E1–E5)* follows.

E1. The conduct of rate setting activities in the subject states should have resulted in more benefits for hospitals than for hospital consumers.

E2. Deregulation should have occurred in Massachusetts, New Jersey, and New York primarily because of a shift in the configuration of interest groups supporting and opposing its continuation.

E3. The shifts identifiable in those three states should not be observable to the same degree in Maryland.

E4. Elected officials should have played only a secondary role in moving the deregulation agenda—with affected interest groups leading the way.

E5. Identifiable shifts in overt political support from affected groups to key legislative leaders should be identifiable in those states that deregulated, and not so in Maryland.

The following set of hypotheses will be explored to determine the applicability of the punctuated equilibrium model *(P1–P6)* to the fate of rate setting in the four states:

P1. In each deregulated state, there should be an identifiable "policy idea" that emerged to accompany rate setting's demise and to replace it.

P2. In Maryland, we should not be able to observe the emergence of the new policy idea, or else we should find clear indications of nonacceptance that differ from the pattern observed in the deregulated states.

P3. In deregulated states, we should observe altered institutional structures to account for the demise of rate setting and the ascension of the new policy idea.

P4. In the non-deregulated state of Maryland, we should observe no indication of significant institutional change.

P5. In deregulated states, we should observe the emergence of new players (groups or individuals) who, by broadening the scope of conflict, were able to undermine the rate setting policy monopoly.

P6. In Maryland, we should either observe no such new players or else see clear indications as to their ineffectiveness.

CHAPTER 3

The Background and Context
of the States

When I sat down and tried to learn the system, it took an
awful lot of effort. Once I did, I thought, "how could a
group of people all over 21 have agreed to play by these
rules?" (Interview with Robert Hughes, Massachusetts
Association of HMOs, Boston, December 15, 1994)

The development of mandatory hospital rate setting in the four subject
states was not accidental. It emerged in its fullest and most distinctive form
in Maryland, Massachusetts, New Jersey, and New York as a result of a
complex mix of economic, political, cultural, and organizational factors
that evolved over long periods of time. All of those factors are also important in understanding the ultimate fate of rate setting in these jurisdictions.

The four states in this study resemble each other in many features,
and they also differ in critical ways that help to explain the genesis, maturation, and disposition of rate setting in each state. This chapter sets the
stage for the analysis of interest groups that follows in chapter 4 and the
analysis of policy ideas pursued in chapter 5 by identifying the context and
development of rate setting in the states. First, prior research that identifies
some predictors of why rate setting was established in these states is discussed. Next, a review of existing data sources presents critical economic
background and other features of the subject states. Finally, the evolution
of rate regulation in the four states will be presented in thematic form.

Prior Research on Rate Setting in the Subject States

While more than 30 states adopted some form of rate setting or budget
controls on hospitals during the 1960s and 1970s, only a smaller group
opted to establish mandatory state controls on hospitals and private payers.[1] Of those states, only four chose to establish long-term mandatory
prospective charge controls on all public and private payers for hospital
services.

As discussed in chapter 2, prior research has attempted to identify
empirically the variables that led some states to adopt rate setting pro-

grams while others did not. The small number of states involved in mandatory rate setting has limited the validity and usefulness of these studies. Sloan identified higher than average ratios of the following factors as potential indicators for adoption of mandatory rate setting: personal per capita income, population density, physician to population ratio, hospital bed to population ratio, and market shares for Blue Cross and Medicaid.[2]

Fanara refashioned the concept of capture embedded in the theory of economic regulation and concluded that public and private payers sought rate setting to control their own health care expenditures. In the traditional "capture" model, the regulated industry, in this case the hospitals, does the capturing; Fanara adapts that framework, focusing instead on the interests of payers. The three significant predictors of rate setting adoption identified in his study include a high rate of change in hospital costs in the two years prior to enactment, a high percentage of a state's budget spent on Medicaid, and a high percentage of for-profit hospital beds in the state. In contrast to Sloan, he found that Blue Cross market share was not a significant predictor. His last category—a high percentage of for-profit beds—does not characterize the subject states at all. We will see, however, that the role of the purchasers and payers was crucial throughout rate setting's existence.[3]

Cone and Dranove rejected Fanara's inclusion of the hospital variables, finding them nonsignificant when Medicaid expenditures were included, and also found that Blue Cross market share was not significant. They determined that "liberal states with budget deficits and large Medicaid expenses were most likely to enact rate setting laws."[4] Cone and Dranove also tested the theory of economic regulation to explain the initial passage of rate setting laws, but they rejected its applicability for three reasons: First, hospitals in rate setting states had lower prices than they would have had in the absence of rate setting; second, because rate setting did not prevent hospitals from charging less than the announced rates, the hospitals that did so could expect to attract price responsive patients; and third, "it is impossible to interpret the empirical evidence . . . as supporting the cartel story." They conclude that rate setting reduced the inefficiencies that had been created by the open-ended federal Medicaid program.[5]

A limitation of the foregoing research, and research on rate setting in general, is that data are limited to the pre-1985 period. As this study will show, rate setting's performance in holding down the rate of growth in hospital costs appears to have deteriorated markedly in the 1985–95 decade, particularly in comparison with its performance during the pre-1985 period. The pre-1985 performance led some researchers to make erroneous predictions about rate setting's future prospects. Cone and Dranove, for example, conclude their 1986 study by suggesting, "we would not be surprised to see nationwide comprehensive rate setting for all privately insured fee for service patients before the end of the decade."

A major difficulty with empirical research on state hospital rate setting is its inability to account for a host of nonquantitative variables that help to explain the program's ups and downs in the various states. Sloan discusses this problem in the following helpful way, making his own off-hand prediction about rate setting's future that has proven remarkably accurate:

> Most studies of rate setting by economists have specified rate regulation as an exogenous variable. This is understandable for the following reasons. To assess why such programs have been implemented in some areas and not in others as well as why the implemented programs differ would require in-depth knowledge of legislative and bureaucratic politics. Outcomes of rate setting will ultimately depend on political decisions as well as those of hospitals and doctors.
>
> In fact, one plausible view of the future of rate setting is that the present emphasis on cost containment will eventually evolve into one of hospital protection in which the rate-setting agency serves the interest of a local hospital cartel. With control over entry and budgets of individual hospitals, such regulation can guarantee a monopoly price to the cartel while insuring that each of the existing producers obtains a specific market share . . . Future research on rate setting should delve into the interplay of forces affecting regulatory legislation.[6]

As we will see, the rate setting programs in at least three of the subject states did shift from an emphasis on cost control to one more concerned with hospital financial stability. Sloan's suggestion to examine the interplay of forces affecting these systems is, in fact, the basis of this study.

Eby and Cohodes followed similar thinking in their review of the literature on rate setting's effectiveness. Their overall assessment of rate setting's performance in 1985 was clear and familiar: "the verdict is unanimous: no matter how cost is measured, every study in this group found that mature rate-setting programs, taken together, constrained hospital costs; and all but one of these findings were statistically significant." However, this record did not leave them sanguine in assessing rate setting's future prospects:

> . . . the states that have tried rate-setting are not representative of the entire country, much less the remaining unregulated states. Most are in the Northeast corridor. They continue to be among the states with

the highest hospital costs in the country. Compared to the West and Midwest, they reflect a greater willingness to apply regulatory solutions to social problems . . .

Circumstances change over time, as well as from place to place . . . the inevitable change in political style and will that accompanies changing state administrations is hard to capture in complex statistical analysis, yet it may be of great importance . . .

The impact of rate regulation on various interests depends on how it is implemented and on local circumstances. Rate-setting systems are not the same everywhere, and need not be the same in the future as they have been in the past . . . the effects of rate setting reflect the motivation (as well as the resolve) of the rate-setting authority. If there are widespread changes in states' priorities, then the performance of new rate-setting programs will differ correspondingly from past performance.[7]

Both Sloan's and Eby and Cohodes's predictions have proven remarkably accurate in light of the ultimate disposition of rate setting in the states. In the case of rate setting, the past (as measured up until the mid-1980s) proved a poor indicator indeed of the system's future performance.

Characteristics of the Subject States

While the major thrust of this chapter examines individual case histories in the states, a number of demographic, health system, and political characteristics are important to evaluate prior to examining the individual stories of rate setting. The indicators included in this section were chosen because they were mentioned in prior research on rate setting, or because they have become important in the development of these systems in the 1990s, particularly the growth in HMO penetration. Data include numbers for the particular states as well as U.S. averages. Categories chosen are organized as follows:

A. Per capita personal income
B. Health and hospital expenditures
    1. Health expenses per capita
    2. Hospital expenses per capita
    3. Average annual percentage change in per capita hospital
      expenditures

4. Hospital expenses per admission
5. Medicaid expenditures as percentage of total state budget
C. Other health system characteristics
  1. Hospital admissions per 1000 population
  2. Hospital beds per 1000 population
  3. Average inpatient days per admission
  4. Occupancy rates in community hospitals
  5. Nonfederal physicians per 1000 population
  6. Health sector employment as percentage of total employment
  7. Nonelderly uninsured as percentage of total population
  8. HMO penetration
  9. Tax status of hospitals
D. Political characteristics
  1. Political culture categories
  2. Political innovation scores

In general, the data will introduce several important themes that will appear throughout the study. All four states currently have high levels of personal income and overall health expenditures; this represents a change only for New Jersey, which had lower levels of health spending before 1982. Massachusetts, Maryland, and New York all began their regulatory periods with high hospital costs (per admission and per capita), but while hospital costs stayed high in Massachusetts and New York during their rate setting years, they declined in Maryland and increased substantially in New Jersey. In all states except Maryland, there was deterioration in rate setting's cost control performance after 1985. The data also show that the rate of hospital admissions increased during the rate setting years and that lengths of stay dropped more slowly than those of the rest of the nation. Medicaid spending is consistently higher than national averages in all four states, but it varies depending upon the measure used.

Regarding other health system variables, all four states have levels of uninsurance below the national average, though their performance has declined in recent years. HMO membership grew faster than the national rate in all subject states except New Jersey during the rate setting years. All acute care hospitals in all four states were not-for-profit during the rate setting years and before. All four states have a high ratio of physicians to population, but not unusually high physician costs. Regarding political characteristics, all four states score highly in indices for innovation in establishing new laws and programs. This is consistent with their historic images as liberal, urban, and high social spending states.

In summary, the data preview themes that will emerge in the case studies. First, Maryland stands out in showing a better-than-average cost control performance during the rate setting years. Second, New Jersey stands out in showing a much worsening performance during these same years. Third, Massachusetts and New York always have, and still do, stand out for high levels of health and hospital spending. These differences emerge despite striking similarities: all four hospital sectors are not-for-profit, and all four states are historically liberal, innovative, urbanized, and high in levels of social spending. Strong HMO growth in Maryland, Massachusetts, and New York led to very different consequences in determining the fate of rate setting. (All dollar figures shown are nominal.)

A. Personal Income per Capita

One strong consistency among the four states is their high per capita income levels over time. Table 3.1 and figure 3.1 show that each of the four states has been among the seven highest states in personal per capita income since the early 1980s.

This pattern of high income is important because personal income has been identified as a significant predictor of state differences in health care spending. The General Accounting Office concluded that differences in personal income may account for as much as half of the difference in health spending rates among the various states. Some reasons suggested for this association are that higher paying jobs typically include more generous health coverage, that higher income persons are more able to afford out-of-pocket health expenditures, and also that higher personal incomes will translate into higher wages for health sector personnel.[8]

The per capita income variable becomes important to consider in evaluating the relative burden faced by the states in meeting their health care needs. While the subject states are among the most expensive states on a variety of unadjusted health spending measures, when health spending is considered as a percentage of average family income, their relative ranking is more mixed: for 1994, New York ranks 11th highest, Massachusetts is

TABLE 3.1.   Per Capita Income

	1982	Rank	1988	Rank	1992	Rank
U.S.	11,481		16,644		20,114	
MD	12,736	6	19,314	5	23,249	5
MA	12,751	5	20,701	3	23,811	4
NJ	13,966	3	21,822	2	26,969	2
NY	12,703	7	19,299	6	23,842	3

Source: 1982 and 1988, Survey of Current Business, April 1989; 1992, Survey of Current Business, July 1993.

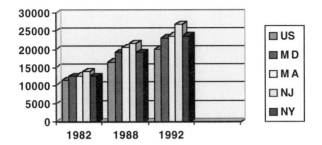

Fig. 3.1. Per capita income. (From 1982 and 1988, *Survey of Current Business*, April 1989; 1992, *Survey of Current Business*, July 1993.)

28th, Maryland is 36th, and New Jersey is only 48th. These figures show why data on ability to pay are as important to evaluate as data on other spending categories.[9]

B. Health and Hospital Expenditure Categories

B.1. Per Capita Health Care Payments. Unlike per capita income, the four states' performance on per capita health care costs is more varied.

These data suggest a number of interesting observations. First, Massachusetts and New York retain their position of having very high levels of per capita health spending in spite of the existence of rate setting during most of the 21-year period in question. While it is true that rate setting only attempted to control inpatient hospital spending, it seems clear that these programs did little to change the relative position of these two states in this broader health spending measure. Regarding Maryland, we shall see in subsequent data a dramatic drop in that state's rates with regard to hospital spending; however, this data indicate that their success in control-

TABLE 3.2. Per Capita Health Payments

	1972	Rank	1982	Rank	1993	Rank
U.S.	381		1,220		3,285	
MD	390	10	1,232	14	3,343	12
MA	489	1	1,508	1	4,157	1
NJ	355	27	1,115	26	3,551	5
NY	488	2	1,417	3	4,111	2

Source: Figures are in nominal dollars. 1972–82, *Health Care Financing Review,* Summer 1985; 1993, *Health Care State Rankings,* Morgan Quinto Press.

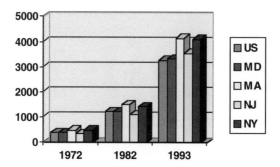

Fig. 3.2. Per capita health payments. Figures are in nominal dollars. (From 1972–82, *Health Care Financing Review,* summer 1985; 1993, *Health Care State Rankings,* Morgan Quinto Press.)

ling hospital spending rates, which is widely quoted by state health policy-makers and rate setting supporters, did not translate into a similar drop in this category. Maryland's performance on this measure raises the question of whether their successful hospital cost control program may have disproportionately shifted costs to other health care settings.

The New Jersey case is perhaps most noteworthy. From a per capita spending position below the national average in 1972 and 1982, the state jumped to fifth among the 50 states in 1993. As we shall see, the New Jersey program, the prototype for Medicare's Prospective Payment System, lost much of its capacity to control costs in its latter years and appears to be associated with a sizable increase in health and hospital spending in the state during the 1980s.

Rate setting defenders do not like per capita health data used in evaluating their systems, chiefly because nonhospital costs are not a target of rate setting regulators. While these data should be included in any evaluation of rate setting's performance, they should not be used alone. Weaknesses in this measure as an evaluative tool include its inability to account for shifts in the numbers of uninsured—because uninsured persons use fewer health services, it can be expected that states with greater than average increases in medical indigency will show lower rates of growth. Also, increases in this measure may reflect excessive increases in costs not associated with inpatient rate setting, such as costs of physician, home health, prescription drug, nursing home, or other services.

B.2. Per Capita Hospital Payments. This measure shows a trend similar to per capita health spending, with one exception.

The trends for Massachusetts and New York (high expenditures then and now) are similar, whether the category is per capita health or per

TABLE 3.3.   Per Capita Hospital Payments

	1982	Rank	1991	Rank
U.S.	577		1,134	
MD	606	11	1,072	24
MA	810	1	1,517	1
NJ	498	30	1,138	16
NY	679	3	1,404	2

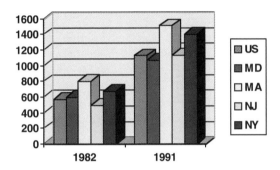

Fig. 3.3. Per capita hospital payments. (From 1982, 1991 HCFA, Office of the Actuary.)

capita hospital spending; similarly, New Jersey's figures demonstrate a clear direction toward greater hospital spending as compared with other states. Maryland, however, shows a different pattern toward a lower rate of per capita hospital spending among the 50 states. This pattern is consistent with data showing per admission rates of spending that indicate a lowered rate of hospital spending under Maryland rate setting. It is a distinct difference from the other three states and an indicator that Maryland policymakers point to when defending their choice to retain rate setting.

B.3. Average Annual Percentage Change in Per Capita Hospital Expenditures: 1980–91. The data on rate setting's performance, however, were not completely consistent, a reality that perplexed policymakers and affected their decisions in evaluating rate setting programs. Table 3.4 makes clear that both supporters and detractors of rate setting could find their own sources of support.

This table must be examined in tandem with table 3.3. Throughout the 1980s, policymakers in Massachusetts and New York trumpeted their rate of growth relative to other states as a signal achievement and

TABLE 3.4.   Annual Change in per Capita Hospital Costs, 1980–91

	Annual Percentage Change	Rank
U.S.	8.9	
MD	7.6	47
MA	8.3	42
NJ	10.7	5
NY	9.0	33

Source: "Health Spending by State: New Estimates for Policy Making," *Health Affairs,* Fall 1993. Data source: HCFA.

justification for the continuation of rate setting. But the Massachusetts data principally seem to suggest that their original spending level was so high that a much more radical shift would have been required to lose its first-place position; the same conclusion would also apply to New York. Once again, the New Jersey data suggest that their rate setting law was accompanied by a significant infusion of new money into their hospital system. We will explore the reasons for this financial infusion in the final section of this chapter. The Maryland figure is consistent once again with that state's 20-year pattern of a lowering in hospital spending relative to other states.

B.4. Per Admission Short Term General Hospital Costs. The spending story unfolds further as we examine "per admission" cost patterns—the rate setters' preferred terrain for evaluation because the numbers were more favorable than per capita indicators.

The data for Maryland demonstrate what regulation supporters regard as their key success, reducing the per admission cost from above the national average to significantly below, along with a substantial drop in their relative position among the 50 states, from one of the highest to number 29 in 1992. Even policymakers in Massachusetts drew satisfaction in the drop in their relative position. During the early 1980s, when the Massachusetts system was at its most stringent, the drop was more substantial. However, the latter part of that decade saw significant hospital reinflation because of political pressure from hospitals, pressure that reversed gains made earlier in the decade.

The data for New York confirm that rate setting did not hold down hospital spending over a 10-year period—this state's data resemble those of Massachusetts, including significant cost pressures during the early and middle part of the 1980s and reinflation in the latter part of the decade. The data for New Jersey confirm again that rate setting—at a minimum—coincided with significant inflation in hospital costs, even on this basic

TABLE 3.5.   **Per Admission Hospital Costs**

	1982	Rank	1992	Rank
U.S.	2,883		5,786	
MD	3,210	10	5,394	29
MA	4,105	1	6,198	7
NJ	2,712	23	5,732	15
NY	3,607	4	7,390	2

Source: 1982, HCFA Office of the Actuary; 1992, AHA Annual Survey of Hospitals.

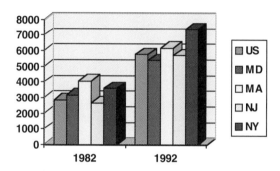

Fig. 3.4. Per admission hospital costs. (From 1982, HCFA Office of the Actuary; 1992, AHA Annual Survey of Hospitals.)

measure. A 1994 RAND analysis of the New York system suggests why the New York and New Jersey records should not be surprising:

> At its broadest level, the success of all-payer rate-setting in controlling unit costs is not terribly surprising. The state, after all, is deciding how much hospitals will be paid per unit. If the unit price is set low enough, payer costs will be contained by definition.[10]

Nonetheless, the data indicate that three of the four states (Massachusetts, New Jersey, and New York) had difficulty making progress on this key indicator. The following section on the case histories of rate setting in the states will seek to answer the question why.

B.5. Medicaid Expenditures as Percentage of Total State Budget. The role of Medicaid costs in pushing states to adopt rate setting is difficult to measure quantitatively. While periods of fiscal stress where Medicaid has been a major budget culprit are easy to identify (Massachusetts in 1975 and 1991, New York in 1975), absolute measures of Medicaid's impact on each state's budget are variable depending on measures used, as the following examples demonstrate.

Depending on the measure, these states are either very high or not high at all in Medicaid spending relative to other states, with only Maryland as very high in both tables. New York's spending levels are lower than others because a substantial portion of the state share of Medicaid costs is paid by counties. The four states appear larger in table 3.6 than in table 3.7 because they only qualify for 50 percent reimbursement of their Medicaid costs from the federal government whereas many other states receive substantially greater levels of federal reimbursements and require less in direct state tax support.

As will be demonstrated in the narrative, Medicaid considerations have played an important role in decisions about rate setting, though not strictly because of the preceding figures. For example, in Maryland—where Medicaid costs are largest in the context of overall state spending and taxes—policymakers were the least interested among the four states in making rate setting decisions based on Medicaid considerations.

TABLE 3.6.   State General Fund Medicaid Spending as a Percentage of State Taxes (excluding gas taxes)

	Percentage of State Taxes	State Rank
U.S.	11.6	
MD	17.2	2
MA	16.0	4
NJ	14.3	6
NY	11.3	20

Source: National Association of State Budget Officers, in State Policy Reports, 12, no. 11 (June 1994).

TABLE 3.7.   Medicaid Spending as a Percentage of Entire State Budget

	Percentage of Budget	State Rank
U.S.	18.4	
MD	24.4	6
MA	21.3	11
NJ	19.6	18
NY	15.2	33

Source: National Association of State Budget Officers, in State Policy Reports, 12, no. 16 (August 1994).

C. Other Health System Characteristics

The data presented below relate to other important hospital and health system characteristics, and indirectly relate to costs and levels of spending.

C.1. Hospital Admissions per 1,000 Population. Hospital admission trends over a 10-year period demonstrate another consistent impact of rate setting in the states.

These data suggest several observations: First, the high cost of hospital care in 1982 in the subject states was not related to a high number of hospital admissions, since all four states were below the national average on this measure. Second, all four states saw their rate of admissions drop during the ensuing decade, but none saw their rate drop as much as the change elsewhere in the nation. In fact, by 1992, all four states had moved from the bottom to the top half of the 50 states in admissions rates. This suggests that rate setting may have kept the rate of admissions higher than it would have been in regulation's absence—a factor that partly explains its poor cost control performance in three of the four states. The lowering

TABLE 3.8. Admissions per Thousand

	1982	Rank	1992	Rank
U.S.	157		125.3	
MD	129	42	125.4	24
MA	152	26	137.8	12
NJ	145	30	144.1	10
NY	149	29	131.1	15

Source: 1982, HCFA Office of the Actuary; 1992, AHA Annual Survey of Hospitals.

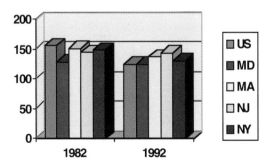

Fig. 3.5. Admissions per thousand. (From 1982, HCFA, Office of the Actuary; 1992 AHA Annual Survey of Hospitals.)

of costs attributable to rate setting in its early years in all four states may have created higher demand and more admissions than otherwise would have occurred.

Also, it was during this period that a pronounced shift from inpatient to outpatient services began to be observable across the nation, with the introduction of Medicare DRGs and the emergence of managed care. Rate setting may have slowed this evolution somewhat in the subject states. If so, this would be consistent with the theory of economic regulation hypothesis that rate setting protected more than squeezed hospitals— at least during the latter half of this period.

C.2. Hospital Beds per 1,000 Population. Hospital inpatient capacity has historically been viewed as important in explaining aggregate hospital costs. State certificate-of-needs laws restraining the growth of inpatient beds were mandated by the federal government in the early 1970s as a way to control hospital spending. Despite this belief, the number of hospital beds per 1,000 does not appear to be a major factor in explaining the expense growth trend relative to rate setting during the 1980s.

TABLE 3.9.   Beds per Thousand

	1982	Rank	1992	Rank
U.S.	4.4		3.5	
MD	3.6	36	2.8	41
MA	4.5	19	3.6	25
NJ	4.1	30	3.7	19
NY	4.5	19	4	15

Source: 1982, HCFA Office of the Actuary; 1992, AHA Annual Survey of Hospitals.

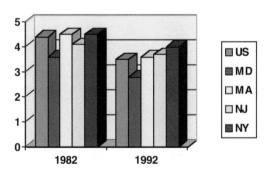

Fig. 3.6. Beds per thousand. (From 1982, HCFA, Office of the Actuary; 1992, AHA 1992 Annual Survey of Hospitals.)

None of the hospital systems in the four states could be considered overbedded based solely on population calculations in 1982 or 1992. Maryland and Massachusetts saw a relative drop in beds greater than the nation as a whole, while New Jersey and New York saw drops somewhat less than the national rate. Clearly all of the rate setting states were in sync with the national trend, and the rate of hospital beds would not appear to explain much of what is occurring in hospital finance in these states.

C.3. Inpatient Days per Admission. The four states stand out among the 50 in average hospital length of stay, though the story is not consistent.

The rates in all four states are consistent with national trends, showing a reduction in average lengths of stay per admission. Once again, the Maryland rate outperforms the nation, dropping from well above to well below the national average during its peak rate setting years. Massachusetts also demonstrates a drop, which may related to the substantial growth of HMOs in the state during the latter half of the 10-year period.

While both New Jersey and New York show drops, they are far less than the rest of the nation, again supporting the observed trend in these two states toward rate setting acting as a regulatory buffer for hospitals in

TABLE 3.10.   Length of Stay per Admission

	1982	Rank	1992	Rank
U.S.	7.6		6.6	
MD	8.3	11	6.1	36
MA	8.9	3	6.9	9
NJ	8.4	9	7.4	3
NY	9.7	1	9.2	1

Source: 1982, HCFA Office of the Actuary; 1992, AHA Annual Survey of Hospitals.

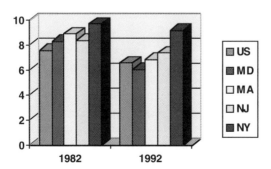

Fig. 3.7. Length of stay per admission. (From 1982, HCFA, Office of the Actuary; 1992, AHA Annual Survey of Hospitals.)

the latter 1980s. As we shall see, New York policymakers were aware that they had the longest lengths of stay in the nation during the 1980s. As we will also see, regulators moved to reduce this rate; however, the AIDS and crack epidemics of the late 1980s have been identified by New York and New Jersey policymakers as developments that frustrated their efforts to reduce this rate to more acceptable levels.

C.4. Occupancy Rates in Community Hospitals. The final hospital-specific indicator examined in the four states is hospital occupancy. In this category, a consistent trend is observable.

Hospital occupancy rates were high in the four states in 1982, and, while lowered, continued to be among the 10 highest in 1993. High occupancy rates may be attributable to several factors: First, during the 1980s, all four states maintained full certificate-of-need programs that, while frequently ineffective, may have had some restraining influence in expanding bed supply; second, rate setting programs provided an opportunity for public discussion about excess hospital beds and occupancy rates that pressed state and hospital officials to keep the occupancy ratios as high as possible; and third, these four states all have physician-to-population

TABLE 3.11.   Hospital Occupancy Rates

	1982	Rank	1993	Rank
U.S.	75.3		64.4	
MD	85.9	5	74.6	4
MA	82.8	4	71.3	9
NJ	81.8	7	77.1	3
NY	87.3	1	82.8	2

Source: 1982, HCFA Office of the Actuary; 1992, AHA Hospital Statistics.

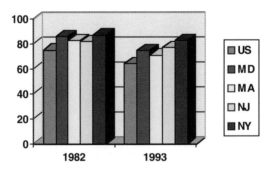

Fig. 3.8. Hospital occupancy rates. (From 1982, HCFA, Office of the Actuary; 1992, AHA Hospital Statistics.)

ratios above the national average, a fact that could lead to higher than average admissions rates and occupancy.

C.5. Physician Data. The ratio of physicians to population in the four states—both total and patient care—are among the highest in the nation.

In spite of the very high rate of physician presence among the 50 states, per capita expenditures for physician services are less extreme.

During 1995 deregulation discussions in New York, it was noted that while their hospital costs—subject to long-term regulation—have been consistently among the nation's highest, their physician costs—not subject to state regulation—are much further down in the pack.[11] This observation contrasts with a critique of New York rate setting made frequently during the 13 years of the that state's system: namely, that the failures of the system were tied to its failure to regulate physician and outpatient costs—the suggestion being that inpatient costs were under control but destabilized by growing out-of-hospital services.[12]

That critique does not wear well given the above data. In fact, we can observe in the four states a reversal of circumstances with respect to hospitals and physicians. Regarding hospitals, the number of institutions and beds is not excessive among the 50 states; nonetheless, costs (except for

TABLE 3.12.   Physicians per 100,000

| | Total and Patient Care Physicians, 1992, Rank per 100,000 | | | |
	Total	Rank	Patient Care	Rank
U.S.	247.2		203.7	
MD	373.8	2	295.2	3
MA	388.4	1	307.2	1
NJ	282.8	7	236.5	6
NY	363.2	3	297.9	2

Source: American Medical Association, 1992; in *State Level Databook on Health Care Access,* Urban Institute, 1995.

TABLE 3.13.   Physician Costs per Capita

| | Physician Costs per Capita, 1991 | |
	Expenditures per Capita	Rank
U.S.	598	
MD	676	9
MA	708	6
NJ	589	16
NY	588	18

Source: Health Care Financing Administration, Office of the Actuary, 1991.

Maryland's) are very high in comparison with the rest of the nation. Regarding physicians, a very large number of them are not accompanied by excessive physician costs. This observation lends support to the suggestion that a higher ratio of providers may provide competitive pressure for lowered rates of overall spending; by contrast, a nonexcessive supply of facilities and beds, constrained by a tight certificate-of-need law, may encourage higher spending, lending weight to the cartel theory as one explainer of high hospital costs.

C.6. Health Sector Employment as Percentage of Total Employment. Data indicate that health sector employment as a percentage of total state employment is higher than average in all four states, though much higher in Massachusetts and New York than in Maryland and New Jersey. According to Bureau of Labor Statistics data, with a U.S. average of 7.9 percent, Massachusetts was near the highest with a 10.3 percent health sector share of total employment; New York was at 8.8 percent, Maryland at 8.2 percent and New Jersey at 8.1 percent.[13]

Higher rates of health care employment may lead to greater concern among policymakers regarding the performance of the health sector as part of the overall economy. The four rate setting states uniformly exhibited concern among policymakers for the stability of the hospital sector, both to avoid large layoffs and to ensure its continued vitality. This is most clearly evidenced by the statutory requirement in Maryland that regulators work to ensure the financial stability of efficient hospitals. Higher rates of health sector employment also create a stronger stake in the sector's performance for labor, both to protect existing unionized workers and to take advantage of future organizing opportunities.

C.7. Population Not Covered by Health Insurance. Rate setting was intended to bring lower levels of hospital spending than would have occurred in its absence; the lower costs were expected to make health insurance more affordable for those without it. The results were more mixed. Data on the levels of uninsurance among the under-65-year-old population add another dimension to our understanding of the context in the rate setting states.

All four states have levels of uninsurance below the national average. Yet in spite of extensive rate setting programs, none of these states is in the top tier of states with low levels of uninsurance. The best performer among the four is Massachusetts, primarily because its drop in levels of insurance coverage in the early 1990s was less than that of other states. (This performance also declined in recent years since 1993.) The other three all saw their rank drop in recent years.

This finding, upon reflection, should not be surprising. Rate setting programs, while paying attention to issues such as uncompensated care to

TABLE 3.14.   Population Uninsured

	1991	Rank	1993	Rank
U.S.	14.4		15.3	
MD	13.2	23	13.5	22
MA	11.1	33	11.7	39
NJ	11.0	35	13.7	21
NY	12.7	28	13.9	20

Source: U.S. Bureau of the Census, Health Insurance Coverage, 1993: Statistical Brief: SB/94-28; October, 1994.

medically indigent persons, are initiatives focused on *institutions,* as opposed to efforts in other states (Hawaii, Minnesota, Oregon, Tennessee) that focused more directly on providing services and insurance coverage to *persons.* Indeed, the genesis of the uncompensated care pools in rate setting states had more to do with institutional bad debt constraints than with the needs of the uninsured. This will be addressed more specifically in the stories of the state programs in the next section.

As we examine the aftermath of deregulation in Massachusetts and New York, more emphasis is evident on finding appropriate means to provide insurance coverage to individuals and families, and less attention is paid to the financial needs of institutions. The record in New Jersey since deregulation is more mixed on this count. As rate setting approaches are abandoned, states seem more likely to move in the directions taken by other reform states. This topic is explored in more detail in chapter 7.

C.8. Growth in HMO Penetration, 1984, 1990, 1993. The final health-related data involve the development of HMOs in the subject states. Penetration refers to the percentage of state residents who are enrolled members in health maintenance organizations. Because of the role that managed care played in undermining the stability of rate regulation systems, the rapid development of HMOs during this period is critical in understanding the fate of rate setting in the states.

A number of observations can be derived from these data. The first is that, with the possible exception of New Jersey, it cannot be asserted that rate setting held down managed care growth in the states. The performance of Massachusetts is the principal evidence for this observation; it had HMO penetration below the national average in 1981 (4.0 vs. 4.5 percent) and saw its penetration rate balloon during its prime rate setting years. In fact, it is plausible that a design feature of the Massachusetts model that permitted HMOs to escape rate setting's charge controls actually encouraged the rapid development of HMOs in the state.

The second observation is that with the exception of Maryland, the

TABLE 3.15.   Percentage of HMO Penetration, 1984, 1990, 1993

	Percentage 1984	Rank	Percentage 1990	Rank	Percentage 1993	Rank
U.S.	6.4		13.5		17.5	
MD	3	21	14.7	15	32.2	4
MA	10.5	6	26.5	2	34.2	2
NJ	4	17	12.5	20	13.1	24
NY	7.1	10	15.5	12	21.5	12

Source: 1984 and 1990, Interstudy, *Managed Care: A Decade in Review, 1980–1990;* 1993, GHAA, *Patterns in HMO Enrollment* 4th ed., June 1994.

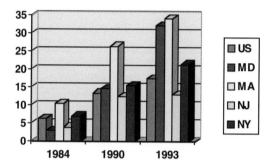

Fig. 3.9. HMO penetration, 1984, 1990, 1993. (From 1984 and 1990: Interstudy, *Managed Care: A Decade in Review, 1980–1990;* 1993, GHAA, *Patterns in HMO Enrollment* 4th ed., June 1994.)

other states maintained their relative position among the 50 states consistently during this 10-year period. New Jersey's rate slipped a little, and Massachusetts and New York held their relative positions. But Maryland went from being below the national average in 1984 (4 vs. 4.5 percent) to having the fourth highest penetration rate in 1993, despite strong rate setting that, unlike in Massachusetts, did not permit excess discounting by any parties. A number of explanations were offered by interviewees for this unexpected phenomenon. These included the state's high proportion of federal employees who were given strong incentives during the 1980s to join HMOs and the state's relatively high cost structure that permitted HMOs to attain profits by outperforming the fee-for-service sector. The former explanation is consistent with data on the numbers of federal employees in the state; the latter explanation does not square with the hospital data presented in this section that show low costs per capita and per admission, and low lengths of stay, but it is consistent with data showing high overall health spending.

The third observation is that, given the performance of Massachusetts and Maryland, it is unclear why New York and New Jersey did not see greater growth in HMO penetration. Interviewees in both states suggested that managed care had difficulty developing in the New York City metropolitan area (including northern New Jersey) before 1996. The observed growth in HMOs in New York can be attributable to upstate/non–New York City population areas; in New Jersey, the non–New York City metropolitan areas hold far less population than the part of the state in the New York City area. In the New York City area, high levels of unionized workers together with a strong fee-for-service culture have been suggested as combining to slow the growth of managed care, a dynamic that did not occur in Massachusetts or Maryland.

C.9. Legal Status of Hospitals. Another feature of the four states does not need tables. As late as 1995, all acute care hospitals in four states were nonprofit. New York has a statute dating back to the 1950s banning for-profit ownership of licensed acute care hospitals. In the other states, the existence of rate setting discouraged for profit corporations during the 1980s from seeking to buy not-for-profits. In 1995, the large for-profit hospital chain, Columbia-HCA, purchased the first acute care hospital in any of the four states—in Massachusetts, which deregulated in 1991. Another for-profit hospital chain, OrNda, made another Massachusetts acquisition in 1996. The emerging role of for-profit medicine in the states will be discussed in chapter 7.

D. Political Characteristics

D.1. Political Culture. Elazar developed a set of political culture categories for all 50 states according to three groupings: the *individualistic* political culture emphasizes the public sphere as a marketplace that places a premium on limiting government intervention and on adopting a businesslike conception of politics; the *moralistic* political culture emphasizes communitarian values, with government as a positive instrument to promote the general welfare, and political participation as a moral obligation; finally, the *traditionalistic* political culture adopts paternalistic and elitist views that are ambivalent toward both the marketplace and public bureaucracies. These categories are intended to define the dominant traditions regarded as proper government activities.[14]

In Elazar's rankings, New Jersey and Maryland are identified as "Individualistic Dominant" while Massachusetts and New York are listed as "Individualistic Dominant, strong Moralistic Strain." This ranking is mentioned here primarily because of the prominence it has attained in state research. Its application here is questionable, especially given the four states' records on innovativeness (see next section). Rather than being reticent about inserting government into the marketplace, the four states are among the most interventionist. While recent moves to deregulation in Massachusetts, New Jersey and New York can be viewed in the Individualistic direction, no broad-based retreat from an activist orientation has occurred, even among the most recent group of Republican governors. Most questionable would be the categorization of Maryland as Individualistic, the state that, for example, has enacted the largest number of health insurance mandates in the nation.

D.2. Political Innovation Scores. Attempts have been made to rank the 50 states according to their track records in adopting new programs and laws that have been approved by other states. Two of the most recognized indices, one from 1969 and the other from 1973, are presented in table 3.16 because of the consistency of the subject states in the rankings.

The results indicate that the four states are among the most active in terms of adopting new programs and laws. These rankings are appropriate because they reflect the general time period when rate setting policies were formed and programs were established. While Maryland's ranking is in the top third of all 50 states, the other three are in the top four in both sets. Walker's index is based on an analysis of 88 different programs in eight areas enacted by at least 20 states prior to 1965. In his analysis, the key variables that correlate with innovativeness are demographic, not political: ". . . the larger, wealthier states, those with the most developed industrial economies and the largest cities, would have the highest innovation scores."[15] Gray's index is based on adoption of new programs in three areas: education, welfare policy, and civil rights.[16] The consistency between the two indices regarding the four states did not hold up regarding the other 46 states, which showed significant variability between the two sets of rankings.

TABLE 3.16.   State Ranking on Innovativeness Indices

	Walker Ranking, 1969	Gray Ranking, 1973
Maryland	no. 16	no. 15
Massachusetts	no. 2	no. 3
New Jersey	no. 4	no. 4
New York	no. 1	no. 2

Source: Walker, Jack L. "The Diffusion of Innovations among the American States," *American Political Science Review* 63, no. 3 (1969): 880–95. 1973, Gray, Virginia. "Innovation in the States: A Diffusion Study." *American Political Science Reveiw* 67, no. 4, 1174–85.

These rankings indicate an openness in the four states toward experimentation with new programs, as well as a liberal and activist orientation on social policy matters. It is not surprising, given this indicator, to find the subject states in the innovator category with regard to establishing hospital rate setting programs, and to setting national models. Even during periods of Republican control, such as the Rockefeller years in New York and the Kean years in New Jersey, the four states maintained liberal, proregulatory political profiles.

Case Histories of Rate Setting in the States

As the previous section suggests, the individual case histories of rate setting in the subject states do not fit into a simple linear pattern. On some variables, the four states are uniform; but on many other characteristics, they group with each other in every possible variation. Our ability to identify these patterns and inconsistencies is helpful in presenting the individual histories of rate setting and in understanding the lessons for health policy from this experience. From our vantage point circa 1997, we can view these data and reach conclusions about the effectiveness of these systems. But state policymakers in 1975 and 1985 had far less ability to predict the directions in which their systems would move. Because data take years to become available, policymakers did not have reliable, up-to-date information on which to base their policy judgments. Rather, their decisions were based on incomplete, anecdotal, and frequently contradictory information. Were the rate setters and their supporters on the cutting edge of a new health system financing structure, or were they holding together the remnants of a failing, outdated regulatory model? In this section, the cases of rate setting in the four states are presented to give the context in which those legislative and regulatory decisions were made.

Rather than relating the full history of rate setting in each state in turn, this overview of the development and history of the four programs will be woven together thematically, so that the similarities and differences can be observed at each stage of development. The structure for this section will borrow from organizational theory, in particular an adaptation of Miller and Friesen's "Life Cycle Stages Model."[17] Their model suggests four stages in the corporate life cycle, which is adapted here to present a "regulatory life cycle." The stages are listed below:

(1) *Birth:* the period leading up to the enactment of the first mandatory rate setting statute;

(2)   *Growth:* the period between enactment of the first statute and the establishment of full all-payer rate setting;

(3)   *Maturity:* the period of mature, all-payer rate-setting;

(4a) *Decline:* the period—including that in Massachusetts, New Jersey, and New York—leading up to enactment of the deregulation statute;

(4b) *Revival:* the period—including only Maryland—during the early and mid-1990s characterized by restructuring and change to enhance long-term survival.

The framework is useful to describe rate setting's development in each state, with one important modification. In Miller and Friesen's model, revival is presented as the stage prior to decline. For our purposes, revival and decline are presented as either/or propositions, with Maryland being the sole example among the four of a potential revival scenario.

One other important feature is that the dates of critical events are not as clear-cut as this model would suggest. For example, three of the four states had statutes relating to hospital and health insurance cost controls prior to adoption of the all-payer model discussed in this research; also, a time lag of several years existed between enactment and actual implementation. In each of the four cases, successor statutes established important modifications to each program. Even deregulation was a phased-in affair in the three states that have pursued that option. Table 3.17 presents the key events in the four states in summary form.

The category "Enactment of First Mandatory RS Statute" is not as precise as it would appear in the cases of Massachusetts, New York, and New Jersey, where mandatory controls were established first for Blue Cross and Medicaid, and later for other commercial payers. The category "key successor statutes" includes statutory revisions that established significant structural changes.

Birth

A review of essential literature on rate setting in the four states makes clear that identifying an actual birth date for three of the four systems is a judgment call. On the most basic level, legislative enactment and regulatory implementation were years apart. Additionally, all states except Maryland had a series of related hospital and insurance statutes, one dating as far back as the 1930s, making clear that the development of rate setting, while clearly a watershed event, was also part of an evolutionary chain.

The explicit motivation for the establishment of formal rate setting differed from state to state. Massachusetts and New York policymakers

TABLE 3.17. Key State Rate Setting Developments

	Key Predecessor Statutes	Enactment of First Mandatory RS Statute	Implementation	Key Successor Statutes	Deregulation
MD	NA	1971	1974	1978: all payer to include Medicare and Medicaid 1980: Congress incorporates Medicare waiver into statute; 1986, 1991: Federal statute modified to protect waiver	NA
MA	1953: Bureau of Hosp. Costs and Finances set up; 1968, 1973: Rate Setting Commission established, reorganized	1975; 1976	1977	1982: all payer rate setting and Medicare waiver; 1985: uncompensated care pool established; Medicare waiver lost; 1988: universal health care law, UC pool capped; rate setting continued until 1991	1991: enacted; 1992: implemented
NJ	1938, 1963; Blue Cross per diem limits; 1969: hospital budget review	1971	1975: DoH control 1976: SHARE	1978: all-payer system enacted; 1980-82: DRG phase-in 1985: UC Trust Fund created 1989: Medicare waiver lost	1992: enacted; 1993: implemented
NY	1966: Article 28 reimbursement framework	1969	1971	1978: Commercial payers added 1982: NYPHRM I, all payer, Medicare waiver; 1985: NYPHRM II, loss of waiver; 1988: NYPHRM III, from per diem to per case payment; 1991: NYPHRM IV, expanded use of pool 1994: NYPHRM V	1996

developed their systems largely in reaction to severe cost crises within their Medicaid programs. Maryland legislators moved in concert with hospital officials to respond to rising private sector hospital costs and to avert more intrusive federal controls. New Jersey had elements of all three at work. While interest groups were involved and aggressive, the search by public policymakers for a better *idea* to control rising hospital costs appeared to rule the day.

Maryland

Among the four states, the genesis of the Maryland system is the clearest to track. In 1971, the state's General Assembly enacted legislation to establish the Health Services Cost Review Commission (HSCRC) to perform rate regulation of inpatient hospital charges. After three years of development, the HSCRC began performing rate reviews in 1974 for Blue Cross and charge payers. The system was modified in 1978 to include all public and private payers including Medicare and Medicaid.[18]

The key motivations for enactment of the new system in 1971 were twofold: First, a desire by legislators to control rising hospital costs, a concern that dates to the mid-1960s with the establishment of Medicare and Medicaid and the accompanying surge in hospital costs; and second, a desire by the hospital industry to avert more intrusive federal controls that they feared were forthcoming.

Bills had been filed to begin rate regulation as early as 1967 when Delegate Rosalie Abrams filed HB515 to establish a Council for Hospital Affairs with broad powers to regulate hospital charges. While unsuccessful, an increasing number of bills were introduced in succeeding years by legislators to address hospital rate increases, most of them demonstrating increasing sophistication. All of the proposals were strongly opposed by the Maryland Hospital Association (MHA), which was, until 1970, an adjunct organization of Maryland Blue Cross, that funded half of MHA's operating budget.[19]

The year of pivotal change was 1971. First, Governor Marvin Mandel announced in his state of the state address that hospital rate regulation would be "the cornerstone" of his consumer protection program. Second, after years of opposition, the hospital industry chose to back rate regulation, writing the bill that became Maryland's rate setting statute. A principal reason for this change can be traced to the reorganization of the Maryland Hospital Association in 1970, which removed Blue Cross's con-trolling interest and also placed hospital trustees in control of the organization instead of hospital chief executive officers—a structure that persists today and is unique among the 50 state hospital associations.[20]

A Baltimore attorney who was an MHA trustee involved in drafting the bill in 1971 remembers the process well:

The dirty secret is that the legislation was drafted by the Maryland Hospital Association . . . The genesis had to do with its [MHA's] desire to avoid national regulation in which the hospitals would be treated in groups rather than individually. There was a strong feeling that national regulation would not be responsive to Maryland's needs. (Interview with Eugene Feinblatt, Gordon, Feinblatt, Rothman, Hoffberger and Hollander, LLC, Baltimore, June 21, 1995)

The new trustee-dominated MHA leadership decided that retrospective cost reimbursement was ineffective and lacking in efficiency incentives, and that prospective rate setting was a more effective alternative. A growing fissure between hospitals and Blue Cross was also at play. Richard Davidson, a future president of the American Hospital Association and a long time MHA executive, noted that prior to state rate setting, Blue Cross exerted "regulation in its most primitive form . . . Third parties had been doing the regulating for years through rules and regulations, application of the reimbursement formulae, and through a general authority that permitted them to proclaim 'We will pay for what we will pay for.'"[21]

The key opponent to passage was Blue Cross, feeling it would be compelled to pay more to hospitals than it did under the prior arrangements. In particular, the insurer objected to provisions allowing hospitals to include bad debts in their charge calculation. According to Blue Cross's lobbyist at the time, Fred Gloth, "The hospitals got together and wrote up the best legislation they could perceive—it guaranteed profit and success." Davidson's stated view was that "Blue Cross viciously lobbied against the bill and used dirty politics."[22]

Two features of the Maryland statute are important, especially compared with the Massachusetts and New York laws: First, the statute did not spell out detailed requirements of the system, but instead left substantial discretion to the HSCRC, a feature that provided important flexibility to the regulators to respond to negative feedback; and second, the statute was not given a sunset, thus requiring no reauthorization by the legislature, enhancing the clout of regulators in setting the rules. The legislature, through these features, took themselves out of the control and governance of the system.

Massachusetts
Massachusetts was one of the earliest states to move in the direction of hospital reimbursement regulation. In 1953, the legislature established the Bureau of Hospital Costs and Finances, which set reimbursement rates for the medical bills of indigent welfare recipients. In 1956, the Rate Setting Board was established to set rates for nursing, convalescent, and rest

homes. In the 1960s, the board began to audit hospitals for Blue Cross. After Medicaid was launched in 1967, legislation was passed in 1968 to create an independent Rate Setting Commission to coordinate and centralize rate making and auditing functions that had been performed by many different agencies that purchased health care services and to assure "that the rates of payment and reimbursement will give both full value received for every taxpayer's dollar spent and at the same time provide the fair and equitable compensation to the hospitals and other vendors of services" (Governor's Special Message, 1967). The new commission was given authority to set rates paid by governmental units as well as industrial accident rates. The RSC was also empowered to approve Blue Cross contracts with hospitals. A 1973 law reorganized the commission, replacing five part-time commissioners with three full-time commissioners and providing expanded authority to approve rates for all social, educational, and rehabilitative programs purchased by government.

The new commission moved rapidly to assume its responsibilities. For example, Massachusetts was one of the first states to receive a federal waiver to set Medicaid rates different from Medicare rates. Beginning in 1974, Massachusetts implemented a prospective per diem methodology for all Medicaid hospital reimbursements. In 1976, the commission received a $1 million federal grant for a demonstration project to develop refinements to the prospective reimbursement system.

For the commonwealth, 1975 was a critical year in the establishment of hospital rate setting. A severe recession, accompanied by a deep budget crisis and a sizable income tax hike, focused attention on the rising costs of the Medicaid program. Because Medicaid represented only about 10 percent of total hospital costs in the state, the legislature decided to give the RSC authority to control the total amount that hospitals charged for their services. Newly elected Governor Michael Dukakis had sought legislation to freeze hospital charges, a proposal strongly opposed by the Massachusetts Hospital Association (MHA). The temporary system (Chapter 424) approved in 1975 as a compromise was followed in 1976 by a longer-term model (Chapter 409). As Kronick notes, "The main reason for enacting this system was to control Medicaid expenditures."[23]

This assessment of the 1975 process is confirmed by an observer who was present at the time:

> In 1975, the idea was, "Let's try and put Medicaid on a better footing." To do it, we had to put controls on the overall system. It's been a consistent theme over 18 years that one of the key drivers had always been trying to control Medicaid: 1975 to 1991 through rate setting, and after 1991 through managed care. (Interview with Steven

Tringale, former Blue Cross, Life Insurance Association, Legislative Staff, Boston, December 21, 1994)

The contrast with Maryland is noteworthy. Massachusetts policymakers sought to control all hospital charges as a means to constrain their own priority, the budget costs related to Medicaid. Maryland policymakers, by contrast, sought to control charges as a means to slow down both hospital and health cost inflation; slowing the growth of Medicaid was not central to their thinking.

New Jersey
In New Jersey, hospital controls were initially related only to Blue Cross rates, dating back to 1938 when the state established its authority to regulate subscriber premiums. By 1963, the first per diem limits on Blue Cross hospital payments were set at $56 following several large rate hikes. Hospitals exceeding the cost limit could appeal through a review process run by the New Jersey Hospital Association (NJHA).[24] In the late 1960s, even with this minimal system, the state had a taste of pressures and challenges to come as hospitals complained of an inability to keep within the $56 limit because of rising medical inflation and the failure of the system to recognize case mix differences among hospitals that served needy populations. Regulators and hospital leaders regarded the retrospective structure of the system as problematic. Also, the regulation of only Blue Cross and Medicaid (added in 1965) led to cost-shifting concerns among commercial insurers and self-pay patients.[25]

Responding to these concerns, the NJHA and the Commissioner of Insurance established in 1969 an oversight process of hospital budgets, with special reviews for hospitals exceeding growth ceilings. The review process was conducted by the Hospital Research and Educational Trust (HRET), an NJHA affiliate, with results reported to an Insurance Commissioner–appointed Advisory Committee.[26] Facing financial distress, Blue Cross found these controls insufficient and began to promote state-run mandatory prospective budget review. Despite hospital resistance to direct state involvement, the 1971 Health Care Facilities Planning Act established mandatory certificate of need and hospital rate setting—Blue Cross and Medicaid hospital rates required approval of the Commissioners of Health and Insurance, with regulations established by a new Health Care Administration Board appointed by the governor.[27]

While Blue Cross and the state achieved their objectives in terms of establishing state control over hospital budgets, hospitals were winners as well, establishing a certificate-of-need program to keep out for-profit health providers who might undermine nonprofit market control. The emergence of mandatory controls thus represented a convergence of interests, including fast-rising hospital costs and overall medical inflation, financial instability for Blue Cross, and rising Medicaid costs on the part of the state government.

In spite of the passage of the 1971 legislation, New Jersey policymakers left the NJHA-affiliated HRET as operator of the budget review system. This relationship was disrupted in 1974 with the publication of a book, *Bureaucratic Malpractice,* which brought attention to the failure of Governor William Cahill's administration to implement effectively the 1971 law that had envisioned a regulatory model independent of hospital control.[28] Newly elected Governor Brendan Byrne committed his administration to correct the state's neglect of its role and appointed Dr. Joanne Finley as Commissioner of Health to stand up to the hospital industry. Finley had served as Commissioner of Health in New Haven, Connecticut, and was familiar with research at the Yale School of Public Health to move from per diem to per case prospective reimbursement methods, referred to as *diagnosis-related groups* (DRGs).[29]

In 1975, the Department of Health took over administration of rate setting, grouping hospitals into comparable categories to hold reimbursement to the median cost of each category plus a modest inflation factor, proposed at 2.5 percent for 1975.[30] A political brawl erupted between regulators, who threatened to provide hospitals with less money than the DoH proposal, and the hospitals, who filed lawsuits seeking retroactive adjustments. In the end, Governor Byrne backed down, and the hospitals received an average 12.5 percent rate increase.[31]

In 1976, the DoH implemented its first full rate setting program known as the Standard Hospital Accounting and Rate Evaluation System (SHARE), which required a complex budgetary review of hospital finances that exceeded an allowable rate of increase. Devine-Perez notes that "the SHARE system represented the dramatic change which had occurred in the state's financing system over a few years. The locus for control over the state's hospital financing system had shifted from the industry, to a state-supervised and increasingly bureaucratic process."[32]

New York

The roots of the New York system can be traced back to 1966 with the establishment of Article 28 of New York's Public Health Law and the creation of the framework for rate setting functions. The State Hospital Review and Planning Council was created at this time to implement the system and given powers to require rate approvals. Adoption of these new structures followed the release of recommendations from Governor Nelson Rockefeller's 1964 Governor's Committee on Hospital Costs that had been directed to examine spiraling hospital costs and the role of state agencies in addressing this problem. Concerns in the state accelerated with the establishment of Medicare and Medicaid and a growing awareness of the need to provide hospital services to uninsured persons.[33]

While earlier attempts to control Medicaid had failed, in 1969 the state adopted its first prospective payment law giving the Health Department authority to certify reimbursement methodologies for Medicaid and Blue Cross. Blue Cross in New York consists of five separate plans, enjoying large market share; for a long time, these plans maintained community rating for all individual and small group policies, and they suffered adverse selection because of that position. (In 1992, the state mandated full community rating on all insurers, with the strong support of Blue Cross.) To aid Blue Cross in maintaining this position, the state established mandatory discounts on the insurer's hospital charges, relative to other carriers, to enable them to price competitively despite its enrollment of sicker and more costly individuals.[34]

As part of the 1969 legislation, the state "coupled" both Blue Cross and Medicaid rates according to the per diem formula. As a result, Medicaid's and Blue Cross's rates were nearly identical and below that of commercial payers who were required to cross-subsidize this arrangement. The rates of the two large payers would remain coupled until the mid-1990s; the coupling had serious consequences for the state's health financing system.[35] The hospital industry, through the Healthcare Association of New York (HANYS), opposed the imposition of these controls, but it was unable to prevent them because of legislative and executive concerns relative to Medicaid spending. Another portion of the 1969 legislation eliminated Medicaid eligibility for 390,000 individuals, or 14 percent of the potential recipient pool. In 1970, the federal government granted a waiver to the state to implement its new system as the basis for calculating Medicaid payments.[36]

Summary Comments at Birth

We can observe during this phase a clear evolution toward broader, more intense, and more complex regulation even during the respective birthing periods in the four states. Most noteworthy is the range and differentiation of experiences of these states in adopting regulatory models that are viewed from afar as similar and comparable. As we shall learn, the variation had only begun.

Viewing this phase of rate setting's developments in the context of the theory of economic regulation, we can observe significant interest group activity at the birth of rate setting—especially by the hospital industry and Blue Cross—but not in a consistent fashion. In Maryland and New Jersey, the hospital industry was hugely influential, at least in the early stages of rate setting development, while the same forces in Massachusetts and New York had these systems imposed on them. Concerns about the stability and solvency of Blue Cross were high in New Jersey and New York, while in Massachusetts those concerns were not evident, and in Maryland, Blue Cross opposition was largely ignored. It is difficult to suggest from these summaries that the systems were created solely at the behest of the regulated industry—the hospitals.

Regarding punctuated equilibrium and policy ideas, we can observe that in Massachusetts and New York, Medicaid was a central, driving concern in moving policymakers toward aggressive, mandatory rate setting. In Maryland and New Jersey, general concerns tied to rising hospital and health costs were of primary importance. In all cases, what emerges clearly is dissatisfaction with the prevailing reimbursement mechanism, retrospective cost-based reimbursement, to address Medicaid and hospital costs. We can observe in the states the deliberate and at times clumsy embracing of a new idea, namely prospective payment, as an organizing principle for hospital reimbursement. We can also recognize the *lack* of voices calling for competition, payer pressure, negotiated payments, or other alternatives to slow expenditure growth. The choice was between doing nothing—thus putting up with unacceptable levels of hospital inflation—versus trying a new system that might slow the growth in costs.

Growth

The following discussion covers the period in the states from enactment of the first rate setting law until the implementation of all-payer rate setting. What should be apparent during this and the subsequent section on maturity is the narrowing of the range of interests involved in the development and maintenance of these systems; the intensity of interest within these groups increased during this period while public attention waned. With the basic policy idea established, policymakers and key interests were required to agree upon and develop the infrastructure necessary to manage these complex arrangements.

Maryland
After enactment, the competition between Blue Cross and hospitals abated. In establishing their rate setting program, Maryland policymakers had both the luxury and the burden of implementing a broadly worded statute requiring only that hospitals be reimbursed based on the "reason-

ableness" of the relationship between costs and services, as determined by the HSCRC. Eight major duties were defined for the HSCRC:

(1) to review and approve all rates, costs, and charges for inpatient hospital services;
(2) to adopt in regulation "uniform accounting and financial reporting systems";
(3) to perform periodic analyses and studies relative to health care costs, the financial status of hospitals, and more;
(4) to "promote and approve alternative methods of rate determinations and payment of an experimental nature" at the commission's discretion;
(5) to receive annual disclosure by each hospital of its financial position;
(6) to issue annual reports on transactions between facilities and trustees;
(7) to make note of certain financial transactions valued at more than 50 percent of a facility's assets; and
(8) to issue an annual report on the commission's activities.

The close relationship between regulators and hospitals was highlighted by wording in the enabling statute that directed the commission to ensure the solvency of all "efficient" hospitals in the state. Even more significant was the appointment of a hospital chief executive officer, Alvin Powers, as the first chairman of the HSCRC. His appointment signaled to hospitals that they had a friend at the helm of the commission, but also ensured that regulators had a leader intimately familiar with the workings of hospital finance. The appointment also created concerns among nonhospital observers that the HSCRC would lean too much in the hospitals' direction.

From 1972 to 1977, the commission implemented their budget review model, while rate reviews began in July 1974. A key part of the growth period included court challenges from segments of the hospital industry opposed to rate setting decisions. Though a few of these challenges played out until 1983, the key decision came from the Maryland Court of Appeals in May 1977 upholding the commission's rate review authority. "The Commission is not required to defer to the hospitals' view of reasonableness in cases of conflict," the court ruled (*Baltimore Sun,* May 5, 1977).

In 1974, the commission began negotiations with the federal Department of Health Education, and Welfare to receive a waiver of Medicare and Medicaid reimbursement rules to permit federal payments according to the state procedures. After three years of negotiation and lobbying by the commission, the governor, the hospital industry, and the Maryland congressional delegation, the waiver was granted effective July 1, 1977. Because of the waiver, all payers, including Medicare and Medicaid, began to subsidizing hospital uncompensated care costs.[37]

At that time, the federal Department of Health and Human Services required annual reapproval of all Medicare and Medicaid waivers, a process that state officials found difficult to face:

> . . . They [HHS] were requiring reapproval each year . . . Each subsequent year we didn't hear from HCFA until after the deadline. It created tremendous turmoil for everyone in the state to be operating after July 1 without knowing. [Congresswoman] Barbara Mikulski came up with the bright idea, why don't we just put it in legislation. The rest of the delegation also became supportive. (Larry Lawrence, executive vice president, Maryland Hospital Association, Lutherville, June 21, 1995)

In 1980, the Maryland waiver became Section 1814(b) of the Social Security Act and required in statute that rate setting not result in greater Medicare expenditures than would have occurred under the prevailing Medicare reimbursement methodology. No other state that received Medicare waivers attempted to place their special status into federal law. This was one of the most significant developments in the history of the Maryland system.

Massachusetts
Unlike Maryland, the Massachusetts rate setting model established under the 1976 statute, Chapter 409, came under rapid, increasing pressure. While the rules provided a ceiling on payments from Blue Cross and public payers, hospitals were allowed to cover their losses from bad debt and free care through add-ons to commercial insurers and self-pay patients. Commercial insurers, who had never been in issues of hospital finance, became increasingly dissatisfied with the payment rules.[38]

Not everyone remembers this period negatively. In spite of the difficulties under the 409 structure, it was also remembered as a time of energy and dedication on the part of the commonwealth's health policymakers. A key hospital official remembers the Chapter 409 period as a special time in the rate setting era:

> [They were] the golden days of rate setting in the late 1970s, when the Rate Setting Commission was able to attract very dedicated and com-

petent people who were strongly committed to doing the job well. (Stephen Hegarty, former president, Massachusetts Hospital Association, Burlington, December 21, 1994)

HMOs, a tiny part of the market before 1980, were not affected by the new 409 reimbursement rules. But they were an object of attention and support from various state officials. In 1978, the state opened an HMO Project Office to encourage the development of prepaid group practice. The Rate Setting Commission led an interagency HMO Task Force to make recommendations concerning HMO applications for federal grants and state licensure.

In 1980, the legislature approved Chapter 540 to tighten the cost control mechanisms contained within the Chapter 409 structure. Rate Setting Commission officials designed the structure of the new law to put pressure on the business community to become involved in health policy and to move the state toward adopting all-payer rate setting. Hospitals were permitted to increase their charges by no more than the rate of inflation in 1981 and 1982, rather than at the prior level that guaranteed their "reasonable financial requirements." Also, a Legislative and Executive Commission was established to develop further recommendations for hospital finance and access reform.[39]

The commission disbanded without making recommendations, and several of the key interests groups (hospitals, Blue Cross, and commercial insurers) backed various pieces of rival legislation. Nelson Gifford, chief executive of a large manufacturer and chairman of the Massachusetts Business Roundtable's Health Care Task Force, organized a select group of former commission members representing the Massachusetts Hospital Association, Blue Cross, the Life Insurance Association of Massachusetts, the Massachusetts AFL-CIO, the Massachusetts Medical Society, and the State Executive Office of Human Services. Consumer representatives were not included. Gifford used business's influence over both Blue Cross and hospitals to block consideration of their legislative proposals and to reach agreement on enactment in 1982 of an all-payer rate setting system that became known as Chapter 372.[40]

In an unusual show of interest group unity, all parties to the coalition signed a joint letter supporting the all-payer proposal that subsequently sailed through the legislature. The MHA, fearing that new federal DRG rules would underpay large teaching centers, requested a Medicare waiver to allow federal participation in the new system. The waiver was granted on September 30, 1982, for a three-year period. It has been suggested that Reagan administration officials looked favorably upon the waiver to assist incumbent Democratic Governor Edward King (known as President

Ronald Reagan's favorite Democratic governor) in his unsuccessful reelection battle against former governor Michael Dukakis.[41]

The Chapter 372 structure contained several important new features. First, it provided that the four major payer categories (Medicare, Medicaid, Blue Cross, and commercials) each pay a set percentage of hospital charges. Second, it created specific incentives to reward hospitals to reduce the intensity of ancillary services per admission. Third, it provided strong incentives to hospitals to reduce admissions. Business supported this structure as a means to reduce the rate of growth in hospital costs and also to ensure that commercial insurers would be able to compete effectively against Blue Cross, preventing a monopoly by the state's largest health insurance carrier. Blue Cross still retained a statutory advantage over their commercial rivals, thus ensuring their support.[42]

One other key feature that differed from the other states was the treatment of HMOs, deliberately left outside of the rate setting structure, free to negotiate any rates of payments that they could. This minor design feature, incorporated as part of the state's strategy to encourage HMO growth and development, would have major implications for the future of the system that were not apparent during 1982. HMO leaders, including Thomas Pyle of the Harvard Community Health Plan, lobbied successfully in the state and in Washington, DC, for exclusion from the new reimbursement rules.

New Jersey

The experience of the New Jersey Standard Hospital Accounting and Rate Evaluation (SHARE) program, which ran from 1975 until 1982, resembled the difficulties of Massachusetts more than the success of Maryland. Research on the SHARE program has found that the program contained hospital cost increases, but also threatened the viability of inner city hospitals and led to cost shifting to commercial payers because the program only regulated Blue Cross and Medicaid.[43] Other research that compared New Jersey hospitals during the SHARE years with a group of eastern Pennsylvania hospitals found that increases in cost per admission and per day were lower in New Jersey, with most of the savings attributable to reductions in length of stay.[44] In spite of its shortcomings, later research by Hsiao and Dunn found that the successor state DRG system did no better (or worse) than the SHARE program in constraining hospital cost inflation in New Jersey.[45]

Dissatisfaction with the SHARE program centered on several factors: First, the cost shifting from Blue Cross and public payers to commercial carriers and self-pay patients; second, the worsening burden of uncompensated care carried by urban hospitals (who, unlike their suburban counterparts, could not shift costs onto their tiny base of commercial payers); and third, the belief that per case payment would provide better incentives for cost-effective care by hospitals than the per diem method used in the SHARE model. These dynamics came together with the legislative passage of Chapter 83 in 1978 that extended rate setting over all payers and hospitals and made explicit that the cost of uncompensated care would be treated as an "allowable financial element." The legislature, significantly, left the choice of reimbursement methodology up to the Department of Health.[46]

As mentioned in the previous section, Commissioner of Health Joanne Finley had worked at the Yale School of Public Health and was familiar with the work of Robert Fetter and John D. Thompson in developing case-based reimbursement called *"diagnosis related groups."* The federal government, interested in encouraging this experimentation, awarded the state a $3 million grant to design alternative hospital cost controls. The grant enabled Finley to attract high caliber personnel at higher than normal state salaries. Bruce Vladeck, who became the DoH Assistant Commissioner in 1979, negotiated agreements with the federal government (assuring financial neutrality) and the NJHA (assuring process rights and aid to urban hospitals) to allow the system to be implemented over three years, 1980 to 1982.[47]

Even before implementation, 10 of the 11 senior DRG project managers had left New Jersey state government both for other career opportunities and because of the election of a Republican governor, Thomas Kean. The impact of this change on the pioneering reimbursement system should not be underemphasized. Weiner and Sapolsky note that "the DRG system was very complex and difficult to run. It had been initially implemented by a task force of outside specialists which had been mandated and funded separately from the existing department bureaucracy. The permanent civil servants had no great affection either for their rivals or for the system they had developed. Because of their high visibility in New Jersey, however, the task force members soon had even better career opportunities as private consultants or in Washington. By the mid 1980s, the rate setting tasks were being handed over to the civil servants. Hospitals, on the other hand, had an incentive to continually expand their expertise."[48]

New York

As was witnessed in Massachusetts and New Jersey, the inclusion of only Blue Cross and Medicaid in early rate setting schemes led to cost shifting, instability, and the mobilization of commercial payers to protect their interests. This dynamic was most pronounced in New York where policymakers proactively "coupled" Blue Cross and Medicaid rates in the per diem prospective payment system initiated in 1970. As a result, Blue Cross and Medicaid rates were kept artificially low and increasingly cross-subsidized by commercial payers.

During the mid- to late 1970s, the system became seriously unstable because the cross subsidy from commercial payers needed to maintain the system was growing, but the base of commercial payers was not. A severe budget crisis hit New York state and New York City in 1975, similar to the economic downslide affecting Massachusetts at this time. To address the budget gap, the state froze income eligibility levels and cut reimbursement rates for Medicaid. As a result, the percentage of New York's poor covered by Medicaid dropped from 79 percent in 1979 to 60 percent in 1982.[49]

A second change heightened the restrictiveness of rate setting, denying routine and ancillary costs exceeding a peer group mean. Because Blue Cross rates were coupled to those of Medicaid, the reimbursement rates paid by Blue Cross to hospitals fell as well. The hospital industry responded by cutting their costs, running deficits, and shifting costs to unregulated commercial payers. The payment crisis led many hospitals to the brink of financial ruin, forcing some to dip into a declining stock of endowments. By 1978, inpatient rates for commercial insurers were on average 25 percent higher than rates for the Blue Cross plans, and the commercial plans refused to write any new policies, threatening to abandon the state.[50]

In response, the state passed Chapter 520 of the Laws of 1978, taking its first steps to regulate commercial rates, capping the Blue Cross–commercial carrier differential, and announcing plans to reduce it further over time. Importantly, the state also established the Council on Health Care Financing to develop a new system for reimbursing hospital care. The Council enjoyed strong leadership from Republican Senator Tarky Lombardi and Democratic Assemblyman James Tallon, both of whom worked cooperatively to overhaul the state's hospital finance laws to stabilize hospitals and to control the growth in costs. Tallon provides perspective on the situation faced by the state in that period:

> In 1978, the hospitals were frantic over a growing problem in urban hospitals in dealing with uncompensated care. If I look at the 1978 chaos, and the fact that New York's health system has survived, and that New York has still maintained the value of trying to provide care for the medically indigent population, I'm not sure that there was a better way to get from 1978 to 1995. (James Tallon, former assembly majority leader, August 6, 1995)

The new system became known as NYPHRM—the New York Prospective Hospital Reimbursement Methodology—pronounced "nifrim." It had five legislatively created versions, each with a three-year life span. The system had the distinct challenges of (1) controlling the growth in hospital costs without creating massive cost shifting; and (2) supporting distressed hospitals and spreading the cost of uncompensated care and graduate medical education in an equitable and politically feasible manner. The structure of NYPHRM I, enacted in 1982 and implemented in 1983, included eight key features:

(1) all payers were included;
(2) payments were prospective, on a per diem basis;
(3) payments were linked to the 1981 base year;
(4) payments were linked to cost of similar hospitals;
(5) payment rates differed among payers, but the 25 percent differential between Blue Cross and commercial payers was reduced to 15 percent;
(6) care for the poor and uninsured was financed through a system of pools;
(7) Rochester's unique payment program was exempted;
(8) regulatory authority was given to the Department of Health.[51]

As part of the last item, the State Hospital Review and Planning Council (appointed by the governor with the consent of the Senate) was given authority to approve regulations. Also, a four-member Independent Panel of Economists, appointed by the Health Commissioner, helped to formulate the yearly trend factor.

The system for charity care and bad debt reimbursement represented a major change. Eight regional pools were formed throughout the state. Medicare participated in the original version with the approval of a federal waiver allowing its involvement and approved in December 1982. The regional pools were needed to convince upstate interests that their needs would not be subsumed by the major problems faced in the New York City region. Each hospital received the same proportion of reported uncompensated care need through pool disbursements, though municipal hospitals were treated separately. The surcharge amounted to two percent of hospital revenues, or $155 million in 1983, three percent or $252 million in 1984, and four percent or $364 million in 1985.[52]

Summary Comments on Growth Period
From the birth period to this one, several changes in the dynamics of rate setting are apparent. Regarding the theory of economic regulation, we can observe a heightening of interest group activity and involvement among key players and a narrowing of interest beyond that central core. Hospitals, whether supportive at birth such as in Maryland, or in opposition

such as in New York, adapted quickly to become central players in the dynamics of regulatory development and attempted to assume the role and behavior of the "cartel" in ways not observable at the birthing stage. Because all four states were moving in the direction of seeking Medicare waivers, and because hospital industry support was essential in winning waiver approval from HCFA, we can observe close collaboration between hospital officials and state regulators.

The insurance industry's involvement shows clear development as the commercial carriers woke up in Massachusetts, New Jersey, and New York to the impact of rate setting on their business. In each state, they moved aggressively to protect themselves from a Blue Cross/public payer cost shift, a trend that mirrored the national support of hospital rate setting advocated during this period by the Health Insurance Association of America.

While it is difficult to assert that rate setting became completely "an insider's game" during this period, it is true that the question shifted from one of "to regulate or not" to one of "how to regulate most effectively and equitably." The details involved in answering the latter question leave out the great numbers of legislators, citizens, and groups unfamiliar with the complexities and technicalities of health care finance. As such, we can observe a narrowing of the field of interest, a narrowing that helps move the agendas and policies of the key interest groups.

Regarding punctuated equilibrium, we can observe that, for the time being, the central policy idea—public utility–like regulation of the hospital sector—went unchallenged. In spite of serious instability in the hospital sector in three of the four states, there is no evidence that anyone suggested dropping rate setting as a policy option. Instead, the policy question was how best to expand the scope of regulatory activity. Other related questions were how to make provisions for uncompensated care in this area, how to support vulnerable institutions that cared for the medically indigent, and how to prevent damaging levels of cost shifting. As was true during the birthing period, there were no voices suggesting deregulation, decreased regulation, or market competition. Instead, what was clearly in evidence was the establishment and refinement of a policy monopoly around the idea of all-payer, mandatory rate setting. The emergence of an alternative idea, as well as the emergence of HMOs, were yet to come.

Maturity

The following section covers the period from implementation of all-payer rate setting to the beginning of deregulation discussions in Massachusetts,

New Jersey, and New York, and the mid-1990s in Maryland. During this period, the life cycle theory suggests that we should see few major changes, the evolution of a more functional structure with professional managers, less delegation, an emphasis on efficiency, and generally incremental decision making. Despite the efforts of policy makers and regulators, we will observe that the developments during this period set the stage for the rate setting deregulations that followed in Massachusetts, New Jersey, and New York. During this period, we see increased interest group competition among hospitals and the mature emergence of new players such as the HMOs.

Maryland

With the approval of the all-payer Medicare waiver, the Maryland rate setting program moved into a long period (between approximately 1978 and 1994) of stability and control among a small core of interested participants. Numerous adjustments to the system were made by the HSCRC, including creating a hospital screening program in 1982, establishing an Inter-hospital Cost Comparison methodology in 1983, stepping up cost pressure on outlier hospitals through the creation of Productivity Improvement Policy in 1985, developing Objective Price Standards in 1986, implementing a Medicare screen program to identify high-cost Medicare providers in 1990, and others.[53]

Health care remained a salient political issue in the state, but in areas not related to hospital spending control. In 1993, the General Assembly laid the groundwork for the expansion of the rate setting model to physician and other nonhospital services with the creation of a companion agency to the HSCRC called the Health Care Cost and Access Commission. The new agency was also charged with initiating health insurance market reforms and undertaking data collection responsibilities for nonhospital providers. In 1994, HSCRC's long-time Executive Director, John Colmers, changed positions to become head of HCCAC, while his deputy, Robert Murray, took over the HSCRC.

The major challenge facing the Maryland system during this period involved the maintenance of the Medicare waiver that many believe is a critical linchpin of the system. Though the waiver was incorporated into federal law in 1980, it established a financial test requiring that the system not result in greater Medicare expenditures than would have occurred under the PPS system over a three-year period. Twice during the past ten years, in 1986 and again in 1990, Maryland system supporters joined together to win approval of changes to the waiver statute, Section 1814(b) of the Social Security Act. The HSCRC's fiscal year 1993 Report relates the following information relative to the 1990 statutory changes:

Although we have been in no immediate danger of losing the waiver, we continue to closely monitor our performance on the waiver test and continue to provide both positive and negative incentives to hospitals to improve Medicare utilization. Through your assistance, and the leadership of the Maryland Congressional Delegation, we were successful in November, 1990 in modifying the language of Section 1814(b) of the Social Security Act, which determines the ability of Maryland to continue its all-payer hospital reimbursement system. The change in the law allows for a more equitable comparison between Maryland's performance and that of the nation by taking into account savings that have been achieved from January 1, 1981 forward. Language was also incorporated into the waiver test that would allow Maryland three years to come back into compliance with the test if, in the unlikely event, we were ever to fail the rate of increase test. The most recent waiver test information indicated that payment per admission for Medicare patients nationally increased 166.78% from January 1, 1981 through March 31, 1992 compared to a 112.5% increases in Maryland over the same time period. (*Report to the Governor, Fiscal Year 1993:* HSCRC)

One observer of the system recalls discussions among interested parties concerning the rationale behind the statutory changes:

For several years they had to go to Congress to change the base . . . they said plainly that if we didn't change the base, we would lose the waiver. (Geni Dunnells, executive director, Maryland. Association of HMOs, Annapolis, June 2, 1995)

A distinguishing characteristic of the Maryland system relative to those of the other three states is the strong positive relationship that has developed between the regulators and the hospital industry. A 1992 *Washington Post* profile of the system included comments from hospital leaders that were unusually positive coming from a regulated industry: Johns Hopkins Hospital Director Robert Heyssel stated, "It's been good for everybody. It's certainly been effective in holding down hospital cost rises." Holy Cross Hospital President James Hamill said, "I've become a big fan." And Charles Seward of Suburban Hospital of Bethseda noted, "I don't know of anyone hurting big time because of the regulatory system" (Rich, S. "Cost Cutting in Maryland Paves the Way," *Washington Post,* December 8, 1992).

Alone among the four states, Maryland set and held to tight controls on hospital price discounting by all parties, including HMOs. Discounts of no more than four percent are permitted to all insurers, but only those meeting "Substantial, Available, and Affordable Coverage" criteria: (1) open enrollment periods; (2) group conversion policies; (3) preexisting condition limitations; (4) limited deductibles and coinsurance; and more. Currently, only a handful of HMOs and Maryland Blue Cross meet the requirements for the discount.

In spite of this tight control, HMOs have flourished in the state in the past decade. From being number 21 among the 50 states in HMO penetration in 1984, Maryland ranked number four in 1993—a development opposite to that predicted by many researchers in the 1980s who thought that such regulation would inhibit HMO growth. Two explanations were suggested for this unexpected development. The first is that the high number of federal and state employees was highly attractive to managed care firms. The second explanation is that the relatively high per capita health and hospital costs provided ample room for managed care entities to make profits by reducing both hospitalizations and lengths of stay (interview with Dr. Gerard Anderson, Johns Hopkins School of Public Health, Baltimore, June 22, 1995).

Massachusetts

Beginning in this period, a clear pattern should be evident that contrasts Maryland with the other three states. In Massachusetts, New Jersey, and New York, the all-payer systems had success holding down the growth in hospital costs during their first half and more of the 1980s; during the latter part of the decade and into the 1990s, the capacity for cost control collapsed for a variety of reasons that will be discussed in turn.

In Massachusetts, the system negotiated under Chapter 372 in 1982 emphasized strict cost controls, allowing hospitals medical inflation increases from the 1981 base year, minus negative adjustments for expected productivity increases. During this period, the business-led Health Care Coalition continued to meet to address discrepancies in the new system, particularly involving treatment of bad debt and charity care, as well as the special status of Boston City Hospital, which treated about a quarter of the commonwealth's medically indigent population.

The system was modified in 1985 in two ways. First, the hospital industry decided to abandon the Medicare waiver that allowed that program to operate according to the state rules. Originally, hospitals were interested in the all-payer model out of fear that a national prospective scheme for Medicare would cost them significant revenue. Instead, hospital officials learned that the Medicare Prospective Payment System in its early phase was most generous to hospitals, especially to academic medical centers that dominated the Massachusetts hospital sector. HCFA officials also made clear that renewal of the waiver was looked upon unfavorably and would include more onerous requirements. The 1985 legislative reauthorization (Chapter 574) of Massachusetts rate setting program thus went from "all-payer" to "three-payer wraparound" with Blue Cross, commercial payers, and Medicaid operating according to the prior rules.[54]

The second change created the state's Uncompensated Care Pool to reimburse hospitals for charity care and bad debt costs. The pool was funded by a surcharge on all payers (including a $20 million addition to private sector charges to account for Medicare's exit from the all-payer system) and was collected by the hospitals. The hospitals had argued successfully that controls on charges did not recognize legitimate uncompensated care needs. The Health Care Coalition agreed, suggesting, however, that the pool would only be a transitional arrangement until policymakers devised a program to provide universal coverage. While the surcharge began at an initial level of approximately seven percent of charges, about $160 million, it ballooned by 1988 to nearly 14 percent and more than $300 million, as hospitals were able to reap significant revenues from a pool with few controls and little accountability.

Because Chapter 574 was seen as a transitional arrangement to a broad, universal coverage program and to more hospital competition, the law was given a sunset of September 30, 1987. A new public Study Commission replaced the private Health Care Coalition. The commission ended its work in June 1987, unable to agree upon either a universal coverage scheme or a replacement hospital financing mechanism. The hospital community began a campaign of heavy pressure to relax the financial controls of the prior regulatory program, culminating in a rally on the Boston Common in early September 1987 with nearly 10,000 hospital workers.

The replacement statute, Chapter 23, known as the Universal Health Care Law, was signed in April 1988 and contained a much publicized "play or pay" employer mandate and other coverage expansions. Less publicized were very different rules governing the continuation of hospital rate setting until September 30, 1991. Hospitals supported the new law because they were permitted to increase significantly their charge bases, with different mechanisms for different groups of hospitals. The Chapter 23 changes gave hospitals charge increases that averaged seven percent above medical inflation for the fiscal years 1988 and 1989. The major changes incorporated in the new law seriously discouraged many of those who had been strong supporters of rate setting:

> The last four years were the worst era of the rate setting system in Massachusetts. It contained features that were guaranteed to be

inflationary such as the percentage add-on for labor costs—hospitals could keep whatever they could prove was spent on labor. It was directly in opposition to what we know about incentives and prospective budgeting. (Interview with Paula Griswald, former Chairperson, Massachusetts Rate Setting Commission, Boston, December 23, 1994)

Large business organizations, including the Massachusetts Business Roundtable, had publicly supported the new law for three reasons: first, private sector contributions to the uncompensated care pool were capped at approximately $300 million; second, they saw the law as a transition to a more competitive financing model; and third, their leaders had committed them to a position in support of universal coverage. Small business outrage and mobilization after enactment led these large business groups eventually to withdraw their support for the universal coverage provisions; and the cost provisions led business eventually to support full deregulation.

In addition to discouragement over the fate of the system's cost containment features, other supporters became frustrated and annoyed with the system's growing complexity and indecipherability. Over time, only a smaller and smaller circle of inside players had any real understanding of the system's dynamics; the hospitals were considered to have a major advantage in understanding and manipulating the system to their own advantage. One of those players describes his own impressions of the actual statutes that he had carried through the legislative process:

The statutes were incomprehensible, like Sanskrit. No one could understand them anymore, even the hospital people themselves. They were incredibly complicated—things like gross patient service revenue plus . . . They were like hieroglyphics. A lot of work for attorneys and accountants. (Interview with Edward Burke, former Senate Chair, Joint Committee on Health Care, Framingham, December 16, 1994)

As the rate setting, charge control system disintegrated into a non-control system, another change was creating a different kind of transformation in the Massachusetts health care market—the rapid growth of HMOs and managed care. That part of the story is best saved for the description of the decline phase.

New Jersey

The DRG system was like a methadone program—a guaranteed bottom line every year, and no one could understand how it worked.

They reconciled money at the end of each year, and then put the reconciliations into their future base rates . . . I remember sitting at one
hearing. The hospitals would say: "These are our shortfalls." The
payers would say: "No, we disagree." The Body would always arbi-
trate somewhere in the middle. (Interview with Dennis Marco, Vice
President, New Jersey Blue Cross, Newark, April 20, 1995)

As discussed in the previous section, the New Jersey SHARE program was replaced by the nation's first DRG reimbursement method
because of problems with the prior program. Commercial insurers
protested the cost shift from regulated Blue Cross and Medicaid rates;
urban hospitals faced potential bankruptcy because of their inability to
shift costs onto their small base of commercial payers, a problem worsened by tightened Medicaid budgets; and policymakers felt that the per
diem SHARE model did not encourage decreases in lengths of stay. The
Health Commissioner's familiarity with the Yale DRG researchers provided the policy link.

Hsiao and Dunn examined hospital expenses per capita and per
admission between 1971 and 1984 (pre-SHARE, SHARE, DRG) and
found that SHARE had restrained the growth in hospital costs relative to
the pre-SHARE period and that the DRG program continued but did not
improve on that performance. DRGs, they concluded, reduced costs per
case and lengths of stay, but increased admissions, thus neutralizing the
reduction in costs relative to SHARE. "Prospective rate setting, DRGs
included, was effective in constraining total hospital expenditures in New
Jersey. There was a marked decrease in hospital cost inflation when the
SHARE per diem rate regulation was introduced . . . rate setting programs
can be designed to achieve health care objectives beyond cost control. The
New Jersey DRG regulation provided for uncompensated care and promoted the financial viability of the state's inner city hospitals."[55]

As occurred in Massachusetts and New York, the latter half of the
1980s saw the gradual disintegration of the New Jersey system. Three
developments worked to diminish public and interest group confidence.
The first was a seemingly inconsequential design feature affecting hospital
bills. While hospitals were paid according to the DRGs, itemized charges
for each hospital stay would also appear on each patient's bill. As one
researcher noted, "the DRGs, which were based on averages, were rarely
equal to the total of itemized charges; and cases for which itemized charges
fell below the actual payment rate were widely publicized as wasteful hospital spending. On the other hand, bills with itemized charges far in excess
of the actual DRG payments did not receive public attention."[56] The

Republican Speaker of the Assembly, who is candid about his own lack of sophistication in health care finance, saw this as a central weakness:

> A lot of members had received complaints from their constituents. A guy breaks his arm, and his hospital bill says it cost $1500, but he has to pay this DRG rate of $3000 . . . This was the old $950 toilet seat all over again. (Interview with Charles Haytaian, Speaker, New Jersey Assembly, Trenton, April 18, 1995)

Second, while the DRG system led to the stabilization of commercial payers and urban hospitals, concerns were increasingly expressed about the financial integrity of the system in holding down costs. Beginning in 1987, a series of measures were implemented to alleviate a severe nursing shortage, a burgeoning AIDS epidemic, and other needs, adding more than $500 million to system costs. A retrospective settlement and appeals process, designed for only outlier cases, became a regular activity for hospitals. The appeals system became so unwieldy that regulators arranged in 1991 a one-time mass settlement of all pending claims to the end of 1988, amounting to about one billion dollars in upward charge adjustments. Another billion dollars worth of claims was pending from the 1989–91 period when the program was deregulated in 1992.[57] A regulator who ran the DRG program sighed in recalling the experience:

> Over 12 years, the system saved the state money, but there was a lot of catch up by the hospitals in the last five years . . . The system was not prospective enough. We were collapsing under the weight of these backup appeals. (Interview with Pamela Dickson, New Jersey Department of Health, Trenton, April 18, 1995)

The hospitals' success in winning battles before the Rate Setting Commission led some early supporters of the system to conclude that they were being taken. A key labor leader recalls his own perceptions:

> DRGs, as originally conceived, was a great idea. The guy that conceived it was Bruce Vladeck. We helped to sell it through the unions as a great concept to stabilize costs. Then we had long discussions with Prudential—they said that hospitals have gone to software companies and melded procedures into coded formulas involving "x" numbers of dollars. They would add a complication here, an extra procedure there. It started to go crazy . . . DRGs had become so corrupt, the insurance companies went to the same software companies

and said, "give us one that neutralizes them." (Interview with Charles Marciante, President, New Jersey AFL-CIO, Trenton, April 18, 1995)

The state's hospital charges were increasing rapidly just as the federal government began to limit increases in Medicare rates. HCFA, which had aggressively pushed the state to create the DRG model in the late 1970s during the Carter administration, actively discouraged such experiments during the Reagan/Bush administrations of the 1980s and only renewed waivers during the mid-1980s because of pressure from, among others, New Jersey's Republican Governor Thomas Kean. HCFA concluded in 1988 that the financial test for the Medicare waiver had not been met and that it would not be renewed. The DoH appealed, but HCFA would not relent, and the waiver was lost in 1989. Hospitals did not see the change as critical because the state had promised to make up the difference through DRG payer differentials.[58]

The loss of the waiver exacerbated the third key ingredient feeding system dissatisfaction, the Uncompensated Care Pool. While hospitals had been permitted to account for charity care and bad debt as part of their charges going back to the SHARE program, the New Jersey Uncompensated Care Trust Fund was established in 1985 as a means to treat all hospitals equitably. The surcharge to fund the pool began in 1986 at 7.8 percent, or $366 million, with Medicare paying 47 percent of that amount because of the federal waiver. By 1991, the surcharge had risen to 19 percent of all hospital charges, totaling nearly $1 billion, with Medicare paying nothing since the 1989 discontinuation of the waiver.[59]

In addition to cost, payers suspected that hospitals were using the pool in a wasteful and inefficient way. While Massachusetts had moved to cap pool contributions to control expenditures in 1988 and 1991, New Jersey continued to permit full reimbursement for bad debts, which in 1989 accounted for more than 80 percent of trust fund expenditures with less than 20 percent going for charity care to uninsured persons.[60] While national data demonstrated that the uninsured used 47 percent less hospital care than did the insured, the uninsured in New Jersey in 1990 used 30 percent *more* hospital care than the insured.[61] "The strong perception, not wholly untrue, was that the hospitals and middle class together were ripping off the system," states Weiner.[62]

With New Jersey Blue Cross facing financial losses of $300 million in 1991, and the New Jersey Business and Industry Association and other groups demanding tighter controls and accountability from the pool, the stage was set for dramatic changes. A lawsuit filed by the state's Carpenters' Union in 1991 began the transformation process.

New York

> If one looks at the whole NYPHRM era, from 1983 to 1995, it would be typified as a period of unique stability in the system where there was no threatening loss of access for an uninsured population that tended to grow . . . Most institutions that were shut out of capital markets for more than a decade were able to reconstruct themselves under NYPHRM . . . (Interview with Ray Sweeney, former New York Department of Health, now HANYS, Albany, July 21, 1995)

> It's father knows best. (Interview with John Rossman, Hospital Association of New York State, Albany, June 29, 1995)

> It's a habit. (Interview with Richard Kirsch, Executive Director, New York Citizen Action, Albany, June 29, 1995)

> It's simply a dinosaur. (Interview with Edward Rinefurt, Vice President, Business Council of New York State, Albany, June 30, 1995)

Not coincidentally, the NYPHRM era coincided with a long-term era of Democratic dominance and political stability in New York. Though the system had roots in the Republican liberalism of Nelson Rockefeller, it came to its zenith during the administrations of Democrats Hugh Carey and Mario Cuomo between 1975 and 1994. Long-term political peace enabled the Department of Health to avoid the rapid staff turnover and discontinuities that plagued rate setting programs in New Jersey and Massachusetts. The hospital associations had far more sophistication and depth than their counterparts in other states. Bipartisan leadership in the Senate and the State Assembly created a convergence of opinion that rate regulation was legitimate and proper for state government. This attitude also was accompanied by a deep mistrust of for-profit entities—indeed, New York law does not permit for-profit ownership of acute care hospitals.[63]

These factors helped the state to enact five distinct versions of NYPHRM since 1982. The original version, implemented in 1983, was shepherded by Lombardi and Tallon with support from hospital, Blue Cross, commercial payers, labor, and the administration. The structure included eight regional pools to provide reimbursement for bad debt and charity care. The first system was all-payer, operated with a waiver from the federal government to permit Medicare participation. Under NYPHRM II, enacted in 1985, the state dropped the federal waiver at the insistence of the hospital associations, who realized $200 million in additional revenue under the PPS system that was designed to be especially generous to academic medical centers, of which New York had many.[64] Both NYPHRMs I and II were per diem reimbursement models.

NYPHRM III's central innovation in 1988 was the switch from per diem to per case reimbursement. DoH officials had wanted to move to per case in 1985, but did not have time to make the transition; they were troubled by long length of stays in New York hospitals, the highest in the nation, and felt that per case payment would address this problem. It did not, though officials believe that new public health crises overshadowed their successes in reducing lengths of stay. The change in reimbursement methods was accompanied by a renewed vigor on the part of DoH regulators to hold down the growth in costs at the same time that the AIDS and crack epidemics were creating major new demands on hospital providers beyond that experienced by their counterparts in other states. Tightening Medicare reimbursements created added pressures on a system heavily dependent on graduate medical education reimbursements. These pressures resulted in operating losses to hospitals of more than a billion dollars in 1988, creating the most significant hospital financial crisis since the mid-1970s.[65]

While NYPHRM IV, enacted in 1990, kept the structure of NYPHRM III intact, the legislature responded to reports of serious financial difficulties among hospitals by adding new funding of approximately $400 million per year, in the form of special adjustments for hospital labor costs. The rates continued to be based on the actual cost experience of each hospital in its 1981 base year—"a lifetime ago in terms of the development of health services."[66]

Beginning with version III and greatly expanding into versions IV and V, policymakers began to use NYPHRM—and the uncompensated care pools, in particular—as a device to create, finance, and expand a variety of health initiatives unrelated to hospital finance controls. These initiatives included: (1) health insurance expansions including the Child Health Plus program to provide primary and preventive coverage for children; (2) primary care expansions to the medically indigent and their providers; (3) community needs assessments by hospitals; (4) rural health networks; (5) education and training support for primary care practitioners; and more.[67] NYPHRM V, enacted in 1993, continued the patterns set in IV of providing additional financial support to distressed hospitals and furthered the expansions in unrelated services funded from the uncompensated care pools.

Three areas deserve attention in forming judgments on NYPHRM. First, the system's complexity was overwhelming: "whatever else one might say of NYPHRM, as it has evolved over the past decade, it is certainly very complicated."[68] This complexity has policy implications that apply to the other subject states. The problem was well summarized in a RAND policy analysis of the New York system: "All parties in New York would stipulate that the system is impossibly complex, with the formulae and methodology changing and growing more intricate each year. This complexity is the subject of considerable black humor within the state, but it has very serious policy and financial consequences for two reasons. First, financial incentives don't work if decision-makers don't understand them. The system reportedly has become so elaborate and arcane that many hospital CEOs and other leaders don't understand how it works at all. Second, financial incentives don't work when they are internally inconsistent . . . the attention of the regulatees becomes riveted on how to change or game the system. Each two years, there is what one participant interviewed terms an 'exercise in war games' in which the players converse to see who will get how much money from the system."[69]

The second set of observations involves the weak financial performance of the system. It is clear that goals other than pure cost containment were part of the rationale for NYPHRM. These goals included access, financial stability for hospitals, and more. As a result, near the end of its rate setting experience, New York's hospital costs were as much an outlier among the 50 states as they had been in 1970. Since 1982, total hospital costs in New York have increased 12 percent more than the nation as a whole. Additionally, New York hospitals continued to be in the weakest financial position of hospitals in any state, despite the fact that New York hospitals reaped more financial rewards under Medicare than those of any other state. "Periods of stringent cost containment, resulting in serious financial losses for hospitals, are followed in an almost oscillating fashion by years in which more money is pumped into the system, in part to compensate for prior year losses . . . New York State possesses an extraordinary armamentarium for the regulation of inpatient hospital services; but like the drunk who looks for his keys under the lamp post because that's where the light is, the state's tools may be increasingly less well suited for the task at hand."[70]

A key legislator involved in many NYPHRM discussions and versions recognizes the turnaround in the system's financial directions:

> The system was originally thought of as a way to keep a ceiling on costs, which is basically why the business community originally supported it. In recent years, it has in many ways served to keep a floor on costs and to keep up revenues to hospitals which is partly why I have supported it and why the business community has done an about face on it. (Interview with Richard Gottfried, Chairman, NY Assembly Health Committee, New York City, July 20, 1995)

The final observations involve the limited ability of the system to provide access for the medically indigent. Thorpe examined the performance of the regional uncompensated care pools and found them to be "a leaky bucket," from which $10 in pool revenue produced about $4 in additional care for uninsured patients between 1982 and 1985. While finding that the pools resulted in increased hospital admissions, hospital days, and outpatient days for the uninsured, "if the goal of such programs is to earmark payments to the uninsured, methods other than the New York system should be employed."[71]

The increased use of uncompensated care funds to finance nonhospital initiatives has been a means to promote valued health initiatives without needing to secure appropriations in the regular state budget. But, increasingly, debates over NYPHRM became fights over distribution of the residual pieces of the pool funds. "It is not clear that the NYPHRM approach to funding nonhospital activities is good public policy."[72] Nonetheless, it has become a central part of the New York health financing debate:

> The rate setting law became the mainframe that a lot of other health financing pieces got attached to that may or may not add to inpatient reimbursement . . . lots of bells and whistles. (Interview with Gerry Billings, Executive Director, State Communities Aid Association, Albany, June 30, 1995)

Summary Comments on the Maturity Stage
It is during this stage that the sharpest differences emerge between Maryland and the other three subject states. Relative to the theory of economic regulation, we can observe a plethora of interest group activity in the states, but not activity that could be characterized as that of a cartel. We can also see that hospitals had their periods of stringent financial pressure and their periods of fiscal relief. In Maryland and New Jersey, the cartel theory would find its greatest support. In Maryland, a tight relationship that dates to the beginning of the system continued between regulators and hospitals, but this relationship was supported by positive financial indicators showing that rate setting was achieving its basic cost control objectives. In New Jersey, the hospitals initially fought the DRG system, but later supported it as an alternative to the PPS model. In that state, regulators had the greatest difficulty in controlling their system.

In Massachusetts and New York, hospitals had their financial limits loosened considerably, but only after documented financial problems and the exertion of strong external political pressures. Other parties, including business, labor, insurers, and legislators, continued to play significant roles in system direction—more resembling the "policy monopoly" or "policy network" structure characterized in the punctuated equilibrium model, where a small core of inside players determines policy moves.

Otherwise, policy ideas were not very much in evidence in any of the four states during this period, with the exception of the "ideas" that developed inside the New York uncompensated care pools. The challenge during this period seemed to be how to make the systems work and how to balance the seemingly contradictory goals of cost containment, access for the medically indigent, financial stability for hospitals, and market stability for insurers. During this period, national policy analysts began a fervent debate on the merits of "regulation versus competition" in health care cost control, with state hospital rate setting often an example for both sides. Nonetheless, none of that debate was observable in any of the four states prior to the beginning of the deregulation experience in Massachusetts in 1991.

Decline

In Massachusetts, New Jersey, and New York, a strikingly similar pattern exists in the circumstances leading up to and accompanying deregulation. These circumstances include: (1) a regulatory collision with managed care; (2) significant in-state political changes; (3) a growing incomprehensibility factor and regulatory failure; (4) a changing interest group landscape; and (5) an anticlimactic legislative process leading to deregulation. We will review all five of these factors in framing our discussion of the deregulation experience in the three states. We will use these same categories in the subsequent section to describe the reasons for Maryland's avoidance—to date—of this experience.

Massachusetts

Managed Care: The overt allowance of HMO-hospital discounting in the Massachusetts rate setting system was only one of a number of factors that fueled the large growth in HMO penetration during the 1980s, but it clearly played an important role. With hospital and health insurance costs among the highest in the nation, businesses and labor anxiously sought lower-cost alternatives as health premiums soared during the 1980s. While commercial indemnity carriers were required to pay 100 percent of hospital charges under the rate setting model, and Blue Cross had to pay 92.5 percent, booming HMOs such as Harvard Community Health Plan and Tufts Health Plan paid hospitals at discounted rates of 20 percent and higher, giving them important leverage in the health insurance market. Two participants recall the changing dynamic:

> Rate setting started out as a form of charge control, but over time charges became less and less relevant because big third party payers were establishing their own rates through negotiations. There were fewer and fewer charge payers actually left . . . Over time, the concept of the consumer changed dramatically. Actual consumers became very large payers and developed organizations of payers. (Interview with Bruce Bullen, Commissioner, Division of Medical Assistance, Boston, January 4, 1995)

> By 1991, we were well on our way to having the most managed care penetration of any state. Everyone could see it coming fast. That more than any other factor changed everyone's historical position on rate regulation. (Interview with Steven Tringale, former Vice President, Massachusetts Blue Cross and Blue Shield, Boston, December 21, 1994)

By the late 1980s, Massachusetts Blue Cross was facing a severe financial crisis, with some analysts predicting potential insolvency in the near future as its market share plummeted. Blue Cross's 7.5 percent discount became less an advantage and more a burden as its market share dropped from 60 to 35 percent of the privately insured market between 1985 and 1990 and as HMOs negotiated significantly better deals.[73]

While private sector pressures were building, state policymakers also felt a governmental interest in changing directions. As we saw in the "Birth" section, Medicaid's role in the 1975 fiscal crisis was a principal dynamic in the original decision to establish rate setting. In 1989, the commonwealth was moving rapidly into its worst economic recession since the 1930s, suffering sharp reductions in tax revenues, and facing Medicaid budget increases of more than 20 percent annually. In 1989, Senate Ways and Means Chair Patricia McGovern labeled the Medicaid program as the state budget's premier "budget buster" (FY91 proposed fiscal budget, Senate Committee on Ways and Means). In 1990, the House Committee on Ways and Means recommended "that all Medicaid beneficiaries be enrolled in some type of managed care program by January, 1992" (FY91 proposed budget, House Committee on Ways and Means). The recommendation was signed into law that year. Though the managed care program was not fully implemented until 1993, it initiated a process by which Medicaid and other state officials began to see the end of rate setting as being in their own interest. The state's Medicaid Commissioner describes his own process in turning against rate setting:

> We really didn't have control over what we were paying. The hospitals told us what to pay by setting a fictitious charge that nobody really

paid and we paid a percentage of that charge. We had a different "payment on account factor" for every hospital, and they would manipulate their charges to generate more or less revenue from Medicaid depending on what their overall revenue target was . . . The payers had no way to know whether the hospital was going to gouge them or not. Deregulation was a shift of control to let the payers set the terms. (Interview with Bruce Bullen, Commissioner, Massachusetts Division of Medical Assistance, Boston, January 4, 1995)

Political Change. A critical factor leading to the Massachusetts deregulation was the election in November 1990 of Republican William Weld as governor replacing Democrat Michael Dukakis. His election was also accompanied by significant Republican gains in the state Senate that enabled Weld to sustain his vetoes—an important point of leverage in negotiating with the Democratic controlled House and Senate.

Though the fate of rate setting was not an issue in the gubernatorial race that year, primary or general, Weld brought to his administration an admiration for free markets in all sectors. Just as important, Weld brought in Charles Baker as his key health policy adviser. Baker had been director of the Pioneer Institute, a conservative Massachusetts-based think tank, and had been an outspoken critic of the 1988 Universal Health Care Law. While his and Weld's orientation were clear, the initial direction to take in the face of a September 1991 sunset of the state's rate setting law was uncertain:

> I met with Weld during the transition and I said to him, "Do you want to delay Chapter 23 for a year? It would be easy to do." He said, "No. You should be thinking a lot between January and February about where people are, and what's important to them, because we really want to fix this right after we get the budget done." I followed up with Paul Cellucci [Lieutenant Governor] and he agreed. So at least on filing a bill, they were on board before they even took office. (Interview with Charles Baker, then–Undersecretary of Health and Human Services, Boston, December 27, 1994)

Virtually all Massachusetts interviewees identified Governor Weld's election as a pivotal event, and Weld, Charles Baker, or the Weld administration as key players in the drive to deregulation:

> Charlie was the most aggressive free marketeer in government and in the debate. That was the single biggest change . . . Also evident was a style change. We had gone through a decade of consensus building with a few groups going back to 1981. It's fair to say that Baker and

the Governor's style was not to soften their position by consensus. The model was directive, leadership—this is where we are. The light bulb went on that the ability of groups to tug at each other was limited. He became the center of gravity. (Interview with Steven Tringale, former Vice President, Massachusetts Blue Cross, Boston, December 21, 1994)

Incomprehensibility and Regulatory Failure. Aside from the direct interests of key players, both inside and outside of government, the complexity of the system, along with the inability to estimate its true effects on all parties, played an important role in disaffecting key players:

It was growing harder to gauge the true financial health of a number of the major participants, whether payers or provider because everybody was carrying lots of potential liabilities on both sides associated with the retrospective settlement process. That was certainly true for Medicaid which ended up carrying very big liabilities down the road associated with ultimate calculations that took years to get to the bottom of . . . In most people's minds, a deregulated system would be less retrospective. (Interview with Charles Baker, then–Undersecretary of Health and Human Services, Boston, December 27, 1994)

While many factors accounted for rate setting's problems, what could not be denied was that the system was failing to hold down large hospital charge increases. The system provided so much authority for hospitals to raise their charges that many began to "bank" charge authority to remain competitive in the increasingly price-sensitive managed care environment. In spite of these increases, the hospital community became factionalized in the quest for specific regulatory benefits for distinct groupings of hospitals. One group called itself the "low-cost hospitals," another the "efficiency hospitals," while another named itself the "sole community providers"; and still other established groups such as the Council of Boston Teaching Hospitals and the public institutions had their own agenda. Each grouping had its own stable of consultants, financial analysts, lobbyists, and legislative proposals to tweak the regulatory system toward its own advantage.[74]

Fatigue with the controversies of a system that required significant exertion for questionable gain played a role in encouraging parties inside and outside of government to look at other options:

Nelson [Gifford] tried to put together an inside game that worked for the first system under 372, and a little bit under 574, but then everyone got into the game and it became a political football. It broke apart because regulators can't get the price right no matter what the system is because they're always trailing the market. (Interview with Robert Hughes, Executive Director, Massachusetts Association of HMOs, Boston, December 15, 1994)

The Changing Interest Group Landscape. The combined weight of dissatisfaction within and without government, from hospitals, insurers (especially Blue Cross), business, labor, and legislative and executive branch officials worked together to bring down the system. As one key participant sums up:

> The system was like a sand castle. A lot of water was getting at it, undermining its basic structure. (Interview with Edward Burke, former Senate Chair, Joint Committee on Health Care, Framingham, December 16, 1994)

Yet despite the number of major interests who saw the system becoming contrary to their interests, groups were not clear on the steps that they wished the state to take in moving away from regulation. The MHA voted in December 1990 to support continued regulation along the lines of the Maryland system, but it had difficulty achieving consensus during 1991 as deregulation gained momentum. Academic medical centers, seeing the deregulated market as working in their favor, actively promoted deregulation; but the state association did not formally back deregulation until September 1991 when the direction was already clear.

Though business groups paid homage to free market notions, they feared the financial risks of immediate deregulation, advocating a three-year phaseout of the system and the establishment of global hospital budget caps in its place. Labor feared a sharp spike in prices following deregulation and advocated a go-slow approach, though their primary attention in 1991 was on nonhealth legislative matters. The insurers paid primary attention to the consecutive debate concerning small group insurance market reforms. Only consumer groups and some of their supporters in academia vigorously advocated continued rate regulation.

Anticlimax. Interest group uncertainty was reflected in the legislative process. The original Weld legislation, House Bill 5900, provided for a three-year sunset period between 1992 and 1995, before the complete elimination of rate setting. The legislature's Joint Health Care Committee reported their version, H.6100, in September that provided for a one-year transition, but adding a new system of ill-defined global budget caps to replace overt rate controls. These versions reflected uncertainty about the pacing of deregulation more than uncertainty with the deregulation decision itself. Edward Burke, Senate Chair of the Health Committee, commented at one hearing, "I favor putting the scorpions in the same bottle and letting them fight it out" ("Democrats Follow Weld on Hospital Bill," *Boston Globe,* September 22, 1991).

Observers agree that the House Committee on Ways and Means made the critical decision to move toward immediate deregulation, with only a loose system of charge controls for one year that most agreed would constrict no hospital in adjusting its charges. The decision for the more aggressive deregulation stance was made by the House Chairman, Thomas Finneran, a conservative, market-oriented Democrat:

> Charlie Baker sent us a bill that spoke to deregulation but they didn't want to climb over the fence immediately . . . I can recall working principally with [Ways and Means budget director] Joe Trainor, and for the life of us, we couldn't quite get it. We couldn't reconcile the public and explicit embrace of a free market, and yet being just a little timid to say it and do it. Our fear was that if you let the old system hang around for a year or two, you were not really preparing people for what Carmen [Buell, House Health Committee Chair] and I thought was appropriate. (Interview with Thomas Finneran, Chairman, House Committee on Ways and Means, Boston, January 21, 1995)

In the House, the Ways and Means version was approved by an overwhelming margin of 119 to 27 in November 1991. An alternative proposal to move the state toward a single-payer financing model was defeated by a vote of 120 to 29. (The single-payer plan was offered by the author.) The state Senate took up the House-approved version with even less controversy, approving its modified version of the financing law on December 12, 1991, on a voice vote.

A committee of conference was established to iron out numerous language and technical differences between the two versions, especially sections pertaining to access and small group insurance reform. The basic deregulatory thrust was not an issue in conference. The final report was approved in the House and Senate on December 21, 1991, and signed by Governor Weld as Chapter 495 of the Acts of 1991 before the start of the new year. After 16 years of controversy and debate, rate setting went out, not with a bang, but a whimper.

New Jersey

On May 27, 1992, Judge Alfred M. Wolin of the Federal District Court in Newark ruled that the federal Employee Retirement Income Security Act (ERISA) preempted some key provisions of the New Jersey rate setting law, including the shifting of costs to pay for indigent medical care, bad debt, and Medicare funding shortfalls (*United Wire, Metal and Machinery v. Morristown Memorial Hospital,* 793 F. Supp. 524 [DNJ 1992]). The suit had been brought in 1991 by a group of building trades unions that had self-insured health benefit plans. While the ruling called for either elimination of or major structural changes to the Uncompensated Care Trust Fund, nothing in the decision required any changes to the DRG payment system. Even though Judge Wolin's decision was immediately appealed by the state's attorney general (and subsequently overturned in 1993), the ruling led to a rapid consensus for the elimination of rate setting and the preservation of the pool under a different financing formula.

Managed Care. As noted earlier in this chapter, New Jersey was the only one of the four states to have HMO penetration consistently below the national average during the 1980s. As such, the collision between managed care and rate setting resembled more a fender bender than the crash experienced in Massachusetts and New York. The other three states attempted to have clear-cut rules relative to HMO discounting: Massachusetts and New York permitted discounting below the statutory charge levels, and Maryland did not allow discounting except within severely constricted authority. In New Jersey, the rate setting statute nominally did not permit discounts beyond the established payer differentials among Blue Cross, commercial payers, and public payers. But most interview subjects confirmed that discounting was widespread in the state's narrow managed care community. DoH officials were aware of the practice:

> There were limits to how far [discounting] could go on the books. Off the books HMOs were negotiating with hospitals not as part of the DRG system . . . DoH set the rates that hospitals have to charge, but we didn't set the rates that payers had to pay, and nothing in our authority permitted us to stop it. It started to become an issue in the very late 1980s. We had internal discussions about the adverse consequences because it took away our power to equalize. (Interview with Pamela Dickson, New Jersey Department of Health, Trenton, April 18, 1995)

Political Change. In 1990, New Jersey state government faced a severe fiscal crisis as part of the national recession. Democratic Governor James

Florio, who promised no new taxes as part of his 1989 campaign, convinced the legislature to approve major income and sales tax increases in 1990; voter dissatisfaction with the hike was evident in November 1990 when then–little known Republican candidate Christine Todd Whitman narrowly lost to incumbent U.S. Senator Bill Bradley by only two percent of the vote. In November 1991 Republicans won control of both the Senate and the Assembly from the Democrats in a serious rebuff to Florio. The change in political control of the legislature had the same effect on the state's political culture that the election of William Weld as governor had in Massachusetts.

The new Republican speaker of the Assembly had wanted since the early 1980s to eliminate the DRG system:

> I came into office in 1981. I tried to undo the DRG system in 1984 and 1985, but couldn't get the votes, so we let it ride. But even then, we did not believe that the DRG system was going to work . . . When we had the opportunity—and Florio deserves a lot of credit; we were talking to him on a regular basis—we said the DRG program has to go. (Interview with Charles Haytaian, Speaker, New Jersey Assembly, Trenton, April 18, 1995)

Equally clear is that legislative Democrats were not ready to abandon the rate setting system. When the final deregulation and Uncompensated Care Trust Fund legislation cleared both chambers on November 30, 1992, it did so without a single Democratic vote. The former Senate Health Committee chair describes his version of what would have happened had the Republicans not taken control:

> I realized that the system was in trouble in 1988–89. If it worked correctly, the system would have been good. But it was a disaster with the public because constituents would ask us to explain why they were charged $6000 for a hospital stay while their bill said it only cost the hospital $3000. How do you explain that? Once the Republicans took over the majority, we knew that they would try to do it. If they hadn't taken over, the DRG system would have been changed. There was no question but that the system was going to change dramatically if we had stayed in power. Since we didn't stay, we didn't have the opportunity to do our changes. (Interview with Senator Richard Codey, former Senate Health Committee Chair, West Orange, April 19, 1995)

Incomprehensibility/Regulatory Failure. The severe stresses on the regulatory system were described in the previous section, including problems with DRG and hospital charges appearing on bills together. The weight of the regulatory morass appeared to accelerate. By 1991, the Rate Setting Commission's special appeals process, designed to respond to extraordinary cost increases at individual hospitals, was handling as many as 2,000 annual rate appeals from the state's 85 general hospitals, some for items as low as $35.[75] During the latter half of the 1980s, the system's ability to control hospital costs has deteriorated badly; while total hospital revenue per capita rose 72 percent nationally between 1986 and 1991, it rose 100 percent in New Jersey, compared with a 64 percent increase in Pennsylvania and an 86 percent increase in New York.[76]

The Interest Group Landscape. The interest groups responded to Judge Wolin's ruling quickly by forming the New Jersey Health Care Reform Coalition that included hospital, insurer, labor, business, and physician organizations. Called together by the New Jersey Hospital Association, which wanted to discuss how to salvage the Uncompensated Care Pool, the other interests immediately placed the fate of the rate setting system on the table. It became clear that the prior support of prospective hospital rate setting by business, labor, and insurer groups no longer existed. The price of support from the nonhospital groups to fix the problems with uncompensated care was an agreement by the hospitals to deregulate the DRG payment system.

Also emerging from the process was a serious rupture within the NJHA between urban and academic medical centers on one side and suburban hospitals on the other. The former group saw rate setting as critical to their own economic survival, remembering the serious financial instability experienced during the 1970s; during the legislative process, this group officially split from NJHA forming the Urban Hospital Coalition. The community hospitals ultimately sided with the NJ Health Care Reform Coalition, seeing the demise of mandatory rate setting as being in their own financial self-interest.

The movement by business to support deregulation was a recent development and not a long-held position. As recently as March 5, 1992, less than three months before Judge Wolin's ruling and less than 10 months before the enactment of deregulation, New Jersey Business and Industry Association President Bruce Coe gave the following testimony at a legislative oversight hearing:

> . . . if you conclude that regulation is better, and we're studying that very point—by the way, we don't have a conclusion. We're studying all the cost data on regulated versus non-regulated states . . . I'm not sure where we're going to come out on regulation versus lack of regulation. My present guess—and it's about 51 to 49—is we may conclude that deregulation is better.

By the time of Judge Wolin's ruling, the business group had decided to support deregulation, but over an indeterminate time period.

In September, the Coalition—which deliberately excluded administration and legislative participation—announced its proposal for deregulation over a three-year period, and refinancing of the Uncompensated Care Trust Fund to $600 million by reinstituting the one cent increase in the state's sales tax that had been approved by the Democratic-controlled legislature in 1990 and repealed by the Republican-controlled legislature in 1992. Their plan did not receive a respectful hearing:

> The New Jersey Coalition was not helpful at all. They would just have a few press conferences. We threw their proposals right out. I had just decreased the sales tax by a penny. The Legislature and the Governor had said no tax hike or their proposal would be rejected out of hand. They responded to union pressure to include it. (Interview with Charles Haytaian, Speaker, New Jersey Assembly, Trenton, April 18, 1995)

When the compromise legislation agreed to by the governor and the legislative leadership was unveiled—deregulating rate setting with one year of backstop charge controls and refinancing the UCTF by diverting $1.6 billion over three years from the state's Unemployment Insurance Trust Fund—a deep fissure split the AFL-CIO from the Coalition. The labor movement fought hard and unsuccessfully to defeat the diversion; urban and academic hospitals fought unsuccessfully to defeat deregulation. The difference was that serious attention was paid to the opposition of labor; little concern or interest was expressed about the need to salvage the DRG system.

Anticlimax. To address Judge Wolin's ruling, the state could have ended the pool and kept rate setting; alternatively, they could have modified the pool and kept or modified the DRG system. Instead, state policymakers chose to eliminate rate setting and refinance the Uncompensated Care Trust Fund. The likely direction was evident from the day of Judge Wolin's ruling. Governor Florio commented: "The court's decision today, while it needs to be reviewed in detail, would appear to finally serve notice on the Legislature that it must face up to this important issue." He said the current system "is an unwieldy system of DRG averages, hospital markups, Medicare surcharges, and appeals. It is part of a health care system that is seriously flawed and that must be changed" (*Newark Star Ledger,* May 28, 1992). In an interview for this study, Governor Florio placed the court's decision in context:

The court decision was the precipitating event. But it was the desire to reduce health costs that promoted changes in rate setting . . . We had the sense that the initial cost efficiencies from DRGs had already come and were now dissipating because people had learned to game the system. (Interview with Former Governor James Florio, New Brunswick, April 17, 1995)

Of principal concern in May and June to policymakers was less the fate of rate setting than securing the stability of the uncompensated care pool that, beginning in 1991, had become the engine from which the state received major disproportionate share hospital payments from the federal government. In late June, with the approval of Judge Wolin, the state extended the life of the UCTF until November 30 to buy time to arrange a new financing vehicle. Republican Senate Health Chairman Louis Bassano indicated that this was one area where both parties were compelled to work together: "Failure to act jeopardizes more than $1.2 billion in federal money available to the state for hospital reimbursement" (*New York Times,* June 26, 1992).

In November, Florio and legislative leaders announced their agreement to tap the unemployment insurance fund for $500 million per year for three years, along with an additional $100 million in the first year to aid hospitals with large Medicare loads. Prospective rate setting and DRGs were ended, with hospital revenue caps in place for a one-year transition. Statutory requirements guaranteeing "efficient hospitals" their "full financial elements" dating back to 1978 were repealed. Two accompanying bills reformed the market for small group and nongroup insurance products. Governor Florio made it clear that the latter two bills were his personal priorities in attempting to reform the state's health system and to care for a growing number of uninsured residents.

The bills passed in both chambers on November 30, 1992. The deregulation/UCTF bill passed the Assembly by a 48–23 vote, and it passed the Senate by a 21–18 vote, with all Democrats in both chambers voting no. But it was the UCTF funding dispute that engendered vociferous opposition. Except for the urban hospital coalition, there were no voices arguing for the rate setting's continuation. When the legislative battle was over, Sr. Jane Frances Brady, President of St. Joseph's Hospital and leader of the Urban Hospital Coalition commented:

There's no question that the [rate setting] system put us on our feet. It gave us the opportunity to build our programs and to go ahead with an expansion that we badly needed . . . Arguably, the judge's decision required a new financing system to repeal the surcharges, but not the dismantling of the whole rate setting plan. But the approach had grown so unpopular that there was little support for keeping it. (*New York Times,* December 6, 1992)

The ultimate irony of the New Jersey rate setting deregulation came on May 14, 1993, nearly one year after Judge Wolin's ruling that had triggered the hospital financing crisis. On that day, a Federal Appellate Court reversed Judge Wolin's ruling, upholding the state's appeal. Also, in April 1995, the U.S. Supreme Court issued a unanimous opinion upholding the legality of broad-based surcharges in a case challenging New York's rate setting system. One other noteworthy post-deregulation development: in November 1993, Governor James Florio was defeated in his bid for reelection by Republican Christine Todd Whitman, thus completing the transformation in New Jersey's political culture.

New York
Unlike Massachusetts and New Jersey, which deregulated in the early part of the 1990s, New York maintained its rate setting system until the beginning of 1997. Nonetheless, the same indicators used to describe the Massachusetts and New Jersey experiences also help to frame the New York process.

The Managed Care Collision. Prior to 1985, for-profit HMOs were considered illegal in New York state under the same statute (Article 28 of the Public Health Law) that prevented for-profits from owning acute care hospitals. Under the threat of litigation that year by investor-owned HMOs, the legislature explicitly permitted for-profit HMOs to operate in New York. There is disagreement among interviewees as to whether HMOs were permitted to discount below state set charges under the NYPHRM I and II per diem arrangements, but there is no dispute that little of it—if any—was going on prior to 1988.[77] In that year, the case-based NYPHRM III statute explicitly permitted HMOs to make negotiated rate agreements with hospitals, subject to the approval of the Commissioner of Health who was required to determine that the arrangements "will result in lower costs to the general hospital and payments approximate to costs" (Chapter 2, Laws of 1988, Section 2807-c, 2(b)(i)).

The DoH official formerly in charge of rate setting remembers the review process well:

The HMOs would send us the proposed contracts for review. One time, I got one in the mail from a hospital, with a little side note saying, "I'm sure that you're going to disapprove this contract because it doesn't meet your test." I wrote back saying it must meet the test or you wouldn't have signed it. I said, "don't use the state as the heavy when you can't negotiate this yourself" . . . In general, we treated the parties like consenting adults. (Interview with Ray Sweeney, former DoH, now HANYS, Albany, July 21, 1995)

Since 1988, HMO penetration had grown rapidly, particularly among investor-owned HMOs, and the level of discounting between HMOs and hospitals was reported to be high by all knowledgeable observers by the mid-1990s. In this context, the Blue Cross plans, as happened in Massachusetts, found themselves at a distinct disadvantage tied to a statutory discount off charges that was much less than HMOs were winning in the market. The continuing financial instability of Blue Cross plans added a special urgency to the need to create a more level playing field.

Also similar to Massachusetts, New York policymakers began in 1995 aggressively moving Medicaid recipients into managed care programs. In writing the fiscal year 1996 budget in June 1995, administration officials were successful in severing the 20-year link that existed between Medicaid and Blue Cross/NYPHRM charges, freezing the so-called trim factor for the public program. A longtime participant regarded this move as a watershed:

It's now just private insurance—meaning Blue Cross and whoever buys commercial indemnity insurance—that is part of the system. So on the price setting side, that part of NYPHRM is diminishing and there is little opportunity to move back. The question is how fast do you want it to go away. (Interview with James Tallon, former Assembly Majority Leader and Health Chair, Portland, OR, August 6, 1995)

The New York Assembly's Health Chairman also recognized managed care evolution as critical in understanding the rationale for NYPHRM's elimination:

The key block pulled out from under the system and leading to its collapse has been the HMO negotiated rate provision accompanied by their enormous increase in penetration in the State . . . They have rapidly grown from being a footnote to being the dominant player in the field, and now hospitals find themselves in a situation where most of their customers pay a negotiated rate designed to barely cover their costs. (Interview with Richard Gottfried, Chair, Assembly Health Care Committee, New York City, July 20, 1995)

Political Change. Decades of political stability that characterized New York came to an abrupt end in November 1994 when Democratic Governor Mario Cuomo was defeated in his bid for reelection by Republican State Senator George Pataki. Unlike the most recent Republic governor, Nelson Rockefeller, the new governor ran on themes of limited government, no new taxes, and deregulation. While NYPHRM's fate was not an explicit topic of discussion in the campaign, a phasing out of New York's rate setting system was fully consistent with the new governor's general perspective.

The change in administrations brought sweeping personnel change to the New York Department of Health for the first time in nearly two decades. Prior to the 1994 election, DoH officials had scheduled a meeting with officials from Maryland, Massachusetts, and New Jersey to discuss their respective experiences with hospital rate setting. By June 1995, all but one of the 15 New York DoH officials present at the November 22, 1994, session had left state government. At the session, some officials candidly admitted that prior to the electoral upset, they anticipated "tinkering" and modest changes in the successor statute to NYPHRM V.[78]

Instead, the entire rate setting system was placed under review by the new Health Commissioner, Barbara DeBuono, and the legislature. In December 1995, a 19-member Task Force, chaired by DeBuono, recommended to the governor that "New York should move toward a system of negotiated rates for all non-Medicare payors."[79] In March 1996, Governor Pataki proposed deregulation to the legislature along with substantial cuts in financing for medical education and indigent care. In July 1996 the Assembly and Senate sent to Governor Pataki legislation to end most of NYPHRM's rate setting functions by January 1, 1997. As occurred in the course of New Jersey's deregulation process, the key battles involved funding for uncompensated care and other important health system needs. The final legislative version restored much of the funding for indigent care and graduate medical education that Governor Pataki had sought to reduce. In all, the final version included nearly $2.6 billion in financing for public goods during the first year of the act. Key hospital organizations that indicated support for deregulation only if sufficient public goods funding was provided expressed satisfaction with the final result. What is clear, however, is that the change in administration precipitated an entirely different dialogue than would have occurred under continued Democratic control of the Governor's Office.

Incomprehensibility/Regulatory Failure. The specific problems with the New York regulatory system were described in the previous section, particularly relative to the RAND assessment of the system's incomprehensible incentives and disincentives. The DeBuono report notes the successes of the system in slowing the rate of growth of hospital costs in the early 1980s, in protecting the financial solvency of vulnerable institutions, and in serving a large population of medically indigent persons. Its conclusions about the current state of NYPHRM reflected a consensus opinion among policymakers about the system:

(1) NYPHRM does not provide the economic discipline to contain costs.
(2) NYPHRM affects a shrinking proportion of the market, thereby limiting its effectiveness.
(3) NYPHRM maintains excess hospital capacity.
(4) NYPHRM provides incentives to train too many physicians.
(5) NYPHRM supports uncompensated care, but the funds are inappropriately targeted.[80]

The RAND Report recognized the extent to which the New York system is simply out of sync with the current needs and requirements: "The health care environment has changed substantially in the past decade, so much so that even New York itself probably would not end up with the same NYPHRM methodology if it were starting from scratch today."[81] The preamble to the deregulation legislation expressed a similar view:

The legislature finds that New York, like the rest of the nation, is experiencing dramatic changes in the organization and delivery of health care services. These changes are occurring as a result of market forces such as the growth of managed care, the integration of providers across the continuum of health care, and the significant shift in the locus of care from inpatient to outpatient setting. In light of these changes in the market, the legislature finds that the inpatient reimbursement methodology established pursuant to the New York prospective hospital reimbursement methodology [NYPHRM] no longer meets the goals for today's health care delivery system. (New York Health Care Reform Act of 1996, Preamble)

The Changing Interest Group Landscape. On May 9, 1995 (14 months before the legislative enactment of deregulation), the New York Council on Health Care Financing convened a meeting of council members along with representatives from New York hospitals, business, Blue Cross, health maintenance organizations, physicians, and consumers to discuss the need to transition to a new health care financing system. All the groups had been supporters and collaborative architects of the five versions of

NYPHRM. At the hearing, with the exception of the hospital representatives who wanted guarantees concerning uncompensated care, graduate medical education, and hospital capital support, all other representatives endorsed the deregulation of the rate setting aspects of NYPHRM. The position of the hospital representatives was not to extol the virtues of continued rate regulation, but rather to argue for the add-ons that have become part of NYPHRM and to cast doubts on an unfettered embrace of free market economics in the health care arena. One participant at the hearing recalled Council Chairman Senator Michael Tully asking: "Can you feel the tectonic plate shifting?" (Recalled by Gerry Billings, State Communities Aid Association, Albany, June 30, 1995).

The year 1995 had been a year of other developments in rate setting that are unusual given New York's regulatory history and culture. On March 2, 1995, key officials from the Business Council of New York State and the State Communities Aid Association (a leading low-income advocacy organization in New York) joined together to send a letter to Governor Pataki urging: "it is time to abandon both rate regulation and the economic components of the certificate of need system." That same month, the Life Insurance Council of New York State (LICONY) and the State Communities Aid Association joined together to release a report whose title is self-explanatory: "NYPHRM's Paradox: How New York's Attempts to Stabilize Hospital Finances Lead to More Uninsured, Increased Health Benefit Restrictions, Reduced Hospital Utilization, and Weakened Hospitals."

By mid-1995, when the New York interviews for this study were conducted, it was not possible to find a single interest group that indicated any degree of support for continuing the rate setting functions of NYPHRM. There were strong voices advocating for remedial solutions to the needs for uncompensated care, graduate medical education, capital support, and the broad range of add-ons that have been funded through the Uncompensated Care Trust Funds. But there was not a visible supporter of continued rate setting among the hospitals, Blue Cross, HMOs, commercial insurers, physicians, labor, business, or consumer/citizen groups.

Anticlimax. NYPHRM V had been scheduled to sunset at the end of December 1995. During the budget debates that lasted into June of that year, the legislature agreed to continue the system for an additional six months to the end of June 1996 when its fate could be determined as part of the broader health agenda facing state government. In some critical respects, the New York situation in 1995 paralleled that of New Jersey in 1992, when the decision to deregulate rate setting was peripheral to the central debate on the future funding mechanism for uncompensated care. Though the final decision on NYPHRM was put off until

1996, the fate of the system became apparent during the course of intensive discussions throughout 1995. The lack of support for NYPHRM demonstrated by the interest groups was also reflected by key policymakers:

> For me, some of the most important aspects of the system have been its ability to force payers to contribute to a variety of what I consider socially important activities such as graduate medical education, payment for bad debt and charity care, subsidies for the children's health insurance program, paying for capital costs of hospitals, and the rest . . . What I support is not so much the price regulatory aspects as much as the system's add-ons or taxes that it requires the payers to pay for. (Interview with Richard Gottfried, Assembly Health Care Committee Chairman, New York City, July 20, 1995)

Gottfried's Senate counterpart was equally blunt:

> There will be no more NYPHRMs. It's just outmoded. (Interview with Kemp Hannon, Senate Health Care Committee Chairman, quoted in *BNA Pension and Benefits Reporter,* July 10, 1995)

On September 12, 1996, hospital, insurer, HMO, and labor representatives joined with Governor Pataki and legislative leaders from both parties at Mount Sinai Hospital in Manhattan to celebrate the signing of the deregulation statute. Having made satisfactory deals regarding the shape of the new health financing system, no voices were heard mourning the demise of the regulatory structure that loomed awesomely for a generation over the New York hospital system.

Revival

Use of the term "revival" to describe developments in Maryland is more speculative than definitive. It suggests that a unique set of circumstances has enabled Maryland's form of mandatory rate setting to survive the same challenges that have undermined the systems in the other three states; it further suggests that the Maryland model potentially may prosper in a new era.

Maryland

> The attitude in Annapolis is that motherhood, apple pie, and rate setting all go in the same boat. (Interview with Robert Kowal, CEO, Greater Baltimore Medical Center, Baltimore, June 23, 1995)

It's the sacred cow of Maryland. (Interview with Deborah Rivkin, Executive Director, League of Life and Health Insurers, Annapolis, June 20, 1995)

It takes on a "salute the flag" connotation. (Interview with Geni Dunnells, Executive Director, Maryland Association of HMOs, Annapolis, June 22, 1995)

The Noncollision with Managed Care. Maryland's approach to HMO discounting was unique among the four subject states. Massachusetts rate setting administrators permitted wide-open discounting of rates for HMOs from its inception; New York rate setting regulators attempted to control the practice through Health Department oversight; and New Jersey rate setting authorities unsuccessfully attempted to prevent negotiated discounts from undermining its system. Through tight enforcement, Maryland rate setting regulators largely have prevented their network of HMOs from engaging in discounting practices beyond the four percent legally permitted under HSCRC regulations.

As has been shown, this regulatory brake does not appear to have discouraged the development and growth of HMOs in Maryland, which in 1993 had the fourth highest penetration rate among the 50 states. While all interview subjects were aware of the strong rate of HMO growth, none had certainty in their explanations. The large number of federal and state employees and the (incorrect) perception of a high rate of hospital admissions were the most common responses. A number of subjects simply shrugged with uncertainty and did not view the high penetration rate as a positive feature of the state's health system.

The presence of for-profit HMOs in the state has made a difference in establishing a new set of voices that now openly question the rationale for continuing the mandatory rate setting system. The most outspoken of these in 1995 was Jeff Emerson, head of New York Life's Health Plus HMO, who points to his and other plans' steady diversion of patients to Washington, DC, hospitals as evidence that the Maryland hospital system is more expensive than it need be in the new managed care environment. A plan representative outlines New York Life's outlook:

If it were less expensive in Maryland, we have very smart people who would figure that out. But that's not the situation. It's not less expensive here . . . Many of my colleagues would love to get rid of it [rate setting]. We murmur it to each other. But they think it would be unrealistic or don't want to spend the political chits. We all have a delicate relationship because we all contract with the state. And there are thousands of state employees who belong to our plans. (Interview with Thomas Goddard, Director of Legislative and Regulatory Affairs, New York Life Health Plus, Green Belt, June 23, 1995)

The pressures from the managed care environment have spilled over into the hospital community. One manifestation of this impact is that some hospitals have not used the full charge authority provided to them by the HSCRC to raise rates to maximum allowable levels. Banking of excess charge authority is becoming commonplace.

Political Stability. In November 1994, in the closest gubernatorial race in the nation, Democrat Parris Glendening defeated Republican Ellen Sauerbray, sustaining the long-term Democratic hold on that office, the legislature, and the state's political culture that was mentioned in the Walker/Gray innovation indices earlier in this chapter. With a high proportion of state and federal workers, along with the highest proportion of African-Americans outside of the Deep South, Maryland has long been known as one of the most reliably liberal states in the nation (*Washington Post National Weekly Edition,* November 13–19, 1995).

This culture has been reflected not only in support for rate setting, but also in the fact that the state has the highest number of mandated health benefits in its insurance statutes of any state in the nation. It is also reflected in the steady pace of intervention in the health sector by the legislature, whether in placing new restrictions on managed care practices such as so-called drive-through maternity deliveries, or in moving to make physician costs part of the rate setting program.

Interviewees were divided on the question of whether a Sauerbray election would have changed the outlook for continuation of all-payer hospital rate setting. But what is undeniable is that the political shift that occurred in the other states where broad deregulation reached the public agenda—with party changes in the governor's office in Massachusetts and New York, and legislative changes in New Jersey—has not happened in Maryland.

Regulatory Stability and Flexibility. Once again, a sharp contrast can be viewed between Maryland and the other states in the management of the regulatory process. The HSCRC has used its statutory flexibility to develop alternative methods of rate determination and payments that allow the system to evolve with changes in the market. Because system changes in the other three states required legislative approval, the other states were unable to engage in broad experimentation at the regulatory level. Indeed, the basic regulatory tools used by the HSCRC today—the Guaranteed Inpatient Revenue and Total Patient Revenue systems—began in the early 1980s as experimental ventures. The most important experiment in recent years has allowed hospitals to develop capitated models that do not undermine the basic tenets of the all-payer system. This is a challenging venture that represents a markedly different vision of the structure and role of hospital rate regulation. HSCRC documents explain the rationale for this new policy initiative:

> The assumption of risk by hospitals is both appropriate and desirable. Hospitals can assume risk and still adhere to the fundamental principals of the Maryland system. In fact, some new payment systems can complement the rate setting system. The rate setting system has been successful in controlling hospital charges per admission, but it has been less successful in controlling the use rates of hospital services. This outcome confirms a belief held by the HSCRC that physicians, not hospitals, dictate admission rates. Payment systems that seek to align the incentives of hospitals and physicians in order to enhance efficiency and the appropriate use of services should redress this shortcoming. (*Alternative Method of Rate Determination: Overview of Proposed Policy:* HSCRC, July 5, 1995)

This latest round of experimentation began in earnest in 1994 with HSCRC approval for an experiment at North Arundel Hospital to deviate from the commission-approved rates for up to 25,000 patients who are covered by area HMOs and under contract with physicians (*Baltimore Sun,* March 3, 1994). Supporters of the HSCRC view this new round of experimentation both as a sign of strength and as vitally important for the future stability of the Maryland system:

> This will very rapidly evolve into a new system as we transition quite rapidly from fee for service into global payments . . . Once we were looking at a ten year horizon for these changes. We now think that in two to three years, we will be where we thought we would be in ten years . . . We're at the cusp of a revolutionary change. (Interview with Larry Lawrence, Executive Vice President, Maryland Hospital Association, Lutherville, June 21, 1995)

Not all are convinced that these experiments with capitation are a sign of strength in the system:

> If they opposed these changes outright, they might have enemies that they really don't need. It keeps the wolf away from the door. (Interview with Livio Broccolino, Chief Legal Officer, Maryland Blue Cross, Owings Mills, June 22, 1995)

Meanwhile, Maryland hospitals are engaged in mergers, affiliations, joint ventures, and other new market strategies, the same pattern visible in all 50 states today. In May 1994, for example, Johns Hopkins Hospital announced plans with seven other hospitals to establish the Atlantic Health Alliance, bringing together 15,000 workers, 4,500 physicians, and $1.3 billion in revenues—all for the purpose of competing more effectively for HMO contracts (*Baltimore Sun,* May 6, 1994).

The Stable Interest Group Landscape. Any individual or group seeking to deregulate the Maryland rate setting system has a substantial obstacle to overcome in the form of the federal Medicare waiver that has been granted to the state since 1978 and that has been part of federal law since 1980. Because the waiver requires the federal government to pay a proportionate share of the state's uncompensated care obligation, the value of the waiver is estimated by the HSCRC at about $200 million, or half of the state's $400 million bill for hospital indigent care. That means that any move to deregulate starts out $200 million in the red as compared to the costs of maintaining the current system. Interviewees were well aware of the importance of the waiver to the state and to the continuation of hospital rate setting:

> It [the waiver] is crucial, vital, the centerpiece of the system. (Interview with Robert Murray, Maryland Health Cost Review Commission, Baltimore, June 21, 1995)

> If we were ever to lose the waiver, we would lose the regulatory system. (Interview with Ernie Crofoot, Maryland AFL-CIO, Bowie, June 22, 1995)

> For several years, they had to go to Congress to change the base . . . they said plainly that if we didn't change the base, we would lose the waiver . . . If you lost the waiver, the reason for the regulatory system would cease. (Interview with Geni Dunnells, Executive Director, Maryland Association of HMOs, Annapolis, June 22, 1995)

> This system has its roots in the waiver. They're inextricably tied. (Interview with Thomas Goddard, New York Life Health Plus HMO, Green Belt, June 23, 1995)

> It's [the waiver] very important. If we lost the waiver, the system would start to disintegrate . . . but the $200 million is not the reason that we maintain the system. (Interview with Casper Taylor, Speaker, Maryland Assembly, Annapolis, June 19, 1995)

Nonetheless, calls have been issued for a renewed look at Maryland's approach to hospital and health sector regulation. In a February 6, 1995, letter to Governor Glendening, Wayne Mills, Chairman of the Board of the Maryland Chamber of Commerce, called for "a fresh approach . . . to questions surrounding the crisis in the regulation of health care in Maryland." Mills urged the appointment of "a consumer-oriented commission" to define the appropriate level of regulation "in an industry undergoing change as rapidly as the health care industry."

The chamber's government affairs representative indicates that the organization is more frequently raising questions about the future of the rate setting system:

> We're moving to an environment that is more cost driven than ever before . . . My discussions with Murray and Cohen [HSCRC] indicate that they know it has to change. It has been because of that they have been giving waivers to hospitals to try different arrangements . . . The concern is always how much better could it be? (Interview with Miles Cole, Maryland Chamber of Commerce, Annapolis, June 24, 1995)

While the call for a reexamination was tentative, it was also heeded by the governor and by members of the legislature.

Anticlimax. A familiar dynamic in the new health system involves out-of-hospital health facilities performing profitable services that were once only done in the hospitals, and doing those services for far less than hospitals' real costs. In 1994 in Maryland, the spotlight landed on the 85 one-day surgical centers taking slices of hospitals' most lucrative procedures. Because the surgical centers are not part of the rate setting system, they are permitted to charge whatever the market will bear and to cut prices far below approved hospital charge levels. Additionally, the "surgi-centers" avoid many of the obligations, such as community benefits, uncompensated care, and open-door policies for the medically indigent, that are thrust upon the acute care hospitals. As the market share of these new facilities began to grow in the early 1990s, hospitals began to demand action from state policymakers.

In November 1994, a special Task Force appointed by then-Governor William Donald Schaefer recommended that one-day surgical centers be obligated to share with hospitals the expenses of uncompensated care to uninsured persons (*Daily Record,* November 22, 1994). Rate setting and hospital allies in the legislature filed bills for the 1995 session, chiefly Senate Bill 639 relative to the Licensing of Freestanding Ambulatory Care Facilities (defined as ambulatory surgical facilities, endoscopy facilities,

facilities utilizing major medical equipment, kidney dialysis centers, and birthing centers), to create a special licensure category for freestanding surgical centers and also to "address the problem of discrimination based on payer class. Ambulatory care facilities should be required to provide access to all patients, regardless of their payer or insurance status as is the case with hospital based ambulatory facilities," according to hospital industry testimony (testimony by Jane Stanek, Senior Director, Government Relations, Johns Hopkins Health Systems, March 2, 1995).

The final version approved by the legislature and signed into law as Chapter 499 by Governor Glendening on May 25, 1995, was vastly changed in the legislative process. The new law requires only a study of the surgical center licensing issue and, responding to critiques issued by the Maryland Chamber of Commerce and other groups, "an evaluation of the all-payor system . . . involving the Governor, the General Assembly, the Secretary of Health and Mental Hygiene, the State Insurance Commissioner, the Health Resources Planning Commission, the Health Services Cost Review Commission, the Health Care Access and Cost Commission, the Maryland Chamber of Commerce, hospital employee unions, and other organized labor groups, health care providers, health insurers, managed care organizations, and health care recipients" (Chapter 499, 1995 Acts and Resolves).

While calling for this review, the legislature also endorsed a preamble that states that "the all-payor hospital rate regulatory system is the cornerstone of Maryland's longstanding history of pioneering, innovative public policy relation to health care delivery that is tailored to the unique needs of the citizens of this State . . . this system serves as a national model that has successfully demonstrated that the cooperative establishment of appropriate incentives can yield enormous social benefits as well as successfully control costs . . . Maryland hospital costs have gone from 25 percent above the national average in 1977, to more than 8 percent below the national average in 1994 and the reduction has saved government, business, labor and consumers in Maryland more than $10 billion . . ." (Chapter 499, 1995 Acts and Resolves).

Thus, the call for a review and assessment of Maryland rate setting was strongly couched in language indicating strong support for the structure and principles of the current system. This assessment was reiterated repeatedly in interviews with key policymakers who see no major changes in the offing:

> If it ain't broke, don't fix it. We feel very protective of our rate setting program . . . There's a lot of trust that policymakers have put into that commission [HSCRC]. (Interview with Senator Paula Hollinger, Sen-

ate Chair, Joint Committee on Health Care Delivery and Finance, Annapolis, June 20, 1995)

We continue rate setting because we believe that we've got a model regulatory system for the country. (Interview with Casper Taylor, Speaker, Maryland House of Delegates, Annapolis, June 19, 1995)

One other related issue that is currently facing Maryland policymakers is the treatment of uncompensated care in the system. Unlike the structures in Massachusetts, New Jersey, and New York that pool funds for redistribution among more needy hospitals, Maryland's rules simply allowed each hospital to build its uncompensated care costs into its allowable charge structure. Thus uncompensated care costs add about 15 percent to bills at Liberty and the University of Maryland Hospitals (both inner city), 11 percent at Johns Hopkins, only 5.3 percent at Greater Baltimore Medical Center, and 3.5 percent at suburban Towson Hospital. In 1996, the HSCRC moved to amend the system to add an additional surcharge to hospital bills that would be used to provide additional subsidies to hospitals (mostly inner city) that provide disproportionate amounts of uncompensated care. While some surburban hospital officials grumbled, the MHA endorsed the proposal that takes full effect in 1997 (*Baltimore Sun,* April 27, 1995).

Overall, Maryland stands in sharp distinction from the other three subject states on the critical factors used throughout this study to explain the deregulation process: managed care discounting, political change, regulatory stability, and interest group support.

Summary Comments
The twin themes of interests and ideas will be dissected in greater detail in the subsequent chapters of this study. While interest groups are strongly involved throughout the lengthy histories of the rate setting programs, we can observe that the predicted patterns and hypotheses of the theory of economic regulation are hard to find. The predicted cartels, so central to the theory of economic regulation, are not at all apparent in the four states, with different interests presenting themselves as potential candidates during each separate phase, including the hospitals, the regulators, the state health purchasing agencies, the insurance industry, and the business community. The only groups that can readily be dismissed from the list of candidates are the labor and the consumer communities.

Regarding policy ideas and the punctuated equilibrium model, we can observe a strong policy idea influence at the birth and decline stages, with less importance during the growth and maturity stages. This disjuncture is consistent with the predictions of the punctuated equilibrium model. Once the policy monopoly and the prevailing ideas are established, the debate on ideas moves to the background. New ideas germinate slowly, and not necessarily in the full view of the public. To determine the fullest applicability of both models, we must return to an examination of the specific hypotheses associated with each theory.

CHAPTER 4

Interests and the Fate of Hospital
Rate Setting

> There are a number of forces that could come together
> that could destabilize everything. The loss would put the
> hospital industry at grave risk. If you have deregulation,
> then it's like road kill—everyone's in here plucking this
> piece or that. (Interview with Dr. Martin Wasserman,
> Commissioner, Maryland Department of Health and
> Mental Hygiene, Baltimore, June 23, 1995)

It should be clear from the preceding case histories that interest groups
have played an important role in rate setting systems throughout their life
cycle. To suggest anything else would be naive. Understanding the actions,
strategies, and *ideas* of interest groups is critical in understanding the
moves and motives of the policymakers. Of specific importance in this
chapter is the extent to which movements by various interest groups led to
the demise of rate setting in three states and the continuation in one other.
We also examine whether the behavior of interests conforms to the predictions of the theory of economic regulation and seek the clearest answers to
the theory's applicability.

The chapter has two parts. First, we review the actions, strategies, and
roles of the major interest groups in turn, from the perspective of all four
states, and during all four time phases. The specific interests discussed
include hospitals, Blue Cross, commercial insurers, health maintenance
organizations, business, labor, consumers, and state government in its
dual roles as regulator and as purchaser of health services. The specific
activities of legislative and executive officials as setters of health policy will
be left for chapter 5, our examination of policy ideas. Physicians are not
included among examined groups because their role in rate setting was not
significant in any of the states.

In the second part, we examine the hypotheses outlined in chapter 2
relative to the theory of economic regulation. Each hypothesis is examined
in turn to determine whether evidence supports or does not support its
validity as an explainer of rate setting policy and politics in the states. The
hypotheses are specified in table 4.1.

Interest Groups' Role in Rate Setting and Its Demise

Hospitals

The discussion of hospitals as the first interest group is not coincidental. Hospitals must be at the center of rate setting discussions if the theory of economic regulation is to hold. As the regulated "cartel," hospitals should have engineered the creation of mandatory rate setting by compliant legislators who were responding to hospital needs. Hospital interests should come first in the distribution of rate setting benefits—before consumers, insurers, government, business, labor, or others. Deregulation should occur for any of several possible reasons: because the objective benefits of rate setting to hospitals have changed, because hospitals were unsuccessful in obtaining needed benefits from the system, because hospitals were politically divided, or because other groups have developed or organized to defeat hospital efforts to maintain the system.

In this analysis, we examine the evidence presented in chapter 3 to seek confirmation of the theoretical hypotheses. One immediate and striking feature of the rate setting case histories from the four states is the variety among them in every phase and on nearly every facet. Perhaps the only consistency among the four states during the four phases in rate setting's life cycle is that hospitals have been central players in each one of the 16 possible cells. Sometimes they achieved their objectives, sometimes not, and sometimes results were mixed. But hospital leaders never allowed their institutions to be taken for granted.

Presented in table 4.2 below is an evaluation of the success record of hospitals in the four states in meeting their objectives during each segment

TABLE 4.1. Theory of Economic Regulation Hypotheses

E1:   Rate setting should work to the benefit of hospitals more than to consumers

E2:   Shifts in the configuration of interest groups supporting and opposing rate setting's continuation should accompany deregulation

E3:   Similar shifts in identifiable support should not be observable in Maryland where rate setting has not been deregulated.

E4:   Elected officials should only play a secondary role in policy decisions about rate setting, with key interest groups setting the policy agenda.

E5:   Identifiable shifts in overt political support from affected interests to key legislative leaders should be identifiable in the deregulation process.

in the life cycle model, indicating whether hospitals achieved their objectives (+) , lost out (–), or experienced a mixed outcome (0) in shaping the direction of their respective state rate setting programs to their own advantage. Hospitals are viewed as having achieved their objectives if the main public policy decisions during the period were consistent with their own aims.

An alternative subtitle to this book could easily have been "Except for Maryland . . ." because—except for Maryland—the results for hospitals in each state under rate setting have been mostly negative or mixed. The two clearly victorious periods in Massachusetts and New Jersey were followed not coincidentally by deregulation. The key period in New York when hospitals attained their objectives was the deregulation period as hospitals were able to negotiate significant financial accommodations. The rationale for the "grade" in each cell is provided in turn.

Birth. Examining the birthing phase of rate setting in the four states, we observe that the Maryland Hospital Association not only supported its establishment, but wrote the enabling legislation in its offices. However, that support came only after major structural changes in the makeup of the association, changes not replicated in any of the other 49 states. Prior to the change, the CEO-dominated MHA vigorously opposed rate setting legislation dating back to the first bill filed in 1967. The newly organized and trustee-dominated MHA in 1971 supported rate setting to avert stronger federal controls, to develop a more effective model than retrospective cost-based reimbursement, and to free themselves from the yoke of the arbitrary rate setting determinations made by Blue Cross of Maryland. *(Grade: +)*

Massachusetts hospitals did not seek rate setting controls; rather they were compelled to swallow Blue Cross and Medicaid charge controls in 1975 and 1976 as an alternative to the Dukakis-proposed charge freeze that they fought. They successfully opposed the freeze. But in the process, legislative leaders became convinced of the need to address structurally a gaping budget deficit and rapidly increasing Medicaid costs by imposing major controls on hospital finances. *(Grade: –)*

TABLE 4.2. **Hospital Experience under Rate Setting**

	Birth	Growth	Maturity	Decline/Revival
MD	+	+	+	+
MA	–	0	+	0
NJ	–	–	+	0
NY	–	–	0	+

New Jersey hospitals were anxious in the early 1970s to win adoption of certificate-of-need controls that would limit entry of for-profit hospitals to their state. In this respect, the New Jersey Hospital Association's activities most resemble those of Stigler's cartel. But the hospital community opposed the budget controls that were part of the state's bargain. State officials were determined to hold down growth in Blue Cross premiums, whose explosive increases were attributed to hospital cost inflation. Once established, the NJHA did their best to direct and subvert the budget controls, but there is simply no evidence to suggest that hospitals sought the establishment of these controls. *(Grade: –)*

As described in chapter 3, the Healthcare Association of New York State (HANYS) actively opposed the establishment of controls on them for Blue Cross and Medicaid charges in 1969 but was unable to prevent legislative enactment because of long-standing state concerns about the growth in Medicaid and hospital costs that dated back to at least 1964. *(Grade: –)*

Growth. Because Maryland hospitals had been central partners in the creation of rate setting, their influence can be seen in the implementation phase leading up to attainment of the Medicare all-payer waiver. The selection of a hospital CEO as the first chairman of the HSCRC lends further weight to the suggestion of cartel-like behavior. Two facts undermine the cartel conclusion. First, the initial implementation period witnessed a spate of legal suits challenging many aspects of the system, with most of these legal actions initiated by hospitals or groups of hospitals dissatisfied with the new regulatory framework. Second, it is during this phase that the system began its steady 19-year descent in hospital costs per admission and per capita. A central assertion of the theory of economic regulation is that the regulated industry should reap more financial benefits under regulation than without it. While Maryland's performance during this phase may not rule out the applicability of the model, it certainly leaves its applicability open to question. Nonetheless, the MHA maintained support for the system during this period and achieved its key objectives. *(Grade: +)*

A key feature of the economic regulation model suggests that the regulatory agency will enable firms to act as a cartel, raising prices, restricting output, and providing firms with higher profits than if regulation did not exist. But the growth period saw Massachusetts hospitals locked in intense and protracted struggle with state administrators, Blue Cross, commercial carriers, and a newly assertive business leadership over the rules of the system. In this and subsequent periods, hospitals attempted end runs around cost-conscious regulators by seeking more favorable treatment from friendly legislators. Rather than victory, the fierce political struggle that culminated in the enactment of the all-payer system under Chapter 372 was the best deal hospitals could win under the circumstances. The advent of national prospective payment in Medicare provided hospitals with a short-lived rationale to embrace all-payer rate setting to avert the threat of more intrusive federal restrictions. But for hospitals, it was making the best of a bad bargain. *(Grade: 0)*

New Jersey hospitals had been able to turn the lemons of state-mandated budget controls into the lemonade of a NJHA-run operation that established ineffectual limits on their growth. But political embarrassment over these loose controls led to the imposition of the state-run SHARE program's strict financial limits and subsequent financial deterioration for urban hospitals. Hospitals reluctantly agreed to the imposition of the nation's first DRG controls to ameliorate the worst aspects of the SHARE program, and—similar to hospitals in Massachusetts and New York— agreed to seek a Medicare waiver to avert feared federal reimbursement changes. *(Grade: −)*

New York hospitals saw a severe financial crisis during their growth period as state regulators and lawmakers used their newly established controls to ratchet down both Medicaid and Blue Cross reimbursement levels. It was little comfort to them that commercial insurers and self-pay patients faced their own drastic financial squeezes. The process that led to the establishment of NYPHRM softened some of the harsher aspects of the prior reimbursement scheme, but did so with a regulatory model that controlled all of their charge authority, not just that of Blue Cross and Medicaid. This phase led to the creation of the eight regional uncompensated care pools that helped hospitals to address charity care and bad debt needs. However, it was not until the maturity phase that the crisis for hospitals began to abate. *(Grade: −)*.

Maturity. Maryland's progress during this phase reflected stability and consensus among the key constituencies inside and outside of government. The major threat to hospitals was the potential loss of the dollars associated with the Medicare waiver. Health care reform appeared frequently on the state's policy agenda, but rate setting was seen as part of the solution, not as part of the problem. Hospitals were major supporters of rate setting during this period. The steady decrease in the rate of growth in hospital charges relative to the national average, however, undermines the cartel thesis. *(Grade: +)*

This phase in Massachusetts consists of two parts. The early phase was one of tight controls on hospital charges. But hospitals organized strongly for the political cycle that ended with the enactment of Chapter

23 in 1988 and won major financial concessions that erased most of the decreases in hospital spending growth that had been achieved earlier in the decade. The Chapter 23 phase was one of major financial infusion for most hospitals—but a victory won from legislators over the opposition of administration officials. *(Grade: +)*

The New Jersey experience during this phase mirrors that of Massachusetts: early successes by the DRG system in holding down hospital cost inflation, followed by massive reinflation as regulators and legislators lost their capacity to hold down system costs. Though Massachusetts's erosion can be tied directly to the decisions of legislators in response to hospital lobbying, the New Jersey erosion can be attributed more to regulatory failure and the inability of system managers to cope with the volume of appeals, retrospective settlements, and structural problems with the Uncompensated Care Trust fund. *(Grade: +)*

The NYPHRM system saw its severest financial pressures in the late 1980s during NYPHRM III, a response to the more generous levels of reimbursement permitted in version II. Policymakers came back and pumped substantial new levels of cash into acute hospitals in versions IV and V, leaving New York with the worst of all possible worlds—hospitals with the highest costs in the nation and the weakest financial condition of any comparable set of institutions as well. *(Grade: 0)*

Revival/Decline. Maryland faces questions about the future of its rate setting system with a strong base of political support and a track record of achievement and flexibility. A strong base of support, though not unanimity, exists among hospitals in support of the system. A large part of this consensus is held together by the estimated $200 million in benefits to the state through continuation of the Medicare waiver. As one longtime observer and framer of the system observed:

> There's no important political voice that wants deregulation to happen. (Interview with Eugene Feinblatt, attorney, Baltimore, June 21, 1995)

(Grade: +)

During Massachusetts's deregulation phase, hospitals had a difficult time deciding on a direction. In December 1990, MHA trustees voted to endorse continued regulation under a Maryland-style framework. During 1991, with the new Weld administration sounding strong pro-market themes, leaders of teaching institutions began to promote a deregulation/market strategy. But other institutions were less certain and feared the economic ramifications of competition. Ultimately, MHA leaders backed deregulation in the fall of 1991, when the likely direction was clear, and only after winning the removal of elements in the legislation not to their liking. The House Chair of the Health Care Committee gives her impressions of hospital political strategy:

> One thing I've learned about hospital CEOs is that they'll go whichever way they think they're going to be successful. They knew that the Weld Administration was hell-bent on this. They thought they had better get on board rather than to buck it . . . they saw the writing on the wall. (Interview with Carmen Buell, House Chair, Joint Committee on Health Care, Boston, December 28, 1994)

The former president of the MHA describes his organization's ambiguity during the legislative process leading to deregulation:

> We would have preferred to see a standardization of discounting and a level playing field with a public utility aspect . . . We did not feel that this model would succeed given the Blue Cross position . . . One thing about competition is that everyone thinks that they'll be able to succeed based upon their own skills. (Interview with Stephen Hegarty, former president, Massachusetts Hospital Association, Burlington, December 21, 1994)

(Grade: 0)

New Jersey hospitals also faced serious splits within their ranks over deregulation proposals. Unlike Massachusetts, the academic medical centers sided with urban institutions in strong opposition to deregulation. Only the suburban hospitals, who dominated the NJHA, strongly backed the removal of regulatory controls on their charges. The result was a split in the organization with urban and academic institutions forming the Hospital Alliance of New Jersey and abandoning the NJHA. Even the NJHA did not immediately seek deregulation, originally calling together the group that became the New Jersey Health Coalition for Health Care Reform only to fix Judge Wolin's ruling that struck down the uncompensated care surcharges. Business, labor, and insurer groups pushed NJHA to back deregulation as a condition for their support of a UCTF fix. *(Grade: 0)*

As New York policymakers moved rapidly toward rate setting deregulation and a new era in health care finance during 1995 and 1996, hospitals officials found themselves divided and uncertain:

> I was at one of the hospital association annual meetings last year [1994]. Jim Tallon asked how many administrators would like to see for profits who could purchase and close hospitals allowed in New York. One third of the hands went up for that and for competitive markets. One third clearly didn't want it. And one third really didn't know. I was surprised. I didn't believe that quite that many would want an open market. This has all happened within the last six months. (Interview with Ed Rinefurt, Vice President, Business Council of New York State, Albany, June 30, 1995)

Some differences in viewpoint were regionally based, with hospitals in the New York City region strongly in support of continued regulation, while hospitals in areas such as the northeastern part of the state "want to negotiate rates tomorrow . . . It's destructive. You couldn't have more extreme positions."[1]

In spite of the hospital community's divisions, the consensus among other key players in the system was that NYPHRM must go and that replacement sources of revenue must be found for uncompensated care, graduate medical education, and the other access add-ons that have been part of the Uncompensated Care Trust Funds. The political challenges to set an agreeable level of subsidization and to find replacement funding sources were met to the hospitals' satisfaction. While they achieved their objectives, for hospitals, there is the additional challenge of finding their way in a new, market-oriented world that will be vastly different from the problems that faced them before:

> The low hospitals margins in New York—you can look back 70 years or the whole 20th century—it's because our hospitals were built under a different ethos. They were all charitable, all non profit, many religious, many funded chiefly by philanthropy and voluntary contributions. The CEOs were rewarded for good community service, not for a good bottom line. Anyone can run a surplus in one year, but over time, people will question your mission. There's a never ending list of things you could spend your money on. (Interview with Ray Sweeney, Vice President, HANYS, former DoH Director of Health Systems Management, Albany, July 21, 1995)

> After some 20 odd years of regulation, we have a whole crop of hospital managers whose job is to manage bureaucrats and not to manage institutions. Part of the convulsions going on now are because we're so used to going up to Albany and trying to handle the bureaucrats—now the focus is more on autonomy and individual responsibility on the part of the managers themselves. So there are withdrawal

problems . . . The New York system was designed to give hospitals no margins. Therefore, any time anybody had a crisis or needed extra financing, there was no surplus and the only way to deal with the crisis was to go to the regulators and look for favors. (Interview with Ken Raske, President, Greater New York Health Care Association, New York City, July 20, 1995)

(Grade: +)

One final feature of the theory of economic regulation that needs attention in light of subsequent hospital performance involves net revenues. A fundamental aspect of the economic regulation model is that the regulated industry should reap profits that are greater than those obtainable in the absence of regulation. Yet in the case of mandatory rate setting, it is clear that hospitals in all four states enjoyed a level of profitability that was far below that realized by their peers in other states. This pattern crosses all four states, through good and bad economic periods. The post-deregulation periods in Massachusetts and New Jersey have resulted in substantially higher net hospital revenues than were realized during the regulatory period. This finding is in clear contradiction to predicted results under the theory of economic regulation.

Over the span of 25 years of rate regulation, we can observe repeated attempts by hospitals to act like a cartel; but we also see their inability to do so in the face of resistance from governmental and nongovernmental sources. Perhaps the best final judgment on the applicability of the cartel thesis to rate setting can be found in written remarks made by Greater New York Hospital Association President Ken Raske after the deregulation statute was signed:

In New York State during the late 1970's and early 1980's, the demand for inpatient services exceeded supply due to the construction moratorium and the nascent AIDS epidemic, which normally would have increased prices. It was in this climate that the State of New York intervened to regulate private sector hospital reimbursement rates. Thus, all-payer regulation was introduced at a time when prices would have been rising.

Today, opposite pressures are at work. The dominant factors influencing hospital pricing are increasing managed care penetration and the continued development of ambulatory surgery, both of which serve to decrease the demand for inpatient services and, thus, to decrease the price of hospital care . . .

Just as the regulatory pendulum swung left (toward increased regulation) at a time of increasing prices, so the regulatory pendulum is now swinging right (toward decreased regulation) at a time of falling prices. Government's motivation is always to decrease the cost of inpatient care . . . It is no coincidence that the State of New York is deregulating private sector hospital rates at a time when prices are falling; deregulation is occurring *because* prices are falling. (Remarks by Ken Raske, "The Health Care Community in 1997 and Beyond," September 1996)

We now turn to other interests to examine their behavior and role in the evolution and disposition of rate setting in their states.

Blue Cross

In the absence of evidence demonstrating a cartel pattern on the part of hospitals, we must consider the possibility of identifying a replacement cartel composed of one or several interest groups involved in rate setting policy. An obvious candidate would be the Blue Cross plans. The non-profit and state-chartered insurer is the only entity that was uniformly part of the original mandatory rate setting statutes. Blue Cross plans were major players in health insurance in all four states, and they were well-positioned political players as well. But in examining the activities of Blue Cross plans in relation to rate setting, we do not find uniformity in behavior, except in the final, deregulation phase.

While Blue Cross was a major interest pushing for establishment of charge controls in New Jersey, the opposite was true in Maryland. Maryland Blue Cross officials were able to take advantage of their structural control of the Maryland Hospital Association to force rates of payment acceptable to their own needs:

They [Blue Cross] started out as a major player and controlled the hospitals. They said, "if you don't give us this kind of discount, we're not going to pay you." They fought the original law. (Interview with Eugene Feinblatt, Attorney, former chairman, Maryland Commission on Health Care Financing, Baltimore, June 21, 1995)

The 1971 battle to establish rate setting included a bitter struggle between Blue Cross and their former partner, the MHA. In the aftermath of rate setting's establishment, they were forced to live with levels of hospital payment higher than they believe that they would have seen in its absence. Some 25 years later, the scars have healed, but the memory of the battle and their ambiguous support for continuation of the system do not mark an organization that regards itself in the driver's seat in establishing health policy for the state:

[Rate setting] works OK for us. But there's another school of thought in the company: We have the largest market share, the largest indemnity base, and an extensive and affordable HMO presence. If the regulations were abolished, we probably could do very well in terms of negotiating with hospitals to obtain significant discounts, deeper than the way it currently works . . . there's deep division. There always has been. It's old and long going. It goes back prior to the commission's establishment when we got much better deals than today. (Interview with Livio Broccolino, Chief Legal Officer, Blue Cross and Blue Shield of Maryland, Owings Mills, June 2, 1995)

Blue Cross of Massachusetts was also involved in bitter struggles relative to rate setting, though these battles primarily involved commercial indemnity carriers more than hospitals. Controlling about 25 percent of hospital business in the state (and more than half of the private sector market), Blue Cross was able to use its substantial legislative influence to win rules under the pre–all-payer system in 1978 (Chapter 409) that resulted in commercial insurers paying about 60 percent of the hospital uncompensated care costs, while they paid only 25 percent. Their principal interest in 1982 was to keep their advantage and to establish the largest possible discount off charges relative to the commercial carriers.[2]

By the late 1980s, their keenest competition came not from commercial carriers but from the state's burgeoning HMOs. Because HMOs were able to offer lower premiums via deep hospital discounts, Blue Cross began to see a hemorrhaging in its subscriber base, in addition to a major financial crisis documented in an extensive and public management review.[3] These related developments, together with a new top management team, brought an about face on continuation of hospital rate setting:

By the fall of 1990, Blue Cross had an almost total turnover in upper management. We had reports from the Division of Insurance and others that the financing model would doom us to failure . . . We were on the top end of the system in terms of the prices that we paid, and we were helping to subsidize the growth of our chief competitors, the HMOs. (Interview with Steven Tringale, former Vice President for External Affairs, Blue Cross, Boston, December 21, 1995)

Thus, Blue Cross became a strong, insistent voice in Massachusetts for deregulation in 1991, recognizing that the possibility of creating a Maryland-like model with no HMO discounting was not a realistic political option. Like other insurers, their primary attention during the deregulation debate was focused on the elements of a separate but related bill creating new, standardized rules for participation in the small group insurance market, a key part of their business. By mid-1991, deregulation was already a given.

Like its counterpart in Massachusetts, New Jersey Blue Cross had been a key part of their state's rate setting system. Indeed, regulation of Blue Cross hospital payments existed before rate setting, dating back to 1938. Competition over the size of charge discounts characterized their relationship with commercial insurers. A difference from their Massachusetts counterpart was that by the time of the deregulation debate, Massachusetts Blue Cross was moving out of its severest financial stress, but New Jersey Blue Cross's crisis was just getting to its zenith. In 1991, New Jersey Blue Cross faced losses of $83 million in its individual and small group lines of business. Seeing their future tied to managed care, the insurer supported the elimination of rate setting, but focused its heaviest lobbying efforts on companion bills to reform the individual and small group insurance markets that were critical to Governor Florio's agenda and central to his agreement with legislative leaders in eliminating the DRG system:

> We supported elimination of the DRG system, but our biggest problem was the amount of losses in the individual market . . . We had an $80 million advantage under rate setting in reduced charges that we would lose, but we were more than willing to give it up. (Interview with Dennis Marco, Vice President, Blue Cross and Blue Shield of New Jersey, Newark, April 20, 1995)

The situation for the five New York Blue Cross plans in the mid-1990s resembled that of the Massachusetts and New Jersey plans far more than that of Maryland. A deep financial crisis, huge subscriber losses, and an inability to compete with dynamic and growing HMOs are familiar themes that characterized the New York situation:

> Blue Cross is now at about 17 percent market share, down from what used to be 38 percent . . . NYPHRM treated them as if they had monopoly status, but they didn't control all the variables. What NYPHRM created at Blue Cross was an inefficient paper pushing operation where all the tough decisions were made externally and they were insulated from them. At the last count, they were big losers. (Interview with James Tallon, President, United Hospital Fund, former New York State Assembly Majority Leader, Portland OR, August 6, 1995)

The New York Blue Cross and Blue Shield Plans supported rate setting's elimination as quickly as possible while preserving some of the policy add-ons of the NYPHRM model:

> It's time to move to a more open competitive market immediately . . . We hear a chorus of voices from all sides—large employers, middle-sized employers, small employers and individuals, increasingly individuals, who now have a sense that rising health insurance costs are related to health care costs. (Dave Oakley, Counsel to New York State Blue Cross and Blue Shield Plans, Albany, June 29, 1995)

There was a time when Blue Cross was effectively the only insurer of last resort in New York—as well as in the other rate setting states. In 1992, the New York legislature adopted a tough community rating law for individual market insurance products that has removed Blue Cross from that role. New Jersey's individual market reforms in that same year had the same effect through a different mechanism. Massachusetts adopted its own nongroup reforms that ended the Blue Cross "insurer of last resort" status in 1996. These developments indicate that Blue Cross plans retain significant political clout, as they evolve into new organizational forms. As plans in all four states examine their future prospects, conversion to for-profit status and development of regional market bases are realistic options.

We can observe in all four states a clear parallel between the profile of their Blue Cross plans and the state's regulatory climate. At times we can observe Blue Cross plans leading, and at other times following, the different transitions. They are always major players, but never dominated the rate setting debates. They operate independently, having only short-term alliances with other health sector players. They cannot be considered a substitute cartel in the context of rate setting.

Commercial Insurers

This combination of interest groups has a fascinating, albeit limited, part in the rate setting story. An important traditional feature of most commercial indemnity carriers was the limited market share of any single carrier in any market. That limited market share provided the insurers with very restricted leverage in winning concessions from acute care hospitals— financial, regulatory, or political. Large national carriers traditionally had been more interested in a large number of subscribers from across the country than in substantive penetration in any one market. By contrast, the new strategy for those carriers choosing to stay in the health insurance market today is to focus on building large concentrated market shares in a limited number of locales enabling them to leverage discounts and concessions that had been going primarily to HMOs and aggressive Blue Cross plans. Because of their limited roles, commercial carriers were left out of original rate setting schemes in Massachusetts, New Jersey, and New York. The cost shift that fell upon them was a harsh wake-up call. Commercial insurers were brought into the rate setting fold only after serious political battles in those three states.

Nationally, the Health Insurance Association of America became one of the biggest boosters of mandatory hospital rate setting in the late 1970s and early 1980s. Indeed, some of the key scholarly articles seeking to demonstrate the empirical value of state-based hospital rate setting were cowritten by economist Carl Schramm, who later became HIAA's national president.[4] While HIAA never formally abandoned its position in support of all-payer rate setting until recent years, it clearly moved away from its prior boosterism. The key reasons for the switch include the industry's rapid embrace of managed care with its different paradigm for running their businesses and controlling hospital expenditures.

Even in Maryland, the loss of enthusiasm for mandatory hospital rate setting is apparent among the state's commercial carriers:

Recently I called a number of my companies that were on record in support of the HSCRC in the early days. They have all changed their position. I understand that HIAA has a paper in draft form changing their position. The principal reason for that is managed care . . . The [Maryland] rate setting program is clearly the best in the country—if you have to have one. (Interview with Deborah Rivkin, Executive Director, League of Life and Health Insurers of Maryland, Annapolis, June 20, 1995)

Nonetheless, the commercial carriers will only embrace deregulation in Maryland if they are convinced that the prospects for that change are realistic.

In 1991 in Massachusetts, the commercial carriers, which had not yet transitioned to managed care, were not ready to break the tie to hospital charge controls, fearing both a cost shift from hospitals and a competitive disadvantage against Blue Cross:

We were concerned that if managed care really led to tight contracts, that hospitals would just shift costs to us, and that fee for service charges would see the brunt of this shifting . . . Removing the compulsion for Blue Cross to contract with every hospital would mean that they could dictate their prices and be even tougher. So instead of an 800 pound gorilla, they would become a 1,000 pound gorilla . . . So our amendments actually proposed continuing the rate setting system . . . We maintained that position, but nobody was buying it. (Interview with William Carroll, President, Life Insurance Association of Massachusetts, Boston, December 29, 1994)

In New Jersey, these misgivings were not apparent in 1992 in a state dominated by large players in the commercial insurance market such as Prudential, Aetna, and CIGNA, companies that "all decided that their future in the health insurance industry lay with managed care." Thus none of these prior supporters of rate setting remained in its favor (similar reasoning led these private companies to leave the national health insurance lobby, which was dominated by small insurers still offering indemnity plans).[5] In addition to concerns about the evolving market for health insurance, officials at the commercial carriers were also fed up with the regulatory failure that characterized the New Jersey system:

It was an idea whose time had come and gone. The reconciliations had become extremely cumbersome. The board had become a giant bureaucracy. The biggest problem for us was the retroactive charges—we couldn't tell what the trend factor would be until the Rate Setting Commission had finished their reviews, and then we had to make 4–5 percent changes to cover past increases and retros . . . We had no ability to predict costs, and we couldn't get moving on managed care. (Interview with Dana Benbow, Vice President, Prudential Insurance Company, Iselin, April 19, 1995)

Four commercial interests (Aetna, HIAA, Multiplan, and Prudential) were members of the New Jersey Health Care Reform Coalition that publicly endorsed a move to deregulation in September 1992.

In New York, the commercial insurers association, the Life Insurance Council of New York State, formally and for the first time voted in the spring of 1995 to support the end of NYPHRM:

There was no big announcement. It may have been April or May before the final vote. It was a long meeting but not heated. One member didn't think we should deregulate right away because they didn't feel ready . . . We realize that going to deregulation may mean the death knell for some of our people, the people who aren't ready to negotiate. Before community rating, we just wanted a level playing field with Blue Cross. Dereg is a big step toward a level playing field. (Interview with Diane Stuto, Vice President, LICONY, Albany, July 21, 1995)

Prior to the actual decision to endorse deregulation, LICONY financed a study on the NYPHRM system by a consultant who formerly had worked for the State Department of Health. As we will review in chapter 5, that study played an important role in promoting the policy idea of deregulation. The study was cosponsored by the low-income advocacy group, the State Communities Aid Association. SCAA's director, as we have seen, publicly advocated deregulation on the same platform and in the same letters as leaders of the State's Business Association. Thus, a three-way collaboration among consumers, commercial insurers, and business was formed for the purpose of moving New York away from its hospital rate setting "habit" (Richard Kirsch, Executive Director, New York Citizen Action, Albany, June 29, 1995).

While commercial insurers only recently endorsed deregulation, they were responsible for a potentially fatal blow to the system in the form of a legal challenge that reached the U.S. Supreme Court in April 1995. In the early 1990s, the state responded to its own and Blue Cross's fiscal crises by raising the charge differential between Blue Cross/Medicaid rates and those of commercial carriers from 13 to 24 percent. In January 1993, a New York federal district court judge ruled that NYPHRM's payer differentials violated the federal ERISA law (*Travelers Ins. Co. v. Cuomo,* 14 F. 3d. 708 [2d Cir. 1994]). While not challenging the entire New York rate setting structure, observers saw a clear parallel between the "Travelers Case" and the "United Wire Case" that precipitated New Jersey's deregulation process in May 1992.

But on April 26, 1995, the U.S. Supreme Court ruled unanimously that indirect effects on employer-sponsored health plans—such as NYPHRM's differentials—were not grounds for ERISA preemption. While the decision gave the state breathing space in deciding the future of NYPHRM (and pleased other state-based health reformers by providing expanded health reform options), it did not lead to calls for a reinvigoration of hospital rate setting regulation, but only a more orderly exit strategy:

We were not happy to be on the losing side. But it had made it easier for lawmakers to work with an add-on type of thing to fund social needs post NYPHRM. (Interview with Diane Stuto, Vice President, Life Insurance Council of New York, Albany, July 21, 1995)

Viewing the range of commercial insurer interests in rate setting, we observe not a cartel dominated by insurers, hospitals, or any other group, but rather an ongoing struggle—or a multiple tug-of-war—that finds different coalitions joining together at different ends of the rope in each phase. As with hospitals, commercial carriers have their wins and losses, but don't resemble dominant winners by any stretch.

Health Maintenance Organizations

Central to deregulation versions of the theory of economic regulation is the predicted emergence of a new interest that upsets the prior equilibrium and changes the dynamics and interests of the cartel. In the rate setting story, that role would clearly belong to HMOs, less than a footnote at the inception of rate regulation in the early 1970s and major institutional players in all four states today.

Prior to the coining of the term *health maintenance organization* by Ellwood, prepaid group practices around the nation were small, not for profit, and insignificant with the exception of the California Kaiser Plans. A series of federal laws beginning in 1973 encouraged their growth as a response to health cost inflation, laws viewed as largely ineffectual.[6] When the Reagan administration ended federal grants for HMOs in 1981, many of these organizations moved into the welcome hands of investors who recognized opportunities for significant financial gain in the burgeoning field of for-profit medicine. Coming at a time of medical cost hyperinflation, the new for-profit managed care organizations experienced rapid increases in growth and development that continue into the 1990s.[7]

The stunning growth of HMOs in tightly regulated Maryland during the past seven years caught many policymakers by surprise in welcome and unwelcome ways:

> I can't quite explain it, but right now Maryland is number three for managed care penetration. The biggest screamers to dismantle our all payer system are the HMOs, out of state entities, and all they want is further discounts, and to get people out of their normal sources of care. There's a war going on. (Interview with Sen. Paula Hollinger, Senate Chair of Maryland Joint Comm. on Health Care Delivery and Finance, Annapolis, June 20, 1995)

Throughout the history of the Maryland rate setting system, managed care organizations have not been influential, a fact that helps to explain why the HSCRC has been able to maintain and enforce tight limits on hospital discounting with HMOs. While some of the new, for-profit organizations talk about the need for deregulation, the Maryland Association of HMOs has not endorsed this position, but is direct in expressing its reservations about the system:

> The system is trying to move hospitals to a more competitive stance, but when you look at one hospital's application—if they're trying to compete with ambulatory facilities down the road—they have to face six months of review by the HSCRC, looking at risk and cost shifting. In the private market, you hire someone to assess what you have to do and you do it . . . I don't think a regulatory system can keep up with market demands . . . We're an industry that supports competition—but our plans want to be satisfied with the results before they recommend dismantling the system. (Interview with Geni Dunnells, Executive Director, Maryland Association of HMOs, Annapolis, June 22, 1995)

Thus while HMOs have gone far beyond the point of critical mass in the Maryland health insurance market, they have yet to make their mark on the state's political system and have not come to terms with the merits of deregulation.

HMO influence has been most apparent in Massachusetts. From the beginning in 1982, HMOs alone were allowed the ability to negotiate discounts of any amount with hospitals under the Chapter 372 all-payer system. Thomas Pyle, the former head of the Harvard Community Health Plan, was an early voice and force for market dynamics in the state's health care policy circles, and he compelled the private Health Care Coalition to bring in HMOs as a member group in 1983, when managed care penetration in the state was still in single digits. The Massachusetts Association of HMOs was formed in 1985, in part to give other HMOs a voice in policy discussions equal to that of Pyle's. But during the fights over the legislation that became the 1988 Universal Health Care Law, the strategy was largely defensive:

> In Chapter 23, we were dancing among the elephants. Pat McGovern [Senate Ways and Means Chairwoman] was just able to take our issues off the table in the negotiations and leave us alone. We stepped away and were very thankful for it. (Interview with Robert Hughes, Executive Director, Massachusetts Association of HMOs, Boston, December 15, 1994)

By 1990, HMOs had become large and strong enough to promote actively a deregulation agenda, casting one of two dissenting votes in a special commission on health finance that recommended the development of a Maryland style regulatory structure as the successor to the failed Chapter 23 rate setting model (Special Commission on Health Care Finance and Delivery Reform, December 31, 1990). With the arrival of the market-oriented Weld administration, HMO leaders were the first and most active interest in promoting deregulation among business groups, in the media, and in other venues. Partly, this was done out of fear that a Maryland style regulatory model would end their existing leverage in negotiating discounts. But HMO leaders also recognized that deregulation was contrary to their own self-interest in comparison to the Chapter 23 model that gave them bargaining flexibility that their rivals lacked:

> We were helped overall [by the regulatory system] because it crippled our competitors. (Interview with Robert Hughes, Executive Director, Massachusetts Association of HMOs, Boston, December 15, 1994)

Nine of 15 Massachusetts interviewees mentioned HMOs as key deregulation advocates, more than any other group outside of the Weld administration. But the effect of HMO support was not to bully or cajole legislators with political pressure, but rather to provide assurances that deregulation would not lead to a worsened health system crisis:

> There was sufficient critical mass in the HMO community to allow members of the Legislature to feel comfortable because so many constituents were already outside of the [rate setting] system. It increased the comfort level . . . In terms of political support [to legislators and the Governor], my groups are pathetic. I wish they would give just half as much more. (Interview with Robert Hughes, Executive Director, Massachusetts Association of HMOs, Boston, December 15, 1994)

In New Jersey, Department of Health officials determined in the late 1980s that they lacked legal authority to prohibit the negotiated discounting that was widespread and undermining the integrity of a badly damaged system. The president of the New Jersey Business and Industry Association testified before a legislative hearing on its effects:

> I know of a specific hospital who recently agreed to a 25 percent discount for US Healthcare. I'm under the impression that in a Blue Cross survey of hospitals, of the 83, that 73 responded indicating, "yup, maybe we'll give a discount, too" . . . Of course, that discount means that I'm getting stuck even harder. So that's the present sys

tem. That's a disastrous system. You have a hospital rate setting commission saying, "this is what the rates should be." Right? Nobody
pays it. (Testimony of Bruce Coe, President, New Jersey Business and
Industry Association Association, Assembly Health Committee,
March 5, 1992)

Unlike in the other three states, HMOs were slow to develop in New Jersey, which was still below the national average in managed care penetration during the 1992 deregulation debate. In the course of that debate, the
state's HMO association participated in the New Jersey Coalition for
Health Care Reform activities, but they also knew their proper place:

HMOs were just part of the crowd. We realized the system wasn't that
great. But we were just coming into our own and were not a
significant part of the market. The issue [deregulation] just didn't
arouse much passion. (Testimony of Dale Florio, Counsel, New Jersey HMO Association, April 17, 1995)

New York's position most clearly resembled that of Massachusetts,
where HMO growth and legally authorized discounting substantially
undermined the rationale for continued rate setting, as did the financial
instability facing both the state Medicaid program and Blue Cross plans.
As was true in Massachusetts and New Jersey, HMO leaders in New York
understood that their sole ability to discount placed them in an advantaged status and a philosophical dilemma:

We are winners [under NYPHRM]. The ability to negotiate rates,
while fair, represents a major advantage for us over our competition.
The Conference [of HMOs] would not fight it, and would support
deregulation as a matter of principle. We certainly couldn't oppose it.
We would rather see it given to others than to have it taken away from
us. (Interview with Harold Iselin, Counsel, New York HMO Conference, Albany, June 29, 1995)

In evaluating the overall impact of HMOs on the deregulation
process, we are faced with a puzzle. The state where HMOs have the greatest rational incentive to push for deregulation is Maryland, where discounting is not allowed and where deregulation is not on the policy
agenda. In the other three subject states, HMOs actually were advantaged
under a rate setting model that allowed only them to have discounting
authority. Deregulation happened in New Jersey with only a marginal
HMO market and political presence. The one state where HMOs clearly

made themselves a part of the deregulation process, Massachusetts, had many other factors pushing policymakers in that direction.

In spite of impressive HMO growth and development in the states, it is impossible to assert that their presence made deregulation happen. There is no evidence to portray them as a replacement cartel. Nonetheless, managed care—which HMOs institutionally personify—played the critical role in undermining rate setting's stability and rationale. But this dynamic is a discussion for policy ideas in chapter 5, not one about interests.

Business

The business community is the first constituency that we discuss out of the inner–health system circle. Business is divided in numerous ways, including the basic division between big and small business, but also among different lobbying groups, sectors, and industries. Their attention is split among a variety of compelling policy issues that reach a state's policy agenda during any given legislative year.

A business embrace of intrusive, large-scale regulation such as rate setting in hospitals was not a position taken casually. Instead, the business community found itself in the 1970s and early 1980s unable to respond to the ability of health providers to increase dramatically the price of their services because indemnity style, fee-for-service insurance did not permit an effective payer response. Rate setting was seen as the only viable short-term alternative to cost-based, retrospective reimbursement, and it was largely welcomed by business leaders in those states that embraced it. In the interim, businesses moved to self-insure, to manage care, and to undertake other initiatives to move the system to the point where overt state regulation would no longer be needed.

In Maryland, business has been a long-standing, though not aggressive, supporter of rate setting. The system was initiated without a major role for business and has survived with their support. Recently, business leaders have been among the leaders suggesting that a fresh examination would be welcome. The chairman of the state's Chamber of Commerce referred to "the crisis in the regulation of health care in Maryland," referring to "overlap, confusion, costs, and delays involved in such a complex regulatory superstructure" and recommending "a new commission to study what is good and what needs to be improved in Maryland's health care regulatory system" (letter from Wayne Mills, Chairman to Governor Glendening, February 6, 1995). But the potential loss to the hospital community of $200 million if the Medicare waiver were not renewed (costs that would be shifted substantially to them) plays into business support:

Our views are clouded here in Maryland because of the waiver. (Interview with Miles Cole, Director of Business Affairs, Maryland Chamber of Commerce, Annapolis, June 24, 1995)

In response to a recent *Baltimore Sun* article asking, "Is Maryland Hospital Regulation Outdated?", a former business representative on the HSCRC responded, "Frankly, no better system is in sight" (*Baltimore Sun,* April 5, 1995).

Massachusetts business leaders were more assertive, dating to the early 1980s, in establishing directions for hospital regulation. Indeed, the coalition able to forge consensus, the Health Care Coalition, was formed and directed by Nelson Gifford, a manufacturing CEO and chair of the Health Care Task Force for the Massachusetts Business Roundtable. But success in the early years of all-payer rate setting in controlling hospital cost inflation did not persist: "The forceful entrance of employers into health care politics was linked to the enactment of a series of policies, each of them supported by employers, which progressively expanded access to care for the uninsured . . . Employers slid down the slope until they reached the point at which support for health care for all was a logical consequence of previous positions they had taken. The center of this story is hospital reimbursement."[8]

One important result of the 1988 Universal Health Care Law—which included a pay-or-play employer mandate and greatly expanded hospital charge authority—was a significant business retreat from state health care politics. By 1991, the business community was splintered. The Roundtable had largely retreated from the stage, though they mildly supported deregulation at the behest of large Boston teaching hospitals that had become organizational members; the conservative Massachusetts High Technology Council also gave rhetorical support to deregulation. Small business groups ignored the issue, continuing to work to repeal the employer mandate and to enact small group insurance market reforms.

The key business group that joined the debate, Associated Industries of Massachusetts, officially supported deregulation by the summer of 1991, but most actively participated in the debate by demanding a systemwide revenue cap on hospitals:

Although the theory behind the Administration bill is that increased competition will keep costs down, there exists significant skepticism on this hypothesis. In fact, there is speculation that costs will increase significantly as hospitals are encouraged to increase volume to compensate for any lost revenue which might result from more competitive prices on individual services . . . AIM strongly urges your adoption of a system-wide revenue cap. (AIM letter to Health Care Committee, September 19, 1991)

AIM repeated this line of advocacy throughout the legislative process in letters and bulletins to the legislature and the media. As the final bill headed for Governor Weld's desk, they continued to sound this theme:

> We are disappointed that the system-wide revenue cap is not included in either the House or Senate bills and we are especially concerned that hospital costs may rise substantially in the next few years without any effective ongoing mechanism to protect employers. (AIM letter to Rep. Carmen Buell, December 17, 1991)

While the overall message from business was supportive of deregulation, it was mixed, and business groups cannot be considered as leading forces behind Massachusetts deregulation.

New Jersey business leaders had only recently come to support deregulation in 1992. As mentioned in chapter 3, New Jersey Business and Industry President Bruce Coe placed his constituency only "51 to 49" in favor of deregulation at a March 5, 1992, legislative oversight hearing. By the time Judge Wolin's decision came down in May of that year striking down the state's uncompensated care pool, business was ready to press the issue. Hospital officials called together a meeting of key interest groups in June 1992 to plan a strategy in light of the federal court decision and were surprised by the outcome:

> While the New Jersey Hospital Association officials only wanted to address the uncompensated care issue, we all wanted to call in the whole question about rate setting . . . Business, labor and insurers viewed the Wolin decision as an opportunity to introduce more competition into the rate setting system. (Interview with Maureen Lopes, Senior Vice President for Health Affairs, New Jersey Business and Industry Association, Trenton, April 17, 1995)

But the end result of the New Jersey Health Care Reform Coalition was a recommendation for a three-year phasing out of the DRG system, a period of time that was unacceptable to legislative leaders and Governor Florio who wanted—and won—immediate deregulation with one year of loose replacement caps. Even more out of touch was the coalition's recommendation to restore uncompensated care funding by adding one cent to the state sales tax that had been cut only months before by the new Republican majority in the legislature. Labor, insurer, and business groups had entered into a coalition with the hospital community—and it was difficult to determine who had won the better part of the bargain. But it is obvious that the business community was not in the driver's seat in New Jersey in 1992 on matters pertaining to health regulation.

The business community in New York shares with its counterparts in the other states a legacy of support for rate setting and now shares with its Massachusetts and New Jersey counterparts a clear sense of a need for change:

> It served us well in the 1970s and in the early 1980s in bringing stability to the hospital sector. But now where you have such blatant examples of HMO discounting as much as 40 percent of a DRG rate, it points to the fact that prices have nothing to do anymore with the market. By allowing the system to continue, it prevents market forces from shrinking the system. Everyone says that shrinking should be done, but no one has the gumption to decide how to do it. (Interview with Ed Reinfurt, Vice President, Business Council of New York State, Albany, June 30, 1995)

The business community has collaborated in coming to its position with the insurers through LICONY, and with consumer advocates through the State Communities Aid Association, along with hospitals and regulators:

> At the business council, everyone has taken a pretty responsible position, and no one has said that they want to turn their backs on the special needs. Nobody wants to throw out the baby with the bath water. (Interview with Ray Sweeney, Executive Vice President, HANYS, former DoH, Albany, July 21, 1995)

The business community was an active voice in the search for replacement revenue sources in the post-NYPHRM era; but they have never been the dominant voice in New York health policymaking. In spite of the new Republican administration in Albany, they are only one of many at the table.

In summary, business is a highly regarded player in health politics—listened to, respected, and feared. There are few times in any of the states where the decisions made by policymakers were substantially at variance with the positions of the business community. Their long-term effect seems most evident in Massachusetts. But, once again, theirs is not the effect of a replacement cartel.

Labor

The house of labor contains at least two distinct points of view on matters relating to rate setting. On one hand, labor as the representative and bargaining agent for hospital workers is advantaged by a regulatory model that provides predictability, the potential for cross-industry bargaining, and the support of political leaders during difficult negotiations. On the other hand, labor as a purchaser of health services has an interest in seeing the health costs held down and in using its large number of members to wrestle favorable rates of payment. Labor interests of the first kind find themselves allied with hospitals on regulatory matters. Labor interests of the latter variety are found with their state Blue Cross plans and other health purchaser groups.

In recent years, both elements of the labor movement have felt their backs to the wall. Hospital workers have seen privatizations and closings of public institutions where they held jobs, and the loss of bargaining leverage and jobs in private health institutions as competitive cost pressures bear down on hospitals. Unions that bargain for health benefits also feel pressures as management has pressed for concessions and givebacks in the form of reduced or restructured health benefits, leading to many strikes over health-related bargaining issues. Building trade unions, which purchase health services through self-funded "Taft–Hartley" plans, have faced near-bankruptcy in attempting to maintain health and welfare funds in the midst of recessions and construction slowdowns that left large portions of their memberships unemployed.

In the four states, the position of the labor movement on matters involving rate setting was heavily influenced by the organizational affiliation of the key union spokespersons on health policy matters. With unions and health policy, where you sit does much to determine where you stand.

The union-as-purchaser pressures in other states have not yet surfaced in Maryland in any meaningful way. The AFL-CIO maintains a strong position of support for the HSCRC and holds a seat on that body. The key spokesperson for the labor movement on rate setting matters is a former executive director of a local public employees affiliate of the American Federation of State, County, and Municipal Employees. He is also a vice president of the Maryland Health Coalition:

> From the viewpoint of a trade unionist, we get good hospital care, at reasonable rates, and the system has an extremely positive social aspect with total equal access. The uncompensated care system is the best in the country. It's a good system, and they monitor the quality and efficiency. It's also a wide open system. You can find out anything

in this system. (Interview with Ernie Crofoot, former AFL-CIO representative to HSCRC, Bowie, June 22, 1995)

In Massachusetts, health policy matters had largely been the province of leaders from the Service Employees International Union, Local 285, representing health care workers at Boston City Hospital and other key institutions. In the late 1980s, construction trade unions organized their own network of health and welfare funds, pooling their resources to bargain with hospitals, emphasizing preventive and primary care for members and families.

In the 1991 deregulation process, both branches of labor found common ground in legislative proposals to establish a single-payer financing system, proposals overwhelmingly defeated in the legislative process. Hospital workers, realizing that deregulation would threaten job stability, preferred any alternative to deregulation. Building trade unions wanted any system that represented a change from the high hospital cost inflation experienced under Chapter 23. But once single-payer proposals were defeated on the floor, labor struggled to find an alternative to support. The position of the Massachusetts AFL-CIO reflected that ambiguity:

> The rising cost of health coverage has been the major cause of job actions and contract disputes in the last five years . . . H6280 [the deregulation bill] takes Massachusetts in the wrong direction. Deregulation of the airline and trucking industries has resulted in lost jobs, company closings, and higher costs to consumers . . . We urge you to vote to defer action . . . (Letter from Massachusetts AFL-CIO to Massachusetts House of Representatives, November 20, 1991)

In fact, organized labor in 1991 had many other issues before the legislature of higher priority to them than the fate of rate setting, including attacks on workers' compensation and Weld administration efforts to privatize large segments of state government. One of labor's key point persons in 1991 on health recalls the uncertainty in the movement:

> Labor was divided. Some in construction were purchasers and provided insurance. Others wanted a more regulated single-payer system. While labor was on the right side in terms of lobbying—they supported regulation as opposed to competition—did they understand the full repercussions? No . . . Construction trades used to eat my head off when we talked about limits on hospital capital expansion. Suddenly people realize that there's going to be a big loss in jobs.

(Interview with Celia Wcislo, President, SEIU Local 285, Boston, January 19, 1995)

In New Jersey, building trades unions held sway on rate setting. The key labor appointee to the Rate Setting Commission was the administrator of the Carpenters Fund who initiated the federal lawsuit against the Uncompensated Care Trust Fund. That suit was in response to UCTF surcharges approaching 20 percent at a time when large portions of construction trades membership were unemployed in the recessionary aftermath of the casino building boom of the 1980s. While the suit is credited by all observers with triggering the chain of events that led to deregulation, the Rate Setting Commission's final labor appointee denies that ending rate setting was their goal:

> We were not looking the topple the DRG system, but looking instead to find a fairer way to finance uncompensated care. The deregulation of rate setting was not my explicit desire . . . The coalition position was for less regulation, not for total deregulation. (Interview with George Laufenberg, Administrator of New Jersey Carpenters Fund, RSC member, Edison, April 19, 1995)

Other labor leaders, however, did desire to get rid of the New Jersey rate setting system:

> Our idea was to get rid of it [rate setting] because of how evil it was in manipulating the charges. (Interview with Charles Marciante, President, New Jersey AFL-CIO, Trenton, April 18, 1995)

While New Jersey labor supported the recommendations of the Health Care Reform Coalition in proposing a three-year phaseout of rate setting, it broke completely when the coalition chose to support the legislative-Governor Florio–negotiated package to fund uncompensated care for a three-year period by raiding approximately $1.5 billion from the state's Unemployment Insurance Trust Fund. When the labor movement brought their busloads of workers to the state capital in November 1992 to weigh in on the legislative debate, their target was the fund diversion, not the preservation of rate setting.

In New York, the labor movement was nonengaged in debates about NYPHRM's future during the critical discussions in 1995. This is unexpected in light of the generally held view that hospital worker unions were key beneficiaries of NYPHRM. As occurred in Massachusetts, deregulation holds significant ramifications for organized labor:

A regulated environment and labor negotiations go hand in glove. Regulation gives organized labor the ability to get things that they couldn't get in a non-regulated environment. The structured payments, the predictability, the lack of volatility, the homogenous solutions that apply to all institutions. Once you figure out the wage rates, it's across the board. So 1199 [the hospital workers union] can structure agreements with groups of institutions which are cross employer. They can achieve multi-institutional bargaining units. The League of Voluntary Hospitals across the hall from here do bargaining with 1199 for about 40 hospitals. Their deals apply across the industry. In addition, the unions have a history of running to the politicians when they get or think they get a bad deal as another way to leverage the industry. The competitive markets are hostile to organized labor. Under competition, one institutional situation will not be replicated at another. (Interview with Kenneth Raske, President, Greater New York Health Care Association, New York City, July 20, 1995)

One New York labor official put the same point of view more succinctly:

Labor doesn't like change. (Interview with Debbie Bell, Coordinator of Policy Development, DC 37, AFSCME, New York City, July 20, 1995)

As was the case with labor leaders in Massachusetts in 1991, New York unions found other fights facing them in 1996 more central to their interests, including the future of the New York City municipal hospital system, the direction of Medicaid managed care, and other health-related budgetary battles. Facing multiple battles, the union-led New York Health Care Coalition began running a series of highly publicized television and newspaper advertisements in June 1996 with the following tagline to characterize Governor Pataki's plethora of health proposals: "It's a killer." While the ads did not specify which proposals fit that description, they were a significant irritant to the administration. The final deregulation legislation included up to $100 million in funds for health worker retraining in anticipation of hospital sector downsizing. At the September 12, 1996, bill signing, standing center stage was Dennis Rivera, head of New York's District Council 37 of the American Federation of State, County and Municipal Employees, one of the state's most influential labor leaders.

Though they were late to the fight relative to other interest groups that abandoned support for rate setting in early and mid-1995, and though they were unable to defend the continuation of the rate setting structure, New York unions were able to exert pressure that led to a more generous package of public subsidies for worker retraining, uncompensated care, and graduate medical education than would otherwise have occurred.

However, we cannot see any pattern suggesting that labor had a disproportionate impact on the fate of rate setting in the various states. With the exception of Maryland, their response to deregulation pressures had been either tentative or ambiguous.

Consumers

"Democratic governments tend to favor producers more than consumers in their actions," notes Downs in discussing the reasons why the presumed beneficiaries of regulation have so little input into the processes that create those structures.[9] Olson posits that in the absence of selective incentives to individuals to act, "the incentive for group action diminishes as group size increases so that large groups are less able to act in their common interest than small ones."[10] Gormley has observed that issues high in technical complexity (such as public utility regulation and, certainly, hospital rate setting) are likely to discourage grassroots consumer participation, while issues that are highly conflictual will discourage the involvement of "proxy advocates" acting in their behalf.[11] Feldstein suggests that the lack of consumer involvement makes sense because the increased prices that must be paid to sustain regulatory structures do not outweigh the costs of personal involvement in changing the structures; consumers have a "diffuse" interest in regulatory matters that reduces their incentive to engage in regulatory politics.[12]

One way to address the need for consumer participation is to require it in statute. But this solution is itself no panacea. Vladeck examined the federally mandated role for consumers in the health planning initiatives of the 1970s and concluded that Congress naively adopted a pluralist, interest-group representation model that they thought would bring all parties effectively into the fray. Instead, he found log-rolling, bargaining, and collusive competition among narrowly defined special interests who often identified themselves as representing broader consumer concerns, while the interests of the public were less well served.[13] None of the rate setting models in this study mandated any direct consumer involvement in decision making.

In Maryland and New Jersey, organized consumer involvement at any stage during the decades-long history of their rate setting programs was largely nonexistent. Interviewees in both states were unable to identify an organized consumer presence that involved itself in the details of rate regulation. Some general interest organizations such as the League of Women Voters, church-affiliated organizations, and senior citizens groups would speak out on broader health matters, but not in a way that affected the direction or shape of rate setting. The author was unable to identify a single consumer representative who was knowledgeable about the intricacies of these systems. The voices of consumers were heard in New Jersey in the form of constituent complaints about hospital bill discrepancies between listed charges and DRG state-approved charges. These complaints had a serious impact on legislators in both parties in an unorganized but highly effective fashion. Consumer voices also were heard in 1995, for example, when these two states became the first in the nation to impose mandated lengths of stay for maternity patients. Once again, unorganized voices occasionally also have the ability to be heard.

In contrast, Massachusetts and New York had sophisticated consumer advocacy groups involved in rate setting and other issues concerning health care finance and insurance. In Massachusetts, Health Care for All, funded through grants and grassroots support, has been a respected voice in health care issues since the mid-1980s, particularly with the news media. They maintain a professional staff and a citizen membership. In the 1991 deregulation debate, they unsuccessfully opposed the move toward a competitive system and supported the union-backed single-payer alternative:

> The Health Care Committee's bill contains even fewer cost containment provisions and less money for access programs than the Weld bill does. The "competitive strategy" is not a new idea. It has been tried in other states without success. It has failed to address adequately the cost problem facing our health care system and has only made access problems worse. (Health Care for All Action Alert, October 1991)

While not able to achieve their objectives in stopping deregulation or establishing an alternative financing mechanism, the group established alliances with sympathetic academics that established a level of debate and dialogue about health system direction that otherwise would have been missing. This aspect of their role will be discussed and analyzed more fully in chapter 5.

In New York, the key consumer organizations are the low-income advocacy organization, the State Communities Aid Association, and the grassroots activist organization Citizen Action. Their perspectives are markedly different. The former moved from a position of dependable support for regulation to vocal support for deregulation. Their executive director formed an alliance with both the Business Council of New York

State and the Insurance Industry in advocating a move away from NYPHRM:

> We initially were very strong supporters of the NYPHRM concept. Back in 1983, we were one of the organizations to initially endorse the so-called Medicaid/Medicare waiver that enabled Medicare to participate in NYPHRM . . . However, over a period of time, and this wasn't an instant conversion, we started to see growing problems with NYPHRM . . . Despite having a mechanism like bad debt and charity care, voluntary hospitals were diverting patients away from their door to public hospitals. (Interview with Gerry Billings, Executive Director, State Communities Aid Association, Albany, June 30, 1995)

Citizen Action had been less directly involved in the NYPHRM debate, but had been very much a part of health care access and financing debates, strongly pushing single-payer legislation that actually passed the New York Assembly in 1991, promoting prior DoH experiments with hospital global budgeting during the Cuomo administration, and promoting restrictions on the managed care industry.

There is nothing like a cartel to be found here. None of these organizations have the financial, organizational, or political clout to dictate the results of health policy debates—on rate setting or any other hospital finance or insurance matters. But these groups do add substance to debates that otherwise can focus entirely on interest group politics and insider issues. The role of these groups will be explored in more depth in chapter 5.

State Administrations

There are at least four distinct and important viewpoints from the state governmental perspective that must be considered in examining that sector's role in rate setting policy: those of chief executives, legislators, rate setting regulators, and health purchasing agencies such as Medicaid and state employee health insurance offices. The particular perspectives and actions of chief executives and of legislators will be examined more closely in the chapter 5 discussion of policy ideas.

While chief executives and legislators have been with us throughout American history, the other two state governmental entities are much more recent in their appearance. Tierney observed that the growth of Medicare and other health entitlements had worked to alter fundamentally the role of government and government agencies in health politics and policy-making: "the federal government has become the nation's largest single source of payment for health care and, thus, is a primary actor with interests of its own. . . . far from being paralyzed, the government is now the driving force in health policy making. The government's information, stakes, and preferences—in short, the government's interests—now increasingly define the interests of private groups, not the reverse."[14] This section analyzes the behavior of both the rate setting regulators who set the rules and run the prospective payment system as well as the government health purchasers who run into conflict with the former group and whose influence and authority have increased along with the size of their budgets.

State Government as Regulator

The political influence and role of regulators has been considered and debated by numerous policy analysts. Niskanen, whose ideas are influenced by the theory of economic regulation and rational choice theory, views bureaucracies such as rate setting commissions as independent actors and interests in their own right. Developing his theory of bureaucratic behavior, he predicts that agencies will seek to increase their budgets as much as possible, and that both legislators and chief executives will be unable to judge the true need for agency resources because of information problems. In short, regulatory agencies become imperialistic and expansionist, searching for more resources and authority.[15]

Wilson, in particular, takes issue with the Niskanen theory, citing example after example where federal, state, and local agencies resisted legislative and executive branch invitations to expand the scope of their operations: "they [bureaucrats] cannot put any surplus revenues into their own pockets; their salaries do not increase with the size of the budget . . . and now it even appears that they cannot even expect to occupy big offices with thick rugs on the floor and a nice view of the city . . . the political environment in which they work powerfully inhibits them from converting their management of a bureau into material gain . . . The truth is more complicated."[16] Noll reached a similar conclusion in examining theories that suggest that agencies want primarily to maximize their own budgets: "In the case of regulatory agencies, the theory does not seem to work."[17]

Gormley, examining the authority and capacity of public utility regulators, found "people who differ markedly in their party affiliation, professional background, and industry experience. Many differ in their attitudes as well." While more independent of gubernatorial and legislative authority than often recognized, regulators' responsiveness to the public and interest groups will vary from issue to issue and from agency to agency depending upon the local political culture, the issue complexity and level of conflict involved.[18]

The evidence from this study lends support to the Wilson, Noll, and Gormley viewpoints. In Maryland, the Health Services Cost Review Commission dominates the rate setting policy discussion because of the trust and broad degree of regulatory discretion that legislators and executive branch officials have placed in them:

> They [HSCRC] are truly expert at what they do. There's a lot of trust that policy makers have put into that Commission. The Planning Commission gets a somewhat different response. (Interview with Senator Paula Hollinger, Chairman, Senate Health Care Committee, Annapolis, June 20, 1995)

Far from being its own special interest, the HSCRC leadership remain highly attentive to the needs and desires of governmental and nongovernmental players, adapting the regulatory model to health market changes needed to sustain the system. Neither their offices nor their scope of regulatory authority have grown. Indeed, when legislators decided to expand the scope of state regulatory authority to physicians and their costs, a new commission, the Health Care Cost and Access Commission, was created to address that policy objective instead of assigning the job to the HSCRC.

The most pointed recent criticism of regulators concerns conflicts among the three commissions with regulatory authority over the health system, the HSCRC, the Health Care Access and Cost Commission, and the Health Planning Commission:

> There are personality conflicts between the agencies that have inhibited their ability to cooperate. The bottom line is that there are two ways as to how one might go about regulation—through a highly centralized regulatory body, or the Maryland way through a decentralized structure. (Interview with Larry Lawrence, Executive Vice President, Maryland Hospital Association, Lutherville, June 21, 1995)

The Maryland legislation approved in the 1995 session calling for an examination of Maryland health sector regulation also required the three health regulatory agencies to develop a more collaborative working relationship. The most important changes in regulatory activity involve the experiments with capitated forms of regulated payments, described in chapter 3. Overall, the interests in the executive branches of the other states in moving away from hospital rate setting are not in evidence in Maryland.

In Massachusetts, the regulators in charge of the rate regulation program were located in the Rate Setting Commission, a separate entity within the Executive Office of Health and Human Services. Rather than assume their own independent outlook, RSC leaders followed policy directions laid down by the governor and the Secretary of Health and Human Services. This occurred across successive administrations, regardless of party or regulatory outlook. When Dukakis officials sought tighter controls on hospital spending in the mid-1980s, RSC officials provided the analyses and backup to document their case; when Weld officials sought to trigger the deregulation process in 1991, RSC officials wrote the initial legislation that put their 15 years of rate setting authority out of business. When the legislature moved for a faster demise to rate setting authority, the agency quietly complied:

> When House Ways and Means came out with a draft that deregulated more than the Governor's bill and took a complete deregulatory approach, it became clear that the Administration would not push back from that. (Interview with Paula Griswold, former Chairperson, Rate Setting Commission, Boston, December 23, 1995)

Bureaucratic rivalry and turf protection existed in Massachusetts between the RSC and the Medicaid program over rate approval authority, a battle that was won finally by the purchasing agency in 1991. Again, there is no evidence of Niskanen-like behavior as regards the Massachusetts Rate Setting Commission and the rate setting program.

In New Jersey, the activities within the administration were also complex. A series of governors dating back to the early 1970s, and including Republican Thomas Kean in 1981, supported the development and evolution of the rate setting model and the Department of Health's regulatory role. As we saw in chapter 3, DoH officials played an aggressive and far-reaching role in the establishment of New Jersey's DRG payment model, a role that comes closer than any other we have seen to Niskanen-like behavior. But the regulatory innovators who designed and implemented the new model left New Jersey state government as quickly as they arrived, leaving the system in the hands of longtime civil service employees.

Rather than an agency attempting to satisfy their lust for budget power, the New Jersey regulators seemed to be overwhelmed with the complexity and difficulties of their task, throwing up their hands in 1991 and giving $1 billion in retrospective rate setting charge adjustments to the hospital industry. Members of the commission seemed as befuddled as the general public in observing these developments:

> Rate setting was not working very well. It was more like a rubber stamp of whatever the hospitals wanted. I don't recall any hospital having a difficult time getting rates increased. There were five com-

mission members and a staff of three. The Department of Health used up other funds for back up services like transcripts. We couldn't address the issues as an independent group because we had to rely on DoH. It was always last minute decisions and a sense of urgency. At one time we were changing hospital factors on a monthly basis. The hospitals became very effective in gaming the system. (Interview with George Laufenberg, Administrator of New Jersey Carpenters Fund and former RSC member, Edison, April 19, 1995)

When deregulation became an obvious part of the policy agenda in the fall of 1992, then DoH Commissioner Bruce Siegel walked a fine line convincing supporters and opponents of rate setting alike that he was on their side. (Five New Jersey interviewees offered different impressions of Commissioner Siegel's position on deregulation.) The Rate Setting Commission that was housed within the Department of Health played no significant role in fighting the deregulation proposal. When the decision came for rate setting deregulation, the bureaucracy that had run the system was left out of the room and out in the cold.

New York's Department of Health bureaucracy that managed the five versions of NYPHRM through the Office of Health Systems Management (OHSM) was large, stable, and powerful. Indeed, hospitals were often characterized as needing to travel to Albany, hat in hand, seeking favors and dispensations from the DoH commissioner and bureaucrats. Nonetheless, it is also apparent that the legislature dictated NYPHRM reimbursement rules and formulas that were often at variance with the desires of the health bureaucracy. There is also no evidence that the department varied from the policies and imperatives laid down by the Rockefeller, Carey, and Cuomo administrations over 25 years of rate setting policy. Perhaps most illustrative of the fragility of such seemingly strong bureaucratic institutions is the speed with which the NYPHRM bureaucracy fell apart with the election of George Pataki as governor in 1994.

The four sets of bureaucracies described in this section varied widely in terms of size, authority, stability, and effectiveness. Rather than viewing them in Niskanen terms as a separate interest, pursuing their own self-interested agendas, and seeking to maximize their own resources and budgets for their own purposes, Wilson's comment returns as the most appropriate summary: "The truth is more complicated."[19]

State Governments as Purchasers
Ever since state governments became major financiers of health services through the creation of the Medicaid program in 1965, they have assumed

an interest that goes well beyond the traditional crafting of public policy through legislation and regulation. States originally were compelled to finance Medicaid services through retrospective, cost-based reimbursement at the inception of the new program. Beginning in the 1970s, the federal government actively encouraged states to experiment with different financing models to constrain the growth in both Medicaid and Medicare. As we have seen, our four states were among the pioneers in experimenting with innovations in prospective payment and other kinds of regulation.

But the rapid escalation in Medicaid costs, along with growth in the use of managed care in Medicaid (voluntary in the 1980s, and expanding to mandatory forms in the 1990s), and finally accompanied by dissatisfaction with the effectiveness of hospital rate regulation, led state government officials to begin to assume different roles in relation to the health sector in the late 1980s. State Medicaid officials moved from being mere payers of health provider bills to being active and aggressive purchasers of health services, with clear outcomes and standards. It is this evolution, more than any other factor, that pushed the subject states to reassess the role of hospital rate setting. It is the growth in the role of state government health purchasing entities that transformed the state's role in relation to health interests.

In Maryland, managed care for Medicaid is a recent phenomenon. Rivalry between Medicaid and the HSCRC has not been an issue for bureaucrats or for legislative and executive branch policymakers. The value of the federal Medicare waiver provides a strong disincentive for policymakers in any branch of state government to abandon the system. Finally, the apparent ability of the rate setting system to hold down the growth in hospital charges provides an additional discouragement to those inside government who would seek another financing structure for hospital care. Interviewees in the Senate, the House of Delegates, and the Department of Health frequently defer to the Health Services Cost Review Commission leadership in discussions about the future of the system. Though the rapid growth in Medicaid managed care may lead to a shift in attitude on the part of policymakers, the current lack of conflict is one more example of how Maryland has found a way to make rate setting work in the current volatile environment.

In Massachusetts, rate setting began because of the Medicaid financial crisis of the mid-1970s. While the state program was affected by rate setting decisions in subsequent years, its officials did not play a significant role in rate regulation decisions throughout the 1980s. The subsequent Medicaid crisis in the early 1990s played an important role in precipitating rate setting's demise. With plans for a major Medicaid managed care program developing rapidly in the early 1990s, the linkage of Medicaid hospital payments to a dysfunctional charge structure was viewed as a key reason to abandon rate setting:

> Medicaid was not the sole reason for [deregulation]. But to the extent that Medicaid was a payer, what really drove the change was the interest of the payers and the changes occurring in hospital finance generally . . . In Medicaid's case, we really didn't have control over what we were paying. (Interview with Bruce Bullen, Commissioner, Massachusetts Department of Medical Assistance, Boston, January 4, 1995)

Rivalry between Rate Setting Commission and Medicaid officials was common during the late 1980s and early 1990s, as Medicaid sought authority to control its own financial destiny. While Rate Setting bureaucrats won a number of the turf battles in the late 1980s, Medicaid officials won the major battles during the deregulation process because of extraordinary budget increases facing their program and because Medicaid officials' positions were consistent with those of other important interest groups such as Blue Cross and HMOs.

In the history of the New Jersey DRG system, Medicaid purchasing decisions had not been a major factor. That began to change in the mid- to late 1980s when the DRG system became more dysfunctional. Even though New Jersey Medicaid program officials were not aggressive in implementing managed care, they came to believe in the late 1980s that the DRG program was wasteful and inefficient and that it led to excessive Medicaid payments to hospitals that were beyond the agency's ability to control. Tensions became apparent between the Medicaid program and the DoH that reached into Governor Florio's office in 1991. The governor and his staff sided with Medicaid, giving it a greater payment differential to reduce acute care hospital expenditures.[20]

In the years leading up to Judge Wolin's May 1992 decision, Governor Florio became increasingly disenchanted with the DRG program and seized upon the judge's decision to place deregulation squarely on the state's agenda. While concerns about the usefulness of the DRG system were foremost in the governor's mind, concerns about the impact of the system on the state's health purchasing systems were also important as the state continued to grapple with the economic recession of the early 1990s.

New York's NYPHRM model was most frequently characterized by consensus decision making and collaboration during the five legislatively enacted versions, even though disagreements and confrontations occurred. A high degree of cooperation characterized decision making among legislative leaders, the governor's staff, the Department of Health leadership, and the regulators. Because Medicaid had not moved forward on mandated managed care until the mid-1990s, tensions between that program, housed in the state Department of Social Services, and rate setting were not substantial.

The strong pressure to move Medicaid into a full managed care system shifted the attitudes toward continued rate setting in New York. The consensus that held NYPHRMs I–V together now has been replaced by an equally strong consensus that the time for mandatory hospital rate setting had passed. Central was the emergence of purchasing rather than regulation as the critical state governmental need. The decoupling of Medicaid and Blue Cross rates in the spring of 1995 was the most tangible evidence of the change before the actual deregulation legislation was approved in July 1996. The new challenge for New York policymakers is to preserve the key health care access elements that have been built into the NYPHRM financing model over the past 14 years:

> What's really so daunting about the task is that it took 12 to 16 years to build up a whole system of health care financing. And it's all converging in one legislative session and in one six month time period. And undoing any piece is going to have a profound impact on other pieces. I look at this as a set of dominoes. (DoH Commissioner Barbara DeBuono, in *Empire State Report,* October 1995)

Summary Comments on Interest Groups
Most apparent from this survey of key rate setting interests is that—with one important exception—each set of interests had its wins and losses. At one time or another, they were all able to influence the shape and direction of hospital regulatory policy in important ways, some more than others.

The one entity that most frequently got what it wanted was state government, in the form of the state's health sector purchasing (chiefly Medicaid) needs, backed up by both executive and legislative branches. In fact, it is reasonable to conclude from this summary that unlike every other group, the state *always*—or nearly always—got what it wanted. Shown below is another version of table 4.2 that shows state government's experience under rate setting, instead of that of the hospitals (+ indicates an attainment of objectives; – indicates failure to achieve objectives; 0 indicates a mixed verdict).

Even during those periods when hospitals were particularly successful in winning large infusions of financial resources (particularly during the maturity stages in Massachusetts and New Jersey), it is clear that legislators and regulators made conscious policy decisions to direct more money to hospitals to compensate for perceived overtightening in prior regulatory periods. Even huge policy direction changes, such as support for deregulation in Massachusetts, New Jersey, and New York, must nonetheless be characterized as wins for the administrations and legislative leaders that pushed for and won these changes in the face of mixed or uncertain positions by many key interests. A key and continuing concern for state policymakers was the health purchasing needs of government. Rate setting programs were initiated largely to protect the interests of the state as purchaser and were abandoned because of a changed approach by those same purchasers.

But is state government, thus, our elusive cartel as outlined in the theory of economic regulation? Not by a long shot. There is simply no support in the literature relative to the theory of economic regulation that would allow government itself to be the cartel. The suggestion distorts a fundamental characteristic of the model whereby legislators, regulators, and governors are directed by the regulated industry and are merely ciphers seeking reelection and job security, aided by cash, volunteers, and support from interest groups. There is even less support for the Niskanen hypothesis that suggests that the regulators themselves become an independent and overly powerful interest group. The health purchaser functions of state government have grown in power and influence, but with the active direction, encouragement, and support of legislative and executive branch officials, not at all on their own.

It can be argued that state government in its multiple roles as purchaser, policymaker, and regulator holds too many of the cards for the public's or its own good. This observation would be most in sync with Tierney's conclusion that "government is now the driving force in health policy making."[21] But that suggestion is the research question for another study.

Now we examine the specific hypotheses presented at the start of this study relative to the theory of economic regulation.

TABLE 4.3. State Government Experience under Rate Setting

	Birth	Growth	Maturity	Decline/Revival
MD	+	+	+	+
MA	+	+	0	+
NJ	+	+	0	+
NY	+	+	+	+

Examination of Theory of Economic Regulation Hypotheses

Presented below is a table summarizing findings from each state (and overall) for each of the hypotheses specified in the theory of economic regulation model.

Evidence explaining the conclusions for each hypothesis and for each state will be presented in turn.

> *E1:* Rate Setting regulation should benefit hospitals more than consumers.

Maryland. There is evidence to suggest that hospitals have been the principal beneficiaries from the Maryland rate regulation system going back as far as 1971 when the original enabling legislation was written in MHA headquarters with the specific purpose of preempting more intrusive federal rules that were wrongly anticipated. The selection of a hospital CEO as the first chairman of the HSCRC adds further weight to this argument. The fact that inpatient admissions in Maryland declined much more slowly than in the rest of the nation between 1982 and 1992 (Maryland's

TABLE 4.4. Theory of Economic Regulation Hypotheses and Results

	MD	MA	NJ	NY	Overall
E1. Rate setting should benefit hospitals more than consumers.	NO	MIXED	YES	MIXED	MIXED
E2. Shifts in the configuration of interest groups supporting rate settings should accompany deregulation.	—	YES	YES	YES	YES
E3. Shifts in interest group support should not be observable in Maryland.	MIXED	—	—	—	MIXED
E4. Elected officials should play only a secondary role, with interest groups leading the agenda.	NO	NO	NO	NO	NO
E5. Identifiable shifts in overt political support from interest groups to key legislative leaders should be identifiable.	NO	NO	NO	NO	NO

position among the 50 states rose from 42 to 24) suggests that this system helped to prop up an unnecessary level of hospital business.

But these points are overridden by strong counterevidence. It is fact that: (1) growth in charges per admission have been lower than the national average for 19 of 20 years; (2) per capita hospital growth between 1980 and 1991 was 47th among the 50 states; (3) length of stay dropped between 1982 and 1992 from 11 to 36; and (4) the operating margins of Maryland hospitals have been consistently lower than margins for acute care hospitals nationally. All of these facts strongly contradict the assertion that hospitals won out at the expense of consumers. The numerous lawsuits facing the system from the hospital community during its early years that were won by the regulators provide further evidence, as does the fact that the trustees who were newly in charge of the MHA in 1971 explicitly wanted a prospective alternative to retrospective, cost-based reimbursement. This conclusion does not suggest that consumers will always be beneficiaries, especially in a new managed care environment. But for now, the evidence strongly contradicts the hypothesis. *(NO)*

Massachusetts. Data suggest that between the years 1976 and 1987 the system under Chapters 409, 372, and 574 actually reduced the rate of growth of inpatient costs per admission relative to the national average. Indeed, Massachusetts's per capita hospital cost growth was 42d among the 50 states between 1980 and 1991—even though the years 1988 to 1992 were ones of hyperinflation for hospitals. Also clear is that Medicaid cost control was a key motivation for the establishment of rate setting, and that—unlike in New Jersey—Massachusetts policymakers moved quickly to place tight controls on the growth in the uncompensated care pool over hospital objections.

Evidence supporting hospitals as the winners include: (1) the extraordinary growth in hospital costs during the Chapter 23 period when the bottom fell out of the rate setting system; (2) Massachusetts remained number *one* among the 50 states in per capita health and hospital costs in 1972, 1982, and 1992; (3) the federal Medicare waiver was abandoned as soon as—and only when—the hospital community decided to give it up. There is convincing evidence on both sides. *(MIXED)*

New Jersey. There is evidence that both the SHARE program and the DRG program in its early years through 1984 were successful in holding down per admission costs below the national average. But on the other side, the evidence is strong that the New Jersey program epitomized regulatory failure: (1) an extraordinary growth in charge control authority in the final six years, including retrospective settlements where regulators simply threw up their hands and threw at the hospitals more than $1 billion in increased charge authorization; (2) New Jersey's rank among the 50 states rose from 27th in 1972 to fifth in 1992 in per capita health costs, and from 30th in 1982 to 16th in 1991 in per capita hospital costs; (3) the state's rank in per admission costs rose from 23rd in 1982 to 15th in 1992; (4) the drop in admissions was far less than the national average, and the state's rank rose from 30th in 1982 to tenth in 1992; (5) added to this was an extraordinary growth in the surcharges tied to the uncompensated care pool, nearing 20 percent in 1991. *(YES)*

New York. Evidence supporting consumers as winners includes the following factors: (1) hospitals faced two major periods of deep financial crisis during the rate setting years, in the late 1970s and 1980s, both the result of aggressive cost containment policies pushed by the state; (2) per capita hospital growth between 1980 and 1991 was only 33d in the nation among the 50 states; (3) New York hospitals have consistently had the lowest operating margins in the nation during the rate setting years, and the state has consistently made Medicaid cost control a central driver in its health system decisions.

Supporting hospitals as winners: (1) only $4 of every $10 going to uncompensated care pools actually went for indigent care in the early 1980s; (2) per capita hospital costs, per admission hospital costs, and average length of stay have consistently been among the top four of the 50 states throughout the 1980s and 1990s; (3) the drop in admissions was far less than the national average, with the state's rank rising from 29 in 1982 to 15 in 1992. The evidence to grant the state a fuzzy grade is clear: *(MIXED)*

Summary. As has been stated before, hospitals had their wins and losses. Rate setting systems have seen periods of strict and loose financial controls. Evidence strongly suggests that consumers were losers in New Jersey and winners in Maryland. It is not as clear in Massachusetts and New York. *(MIXED)*

> *E2:* A shift in the configuration of interest groups supporting and opposing rate setting's continuation should accompany deregulation.

Massachusetts. The clearest switch was observable in the executive branch with the transition from Governor Michael Dukakis to Governor William Weld on downward, including the Secretariat of Health and Human Services as well as the Medicaid program. Massachusetts Blue Cross had been a long-term supporter of rate setting, but joined the opposition when it became apparent that a Maryland-type model that would end HMOs' right to unlimited discounts was not in the offing. The business community moved more slowly and hedged its support for deregulation with calls for ill-defined global caps, but was clearly counted in the column supporting deregulation. The HMOs were not part of the original rate setting coalition, but strongly pushed for deregulation as newly formidable players. Some hospitals, especially large and powerful academic medical centers, were strong early supporters for deregulation; the MHA waited to see the likely direction, and followed rather than led, but clearly did not push for continued regulation. *(YES)*

New Jersey. Again, the clearest switch involved the administration, as Governor Florio became a strong advocate for dropping the DRG model, along with his key health policy aide, Brenda Bacon, and the Medicaid program; the DoH stance was noncommittal on continuing its own program. The hospital industry literally divided itself over the issue, with suburban and community hospitals promoting deregulation, while urban and teaching institutions worked against the plan. The insurance community—including Blue Cross, commercial plans such as Prudential, and HMOs—all wanted to move away from rate setting with its burdensome and unpredictable retrospective settlements. The business community changed its position in the spring of 1992 to favor deregulation. Most unusual among the subject states, the New Jersey labor movement placed itself squarely on the side of those seeking to dismantle the system. It is noteworthy that the nongovernmental interests all defined deregulation as a three-year transition out of the DRGs, and that the governmental players—Governor Florio and the legislature—moved for the sharper break. *(YES)*

New York. The change in support for NYPHRM starts at the top, with newly elected Governor Pataki and his Commissioner of Health, Barbara DeBuono who led the process to find acceptable replacement revenue sources for the parts of the rate setting system to be salvaged. The hospital industry, as in New Jersey, appeared divided over NYPHRM's fate, with Long Island and New York City institutions initially promoting continuation, and upstate hospitals looking toward a market future. Ultimately, the industry supported deregulation as long as adequate funding was provided for uncompensated care, graduate medical education, and other ancillary needs. The insurance community, including Blue Cross, the commercial payers, and the HMOs, all supported deregulation. Business also weighed in to support deregulation, a change from its long-term support. Labor was largely silent on the basic deregulation question, seeking adequate support for worker retraining and uncompensated care instead. Perhaps the most unique development was the strong deregulation advocacy by the low-income consumer group, the State Communities Aid Association, which had a long history of NYPHRM support. *(YES)*

> *E3:* Shifts in the configuration of interest group support for regulation should not be observable in Maryland.

Maryland clearly does not exhibit the sharp changes in the interest group landscape that appeared in the other deregulated states. However, a close examination reveals a series of subtle shifts that produce a more clouded picture, chiefly in the business and insurance industries. The business leadership has clearly sounded its intention to open a dialogue on the future of hospital rate regulation in the state and is talking about the changes in the state's environment wrought by the strong emergence of HMOs. The Chairman of the State Chamber of Commerce used the word "crisis" in his letter to Governor Glendening calling for a "fresh" look at the regulatory structure.

In the insurance community, Blue Cross has always had an ambivalent attitude toward Maryland rate setting, a stance very much in evidence today. But commercial insurers, who have been long and vocal supporters, now openly question the need for rate setting in the managed care environment—and privately admit that all their key companies would like to see it go. The HMOs, similarly, will not call openly for abandonment, but clearly indicate dissatisfaction with its restrictions. In Maryland as in other states, fissures are also in evidence in the hospital community, with suburban hospitals talking quietly but openly about the need for a less heavy-handed approach and an ability to compete on a more even footing with the new players such as the one-day surgical centers.

All of these groups have been stopped in their tracks by a strong resistance on the part of the legislature, hospital leadership, and the HSCRC/DoHMH bureaucracy to suggestions of deregulation. Thus far the legislature's stance clearly has prevailed. But it is equally clear that the ground is beginning to shift. *(MIXED)*

> *E4:* Elected officials should play only a secondary role in decisions about rate setting and deregulation, with interest groups leading the agenda.

Maryland. The key health policy leaders in the House and Senate do not want to shut out any dialogue about the value and direction of the rate regulation system. But they make it abundantly clear that Maryland's unique model fits well with the state's values and political culture and that they will fight hard to keep it if that becomes necessary. Thus far, the administration of Governor Glendening has issued the same signals, though the governor himself has not become directly involved. The leadership of the HSCRC is proactive in its work, seeking to forge consensus within the current policy framework and allowing experimentation that does not undermine the basic structure.

Rather than suggesting that legislators and administration officials work for them, key interest groups are wary of saying things and taking positions that would receive a negative response from those public officials. The suggestion that the legislators and regulators dance to the tunes played by the special interests is not credible. *(NO)*

Massachusetts. Throughout the history of the Massachusetts system, legislators and administration officials have had an active role. The chief exception to the trend was in 1981–82, when the Business Roundtable filled a policy vacuum during the years of Governor Edward King and drove the process that created the Chapter 372 all-payer model. The deregulation process, though, provides the clearest evidence relating to the hypothesis.

In December 1990, the Massachusetts Hospital Association surprised most observers by voting for a continuation and modification of rate regulation after the Chapter 23 sunset date of September 30, 1991. Later that month, a Special Commission voted by a wide margin to back a Maryland-style regulatory model. Newly elected Governor William Weld and his chief health adviser Charles Baker are credited by all observers with turning that wobbly consensus on its head and starting the march toward deregulation. When the administration tried to mollify critics by proposing a three-year phaseout of rate regulation, House Ways and Means Chairman Thomas Finneran changed the dynamic by producing a bill calling for immediate deregulation. His form is what reached the governor's desk for signing.

The key interest groups, while endorsing a move to deregulation, were far more tentative and cautious than were key governmental officials. Included in this characterization are the hospitals who initially favored a Maryland-style alternative, business leaders who sought an elusive form of global hospital caps, insurers seeking a longer transition, and labor leaders who were unable to articulate a clear position on the matter. The deregulation decision in Massachusetts was driven overwhelmingly by state policymakers, legislative and executive, and the key interest groups largely went along for the ride. *(NO)*

New Jersey. Administration officials, more than legislators, were in the lead in establishing and running the New Jersey rate setting system. The move to create DRGs was very much governmentally driven by the Department of Health and the core of specialists they hired, including Bruce Vladeck. Once again, the deregulation period provides the most useful portrait of public officials' involvement.

During his first two years in office, Governor James Florio became increasingly disenchanted with the DRG rate system, as did his key health adviser, Brenda Bacon. On the day of Judge Wolin's ruling, Governor Florio spoke first about the need to dismantle the system, before the affected interests weighed in. The new Republican majorities in the Assembly and Senate had wanted to dismantle the system for some time and seized on the opportunity created by the Uncompensated Care Pool crisis. Rate setting did not have to go in 1992—it was a deliberate, policy-driven decision.

The interests represented in the New Jersey Health Care Reform Coalition helped to develop the public consensus behind deregulation. But their key recommendation called for a three-year phaseout of the system and reinstitution of the one cent increase in the state's sales tax, proposals rejected out of hand by both the governor and the legislative leadership. *(NO)*

New York. The names involved in establishing and maintaining NYPHRM and its predecessor statutes belie any notion of government officials as passive: Assembly Majority Leader James Tallon, Senator Tarky Lombardi, Governor Mario Cuomo, Health Commissioner David Axelrod, and others. These were individuals with sharply defined and commonly shared visions for the health system, visions that they worked aggressively to impose on an often reluctant system.

In the most recent process leading to deregulation, Governor Pataki set the tone by establishing a deregulation mandate throughout state government. His Health Commissioner, Barbara DeBuono, took the lead in attempting to define how access provisions would be defined in the post-NYPHRM environment, an approach affirmed by the governor in his March 20, 1996, call for NYPHRM's complete deregulation (*New York Times,* March 21, 1996, 1). The new Senate Health Committee Chairman, Kemp Hannon, proclaimed "no more NYPHRM's" early in the process in 1995. And his Assembly counterpart, Richard Gottfried, made it clear that he would fight aggressively to preserve maximum access guarantees, despite whatever deals could be cut by the involved constellation of interest groups.

These directions are all taken in an environment where the hospital organizations were divided and at odds with each over the parameters of the coming debate. In the end, it was a debate about the amount of money put into the system to care for access obligations. Those decisions were overwhelmingly governmentally driven. *(NO)*

> *E5:* Shifts in overt political support from affected interests to key legislative leaders should be identifiable.

This hypothesis will be discussed grouping all four states together, because the results are similar for all four. First, in no state did any of the 60 interviewees—inside or outside government—answer affirmatively that decisions by public officials about the fate of hospital rate setting were driven by campaign donations from affected interests or similar electoral/politically motivated concerns. Additionally, interviewees were unable to report any awareness of changes in patterns of political donations from key interest groups during the period leading up to the deregulation process. Also, interviewees (a politically savvy and well-connected set of individuals) were widely inconsistent in their judgments concerning which groups and interests provided the most important levels of political support, financial or otherwise.

Second, in all four states, reports of political action committees filed at offices that regulate campaign finance matters were examined in the three-year period before, during, and immediately after the deregulation decision. Political committee records examined included those of hospitals, insurers, HMOs, labor, and more. There was no evidence that could be gleaned from these filings to suggest any overt shifts in the kind or amount of campaign donations from interest groups to key legislative decision makers.

Third, individual reports of several key legislators in each subject state were examined to observe any identifiable shifts in levels of support from key interest groups. Again, no pattern could be observed reflecting any shifts in support from political action committees or other sources that could be identified. A limitation to this third observation is mentioned below.

Finally, the summary of rate setting developments in each state outlined in chapter 4 suggests a clear rationale for the directions taken based upon both policy considerations and the input provided by key constituencies. The strikingly similar patterns observable in the deregulated states, together with the contradiction to that pattern observable in Maryland, undermine the notion that decisions by key policymakers about the future of rate setting were up for sale to the high bidders. No evidence could be found that would lend support to the hypothesis, and thus the conclusion for all four states, as well as the summary judgment, is *(NO)*.

However, the following three caveats must accompany this conclusion to hypothesis *E5*. First, there is no ability to track the occupation and organizational affiliations of individual campaign donors; thus, shifts in the levels of support from individual contributors associated with affected interests would not be detected by the examination means utilized. For example, individual contributors who give because of their ties to insurance, hospital, or business interests cannot be identified simply by examining campaign finance documents. Second, campaign finance record reporting requirements vary from state to state, and the consistency in the materials examined was not uniform, making cross-state observations risky and unreliable.

Third, and most important, an examination into campaign finance documents of this sort fails to capture the impact of changes in those occupying leadership positions. For example, in the year of New Jersey's deregulation, the Assembly elected a new, Republican speaker for the first time in many years. That individual was always opposed to the state's DRG system, but only in 1991 from the speaker's vantage point. Thus, the change in the speakership was a key factor leading to New Jersey's deregulation—but not any particular change in the level of interest group support to that individual.

From this survey and analysis, we can conclude that interest groups played a critically important role in the development and disposition of rate setting in the subject states, even though the hypotheses of the theory of economic regulation are not largely supported. Next we will examine the role of ideas and the specific hypotheses of the punctuated equilibrium model.

CHAPTER 5

Ideas and the Fate of Hospital Rate Setting

> It wasn't partisan. There was no legislative/executive distinction. There was no inside/outside government distinction in our mindset of how the world of health care economics worked. Then, all of a sudden, people went: "Oh, maybe it doesn't work that way. Maybe the emperor has no clothes." (Interview with Gerry Billings, Executive Director, State Communities Aid Association, Albany, June 30, 1995)

Ideas matter . . . sometimes. When and how they matter is a central question of this chapter and this book. There are times in political battle when the competition of interests prevails, and ideas are secondary or nonexistent. At other times, it is ideas that are in competition, when a more fundamental level of discourse concerning policy directions is held. At those times, interests often play only supporting roles and must accommodate new or prevailing policy ideas. When prevailing policy ideas are generally accepted and largely unchallenged, interest group politics prevail. But when the central policy idea is up for grabs and the competition for dominance is serious, then interest group rivalry stands to the side while the idea rivalry is settled.

This framework fits well with the rate setting case histories from the four states. Rate setting systems were established when the prevailing policy idea for how health providers should be paid—cost-based retrospective reimbursement—was under attack as inflationary and inefficient. Prospective payment, a method to rearrange the incentives faced by medical providers, was proposed during the 1960s and 1970s as a replacement policy idea. The agent to manage and enforce the new system at that time was government, largely because no other party held sufficient leverage over providers. Interests outside government—including business, labor, and insurers—accepted this role for government without objection. During the succeeding decades of state-based rate setting, when the reigning policy idea went largely unchallenged, battles over rate setting became battles among key interests over the rules of the system.

Gradually, a new idea emerged to challenge rate setting—not a return to cost-based reimbursement, or the elimination of reimbursement regulation. The new idea, rather, was that the private sector—using managed care, capitation, and other advanced forms of prospective payment regulation—had reached a stage where it could outperform government in controlling and even reducing provider payments. Further, the new policy idea proposed that a system emphasizing competition among payers and providers would be more efficient than the prevailing system that emphasized uniformity and equity. The ensuing competition between the old and new policy ideas most characterizes deregulation.

On the national level, a debate between competition and regulation proponents raged fiercely from the late 1970s into the 1990s. While this debate focused on many areas of the economy, health care received a good share of attention. Regulation advocates described health care as an inevitable example of market failure, with government intervention needed to control costs and to address growing access gaps. Competition advocates accepted the diagnosis of market failure, but focused their attention instead on changes in the structure of the health economy needed to correct it. Substantial research and policy writing on the topic was published during this period, with both sides citing the alternative examples of mandatory hospital rate setting versus market competition.[1] A key article by Goldsmith in 1984, "The Death of a Paradigm," pointedly noted the emerging shift in the balance of power between providers and purchasers in the health sector and the ramifications of the change: "The economic power of providers, nurtured for decades, has begun to shift from those who provide care to those who pay for it . . . The health sector is a vital active enterprise in the midst of revolutionary change."[2] By the late 1980s, the national debate over rate setting had largely subsided without an apparent winner. (For example, the five-year *Health Affairs* index, 1982–86, contained a separate category entitled "State Rate Setting" with 17 references; the 1987–91 index contained no such category and only two state rate setting references, both of which were from the year 1987.)

While the results of the national debate were inconclusive, the health system changes noted by Goldsmith gradually began to develop significant momentum in various states. It took some years for the implications of Goldsmith's observations to become apparent in the rate setting states that eventually deregulated, and the results were not uniform over time. This time lag can partly be attributed to the differential rate of growth in managed care in the various states, as well as to the normal variation in the rate of diffusion in policy ideas in regions and states. Mitnick notes that the political and legislative processes involved in deregulation can be as burdensome and time consuming as those involved in initially establishing regulatory forms: "Deregulation . . . is itself a policy that must reach an institutional agenda, be subject to decisions on that agenda, and experience implementation . . . The characteristics of the policy formulation and implementation process for deregulation are therefore similar in many major respects to that of the process for regulation."[3]

This chapter's investigation into policy ideas and rate setting utilizes Baumgartner and Jones's punctuated equilibrium model of policy change that was outlined in chapter 2 as a rival to the theory of economic regulation in explaining the fate of rate setting in the states.[4] In this chapter, we will examine the policy ideas debate in each of the states, and examine the specific hypotheses of the model in light of the evidence collected. Table 5.1 specifies the hypotheses for this model that were originally presented in chapter 2.

Policy Ideas in the Subject States

Maryland

> The people want to keep the system as long as the philosophical underpinnings can be carried through and maintained in this era of HMOs and competition. The key is equity, that charges should bear a reasonable relationship to costs. Also fairness, to avoid cost shifting, so that everyone pays the same as every other person. This was a great departure from what was going on at the time . . . The Commission has held fast to the basic concepts, but the methodology has changed

TABLE 5.1.   Punctuated Equilibrium Model Hypotheses

P1.	There should be an identifiable "policy idea" accompanying deregulation.
P2.	In Maryland, we should be able to observe the nonemergence of the new policy idea or clear indications of nonacceptance.
P3.	In deregulated states, we should observe altered institutional structures to account for the demise of the old idea and the ascension of the new one.
P4.	In Maryland, we should observe no similar institutional change.
P5.	In deregulated states, we should observe the emergence of new players who, by broadening the scope of conflict, undermined rate setting's policy monopoly.
P6.	In Maryland, we should observe no such no players, or clear indications as to their ineffectiveness.

significantly. (Interview with Eugene Feinblatt, Attorney, former
Chair, Maryland Commission on Health Care Finance, Baltimore,
June 21, 1995)

Rather than a response to the demands of key interest groups, the original
bills filed in the Maryland legislature in the 1967 to 1970 period were the
response of concerned legislators to rising health and hospital costs. Those
early bills were not sophisticated in their structures, but laid the groundwork for the policy debate that ensued in 1971 over legislation that established the Maryland Health Services Cost Review Commission (HSCRC).
Consistent with Baumgartner and Jones's model, the Maryland rate regulation structure was established during a period of significant political
upheaval. In 1971, newly elected governor Marvin Mandel made the adoption of hospital rate regulation a centerpiece of this consumer protection
agenda. By that time, a large number of legislators were filing bills to craft
one type of rate regulation or another. While the Maryland Hospital Association supported (and wrote) the bill that became law, they did so under
the direction of trustee board members who rejected their CEO's prior
opposition for several reasons. One of their key reasons was to establish a
more predictable and prospective form of reimbursement. The political
upheaval included a pitched battle between hospitals and Blue Cross, with
legislators and administrative officials attempting to mediate the dispute.

There is no evidence from journalistic accounts, documents, or interviewees that any other competing policy ideas were part of the 1971
process. Rather, the choice was to continue with cost-based retrospective
reimbursement, with its inflationary incentives, or else to move to a regulated and more predictable prospective structure. There is evidence from
all three sources that the adoption of this new idea was an essential part of
the discussion and process in 1971.

Following adoption of the new system, we can clearly observe the
development of an institutional structure to carry out the objectives of the
new idea, as well as the formation of a narrow policy monopoly to channel
feedback and to maintain and protect the structure. The structure was the
Health Services Cost Review Commission, housed within the Department
of Health and Mental Hygiene, but granted independent authority to pro-
mulgate its own rules and practices, within a framework of broad discretion granted by the legislature. The policy monopoly consisted of the following primary and secondary key players: primary players were the
hospital association, and the leadership and staff of the HSCRC; secondary ones were key executive branch officials such as the Commissioner
of Health, the few senators and delegates with a sophisticated understanding of the system, the AFL-CIO, Blue Cross, and commercial carriers.

During the ensuing 25 years, the Maryland rate regulation has undergone substantial changes in its reimbursement methodology, as outlined in chapter 3. The changes have been attempts to respond to negative feedback on the operation of the system as well as to keep up with changes in the health sector environment. Without exception, these changes have been negotiated within the structure of the prevailing policy monopoly. (For example, there have been no statutes enacted since 1971 modifying the system in any significant way.) Even the activities involving the federal Medicare waiver legislation were restricted to the closed circle and the Maryland congressional delegation. Fitting with the punctuated equilibrium model, these changes have all been incremental and evolutionary in nature. The "fit" of the change with the principles laid out in the original enabling statute is always a concern of regulators:

> We go back to the original goals of the Legislature: cost containment, equity or fair payment for the system, access and accountability. Those are always what we go back to in assessing any given project . . . When you get people in the room and talk about principles, you get remarkable consensus on what are the public policy issues from the overall state standpoint. (Interview with Robert Murray, Executive Director, HSCRC, Baltimore, June 21, 1995)

Virtually every individual interviewed could identify their version of the "policy idea" associated with the Maryland rate setting system. The key themes mentioned most often included equity, a mechanism to control the growth in costs, fairness in the treatment of poor people, and correction for "market failure." Every interviewee for this study could also identify the replacement idea that would succeed rate setting in a deregulation scenario—this was most commonly referred to as "the free market," whether the interviewee supported or opposed this notion. While interview subjects are not uniform in their assessment of the prospects for structural changes in the future, all agree that the market is the alternative:

> We fought the major interest groups to get rate setting enacted. And some groups are itching to fight again to open it up to the free market. This is about ideas. (Interview with Casper Taylor, Speaker, Maryland House of Delegates, Annapolis, June 19, 1995)

Interview subjects in all four states were asked to assess whether debates over rate setting in their states were more about ideas or competition among interests. Generally, Maryland opinions followed a pattern exhibited among subjects in all four states—government officials view rate setting as being fundamentally about policy ideas, and interest group spokespersons view it largely as being about interest group competition. There is also agreement that the fate of Maryland's long program in setting hospital rates of payment is not a compelling issue on the public agenda in the state at this time:

> Rate setting is not a front burner issue in this state . . . Overall it's a plus, but it's not the panacea that the HSCRC says that it is. (Interview with Gerard Anderson, Professor, Johns Hopkins School of Public Health, Baltimore, June 22, 1995)

> Health policy is not debated on the policy level in Maryland. There are two important things missing. The first is serious substantive debate at the legislative level. And second is an appreciation for the value of the free market. The free market doesn't get much sway here. (Interview with Thomas Goddard, Director of Legislative and Regulatory Affairs, New York Life Health Plus, Green Belt, Maryland, June 23, 1995)

The description of rate setting as a secondary issue in Maryland politics fits well with the punctuated equilibrium suggestion that successful policy monopolies are able to keep broad discussions of structural change away from the primary policy agenda. Much to the frustration of those who would like to change the system, its defenders have been able to prevent the acceptance of an adverse issue redefinition and to respond on their own terms to changes in the health care marketplace.

The key modification to rate setting in recent years has been the HSCRC's experimentation with capitated payment plans under a rate regulation umbrella. This is an evolution that has never been attempted within any rate setting structure. It represents Maryland regulators' unique response to new ideas about efficient ways to pay for health care services. It also helps to disarm critics who would complain that the system is unable to respond to changes in the market. Again, these changes are designed to conform to the basic principles of the regulatory system:

> The objectives for us are to still allow for hospitals to compete on the basis of efficiency—but to hold them harmless for price differences other than those based on efficiency, i.e., for differences in uncompensated care and graduate medical education. We want to hold them harmless for differences in severity. (Interview with Robert Murray, Executive Director, HSCRC, Baltimore, June 21, 1995)

While all Maryland parties, in and out of government, watch developments in other states and create room for experimentation and change in their model, they do so affirming the basic ideas written into the original enabling statute 25 years ago:

> The all-payer hospital rate regulation system is the cornerstone of Maryland's long-standing history of pioneering, innovative public policy relating to health care delivery that is tailored to the unique needs of the citizens of this state . . . this system serves as a national model that has successfully demonstrated that the cooperative establishment of appropriate incentives can yield enormous social benefits as well as control costs . . . (Preamble to Health Care Reform Act of 1995)

The punctuated equilibrium model recognizes that any policy monopoly is more unstable than it might otherwise appear; the potential splits among hospitals and the possible desertion of key insurance-affiliated allies could also undermine the system. Political change, from Democratic to Republican control, would also place the system at risk. But, for now, the Maryland system remains the sole example of a continuing and thriving rate setting policy monopoly.

Massachusetts

The hospital rate setting program in Massachusetts was born from a disruptive and intense fiscal crisis and recession, and the need for policymakers to rein in skyrocketing Medicaid costs. A series of pitched and broad-based battles that included legislators, administration officials, hospitals, business, Blue Cross, and commercial payers over a six-year period finally led to the establishment of the all-payer rate regulation policy monopoly under Chapter 372 in 1982.

The essential policy idea behind Massachusetts rate setting, according to interviewees, had several facets: to control Medicaid spending by controlling all hospital costs; to minimize cost shifting among payers; to provide an honest broker between providers and payers to guarantee an honest price; and, more fundamentally, to respond to market failure in the health sector by creating a "public utility" form of regulation. As with Maryland's genesis, in Massachusetts we can observe dissatisfaction with the ability of retrospective methods to control spending, along with the "idea" that controlling charges to all payers was necessary to provide effective controls on the rate of growth in Medicaid spending.

The institutional structure that accompanied the new system was an expanded and strengthened Rate Setting Commission with three full-time commissioners and a professional staff. As was true in Maryland, the structure was located inside the larger governmental health structure, but provided with independence from direct day-to-day pressures. Institutional separation from the Medicaid program also guaranteed some degree of bureaucratic rivalry. Unlike similar regulatory bodies in Maryland and New York, the Massachusetts overseer suffered from mediocre staff salary levels and a rapid and regular degree of turnover that left regulators weakened relative to better-paid professional staff from the hospitals. Indeed, it was common for hospitals to hire some of the best staff away from the Massachusetts Rate Setting Commission.

The new rate setting policy monopoly consisted of regulators, hospitals, Blue Cross, commercial payers, labor, HMOs, and business. In the early 1980s, this monopoly revolved around the activities of Nelson Gifford, chairman of the Health Care Task Force for the Massachusetts Business Roundtable and the CEO of a manufacturing company. The informal, closed-door Health Care Coalition became the locus of discussion for any and all changes in the hospital regulatory environment between 1980 and 1985. HMOs and labor were added to the coalition after its initial formation, only after complaints about their exclusion were lodged. Consumer groups argued for admission and were left outside the door.

Between the years 1982 and 1987, disputes concerning the rate setting system were dealt with quietly and without major controversy. But the process leading up to Chapter 23, the Universal Health Care Law of 1988, was open and confrontational. While much public attention was focused on the access debates relative to the uninsured, hospitals sought to expand the scope of conflict around hospital rate setting rules by bringing more than 10,000 hospital workers to the Boston Common in September 1987 for a rally to demand more money for their institutions. To be sure, the intricacies of hospital finance that are part and parcel of the rate setting dialogue went over the heads of the vast majority of citizens reading about the health care controversies at the state House. The essential regulatory design questions still were discussed and understood by a small number of players, but the policy process in no way resembled the serene negotiating process in evidence during 25 years of Maryland rate setting.

In Massachusetts, the policy monopoly's days of peaceful and restrained "equilibrium" were short-lived. We can attribute this difference from Maryland to a number of factors: first, the short-lived nature of each enabling statute, lasting only between two and four years; second, the lack of leeway provided to rate setting professionals, leaving all major policy questions up to the legislature; and third, the large number of major hospitals that competed for financial and political leadership.

Following enactment of Chapter 23, hyperinflation developed in Massachusetts hospital costs that further eroded much of the remaining support for continued rate regulation. A severe fiscal crisis gripped the commonwealth in 1989, leading to a major budget shortfall exacerbated by double-digit increases for the Medicaid program. A Special Commission in 1990 was unable to agree on the precise outlines of a regulatory system to replace Chapter 23 after the law's September 1991 sunset. An accompanying crisis affecting the financial solvency of Blue Cross of Massachusetts created an additional rationale for major policy changes.

While the controversy that accompanied rate setting deregulation was not intense, there were efforts by consumers, labor officials, and academics to prevent or to modify the move to abandon rate regulation. The consumer organization Health Care for All, hospital worker unions, and health policy academics from Harvard, Brandeis, and Boston University all worked in various ways to challenge the growing consensus in favor of rate setting deregulation. Health Care for All organized press conferences, events, and other grass roots initiatives to win support for their single-payer alternative plan. The labor groups, chiefly Service Employees International Union Local 285, produced their own report about the increasing corporatization of community hospitals and the implications for community care.

Academics played a more prominent role in the Massachusetts deregulation process than can be observed in any phase of rate setting regulation or deregulation in the other subject states. Researchers from the Harvard School of Public Health and the Gordon Public Policy Center worked with House Health Care Chairwoman Carmen Buell during the summer of 1991 to craft a hospital global budget cap to add to the deregulation legislation, described as follows:

> H.5900 [Governor Weld's bill] is designed to lower aggregate hospital costs through increased competition. The proposed fail-safe mechanism is triggered *only* if aggregate hospital costs *increase substantially* under H.5900 . . . Supporters of the competitive approach should in fact enthusiastically support such a fail-safe mechanism, exactly because it effectively removes one of the serious concerns which might otherwise be raised against H.5900. (Draft memo to Representative Carmen Buell from Martin Levin, Gordon Public Policy Center, Brandeis University, August 26, 1991)

The proposals made by the Harvard and Brandeis academics, incorporated into the Health Care Committee's version, were dropped at the next stage in the House Ways and Means Committee and never reappeared.

At Boston University, an "Access and Affordability Monitoring

Project" affiliated with the School of Public Health had been producing reports on the Massachusetts health care market since the fall of 1988. In the summer and fall of 1991, they contributed a series of reports all of which sought to undermine the direction and support for deregulation. Some titles included "Paying for Our Mistakes" (July 2, 1991); "A Reckless Miscalculation" (September 16, 1991); "No Scorpions Needed: Building Fair, Simple and Affordable Hospital Payments in Massachusetts" (October 1, 1991); "California's Catastrophic Competition" (October 28, 1991); and "Manipulating the Minnesota Marketplace" (October 28, 1991).

The AAMP's most controversial contribution to the debate was a report also issued on October 28, 1991, entitled "Which Hospitals Are Vulnerable? Characteristics That Might Endanger Massachusetts Hospitals under a Competitive Payment Plan." Noting that "several experts have estimated that *10–20 additional hospitals will close* within three years if the fully competitive method of paying hospitals now making its way through the legislature were to pass," the report ranked the state's 91 acute care hospitals according to seven financial characteristics.[5] While the activities of consumers, labor groups, and academics generated some media attention and responses from pro-deregulation supporters, there is little evidence that their proregulatory activities made a significant mark on the process.

On the other side of the deregulation debate, interview subjects all agreed that a change in the prevailing policy idea was at the root of the deregulation decision, from start to finish. The administration's point person, Charles Baker, saw dissatisfaction with the prior system as a primary cause for deregulation:

> There was a willingness on the part of a lot of people to try something new, which is not always there . . . A big reason why [deregulation] happened was just because there were a lot of things that many people couldn't stand about Chapter 23. A lot of people were punished for doing the right things. There were a lot of weird incentives for people not to do the right thing. Rate setting lost the capacity to represent a broader public purpose. What people want more than anything out of these processes is a level playing field. (Interview with Charles Baker, Undersecretary for Health and Human Services, Boston, December 27, 1994)

There is evidence that the administration was concerned about the broader policy ideas and implications throughout the process. A September 2, 1991, file memo by Baker discusses "Johns Hopkins Professor

Gerry Andersen's Presentation on Maryland and Minnesota Hospital Systems":

> In 1971, Maryland and Minnesota both had per capita hospital costs of about $140. This was about 10 percent above the national average. In 1989, Minnesota's per capita hospital costs had risen to $818, while Maryland's had risen to $862. These numbers, in both cases, were below the national average. Conclusion: competition or regulation both work—as long as one is consistent—although they accomplish different things. (Memo to files, from Charles Baker, September 2, 1991)

At the other end of the process, the House Chairman of Ways and Means who crafted the bill that led to a quick deregulation talks about his own developmental process in moving toward an end to rate regulation:

> I thought the deregulated market would be more coherent than the regulated market which was criticized for being inequitable, not fully factual, sometimes political . . . As I recall, we caught the industry by surprise. This was a battle of ideas. This one I personalize. I struggled with it inside. I was not aware of anyone's interest on it outside. I spent the greatest amount of time on this one talking with Joe Trainor [Budget Director], not far behind that talking to you [author] and talking to Carmen. Testing myself, asking your thoughts and opinions. It was all ideas. (Interview with Thomas Finneran, Chair, House Committee on Ways and Means, Boston, January 21, 1995)

Other participants and observers in the deregulation process had similar impressions that—at least during this debate—ideas counted:

> A lot of education went on with the [House] members. It was a debate about the shift in ideas, and the sense that it was time to try something new. (Interview with Carmen Buell, House Chair, Joint Committee on Health Care, Boston, December 28, 1994)

> I remember the hearing before the Health Care Committee that summer when Baker spoke with such assurance, and the hospitals were supportive as well as the representatives from the business community. It was the first public manifestation that this was an idea that had come of age. It was clear that the idea had arrived. (Interview with Elizabeth Rothberg, Issues Director, Life Insurance Association of Massachusetts, Boston, December 29, 1994)

It's always about interest groups from day one. But it was also an idea thing. The Weld people brought a philosophy and a perspective about markets that was different than the Dukakis people and Democrats in general. To them, market failure wasn't one word. (Interview with Robert Hughes, Executive Director, Massachusetts Association of HMOs, Boston, December 15, 1994)

We can thus observe that a clash of ideas accompanied the Massachusetts deregulation experience—whether or not that debate had any major impact on the final deregulation statute. The final element in this part of the story is the punctuated equilibrium model's prediction of an altered institutional structure in states undergoing deregulation. In Massachusetts, this altered structure is apparent on several levels. First, the Rate Setting Commission lost its authority to establish prospective hospital charges. The agency's role was downgraded to that of an information gatherer in the deregulation statute. At the same time, the Medicaid Program saw its status increased from a agency within the Department of Public Welfare to a special division within the Secretariat of Health and Human Services; the Medicaid Program was authorized to negotiate its own rates of payment without rate setting oversight or approval. The Department of Mental Health was granted authority for the first time to conduct its own rate negotiations with hospitals. Finally, a new oversight agency—called the Hospital Payments Advisory Commission, or HOSPAC—was created in 1992 to monitor developments in the new competitive marketplace and to report on developing trends to the legislature. That new entity was eliminated in mid-1995.

New Jersey

The creation of the New Jersey system of hospital rate regulation was spread out over the longest period of time, with initial forays directed at Blue Cross more than at the hospital sector. As hospital costs began to escalate at a faster rate, the Blue Cross mechanism was seen as a convenient point of entry to broader controls. Mandatory hospital budget controls were adopted in 1971 that were left in the hands of an organization affiliated with the New Jersey Hospital Association. A 1974 book that exposed the ineptness of that model led to the enactment of Department of Health controls in 1975 and the establishment of the SHARE program in 1976.

There is strong evidence that ideas played a prominent role in the creation of the DRG, all-payer system between 1978 and 1982—perhaps even too much so. The newly appointed Commissioner of Health, Joanne Finley, in 1975 used her authority to attract $3 million in federal funding to enable the state to launch the nation's first experiment with case-based prospective payment. Analysts who have studied the New Jersey system have noted the importance of policy ideas in that model: "The prominence that DRGs have gained in current health policy is partially explained by the seductiveness that economic incentives hold for policy analysts. Economic logic appeals to common sense and its prescriptions appear to be self-executing: change the financial rewards and behavior changes . . . An alternative perspective, that of organizational theory, describes hospitals as complex, and dominated with multiple objectives and well established routines. Such an institution can be expected to resist externally imposed pressure to change in directions that threaten preferred values and relationships."[6]

There is also evidence that dissatisfaction with the SHARE program's structure played an important role in the DRG experiment: "Prospective payment on a per diem basis is often criticized for its encouragement of longer length of stay, because days of care at the end of a stay are often less intensive and costly than earlier days. Other alleged problems with the SHARE system were that it ignored hospital case mix differences, did not effectively link clinical and financial decisions, encouraged hospitals to shift costs to unregulated payers, and failed to fully compensate New Jersey hospitals for care rendered to indigent patients."[7]

Rather than turning the DRG design challenge over to the affected interests, New Jersey policymakers recruited a skilled team of health policy specialists led by Bruce Vladeck (President Clinton's HCFA Administrator) who served as Assistant Commissioner between 1979 and 1982. In the recruitment story rests an important lesson for policymakers: "We conclude that it is less difficult to bring together a talented group for designing a new program than it is to hold one together for the arduous task of program implementation and refinement . . . By 1982, the Department of Health had suffered almost 100 percent turnover of DRG project personnel . . . If government is to be effective, the limits of its administrative capacity must be recognized."[8]

One reason why so many of the original framers of the DRG system left was the election in 1981 of Republican Thomas Kean to the governor's office. Many suspected that the new governor would thwart DRG implementation before the final phase-in was completed. He didn't, and in fact he played the key role in convincing a very reluctant Reagan administration and HCFA bureaucracy to renew the state's Medicare waiver.[9] He did so for two key reasons. First, the NJHA decided to support the state prospective payment model as an alternative to the looming federal PPS structure. But also, no alternative method to control hospital cost inflation was in sight of the governor. Governor Kean bought into the idea of prospective payment regulation, much in the same way that the free-market Reagan administration bought into national prospective rate setting for Medicare—because of the lack of viable alternatives.

A new institutional structure was created through a Rate Setting Commission to implement prospective payment. The policy monopoly included regulators and hospital officials first and foremost. While other groups such as business, labor, Blue Cross, commercial payers, and others had seats at the table, as described in chapters 3 and 4, all felt outside of the inner circle of decision making. While throughout the state, hospital consumers complained to legislators about the size of their hospital liabilities in relation to hospital's charges, at meetings of the Rate Setting Commission it was apparent that the system was an insider's game:

> I remember sitting at one hearing. The hospitals would say: "These are our shortfalls." The payers would say: "No, we disagree." The body would almost always arbitrate somewhere in the middle. (Interview with Dennis Marco, Blue Cross and Blue Shield of New Jersey, Newark, April 20, 1995)

> Rate setting was not working very well. It was more like a rubber stamp of whatever the hospitals wanted. I don't recall any hospitals having a difficult time getting their rates increased. (Interview with George Laufenberg, Administrator, New Jersey Carpenter's Fund; former Rate Setting Commission member, Edison, New Jersey, April 19, 1995)

Unlike the deregulation process in Massachusetts and New York, the abandonment of rate setting here did not so much involve the understanding that a system based upon negotiated rates would be more effective as it did the sense that the New Jersey regulatory structure had simply failed.

> The benefits of rate setting were that it was not the previous system— fee for service running up bills without any constraints. It worked well at first and still would be regarded as an improvement on the prior situation. But it was starting to yield less and less. (Interview with James Florio, Governor, New Brunswick, New Jersey, April 17, 1995)

Governor Florio is regarded by most New Jersey interviewees as the individual who most brought ideas to the deregulation process. Prior to Judge Wolin's ruling in May 1992 that threw out the state's method of financing uncompensated care, Governor Florio had organized commissions and other groups seeking changes in uncompensated care and rate setting. He had been examining health system reform efforts in other states and had put forward ideas to deal with a growing number of the state's citizens without health insurance coverage. While much attention during the summer and fall was focused on finding a replacement source of financing for the Uncompensated Care Trust Fund, Florio himself placed considerable weight behind companion bills to reform the state's small group and nongroup health insurance markets. He had already decided that the rate setting structure should be eliminated, but used his agreement with the legislature on deregulation to leverage legislative support for his insurance reform initiatives:

> Governor Florio is one of the people who most consistently had some vision of where he wanted to go, and found ways to drive the processes. Florio clearly had vision. (Interview with Maureen Lopes, Senior Vice President for Health Affairs, New Jersey Business and Industry Council, Trenton, April 17, 1995)

But perhaps because managed care penetration in New Jersey was far less than that of other rate setting states, the precise replacement idea was far less clear than in the other two deregulated states. New Jersey interviewees varied in their assessment from "no policy idea—I couldn't come up with one" to "we were prepared to let the market work" to "the regulatory system didn't work." Though some members of the New Jersey Health Care Reform Coalition saw a need to bring more market forces into the hospital regulatory environment, even their position was somewhat muddied, advocating for a three-year transition to deregulation. Their preamble and problem statement highlights the ambiguity:

> . . . to develop and propose a new, long term approach to the structure and financing of health care in New Jersey. Our goals have been to replace chaos with order, provide universal access to "high" quality care at an affordable and equitable cost, and to reexamine (and possibly reorganize) the complex and interrelated web of health care issues which together comprise the health care system . . . (New Jersey Health Care Reform Coalition, June 1992)

The coalition and its constituent organizations' agendas were foggy. The legislature primarily wanted to get rid of rate setting and to find a politically acceptable way to finance uncompensated care. The driving vision, and the one realized, was Governor Florio's—to replace a dysfunctional regulatory structure that failed in its efforts to control hospital spending with a new structure that focused on providing affordable health insurance choices to individuals and small business. The switch in governmental focus—from institutions to individuals, and also from institutional subsidies to individual insurance coverage—was critical in understanding Florio's vision.

In the wake of deregulation, key structural changes were made in state government. The Rate Setting Commission and the state's role in establishing hospital charges were eliminated. New state agencies were established to meet the new state agenda. The key one was called the New Jersey Essential Health Services Commission. Its principal duties were: first, to oversee payments to hospitals for uncompensated care; second, to develop a subsidized health benefits program for low-income and uninsured New Jerseyans who are working or temporarily unemployed. Unlike the prior uncompensated care arrangements, payments to hospitals for bad debts were no longer permitted, and only payments for income-eligible uninsured persons were allowed. In addition, advisory boards were established to oversee both the small group and nongroup insurance market reforms.

Since deregulation, New Jersey's agenda of reforms has experienced a series of ups and downs and modifications. But the disappointing aftermath should not obscure the achievement made in 1992 in turning a federal judge's narrow ruling on uncompensated care funding into a mandate for broader, systemic health reform:

> This was one time where the policy makers made a bold move and instituted a good reform that went beyond what any of the groups wanted. It was about an idea. There was a common thread through all three of the bills—the system is broken. (Interview with Dennis Marco, Vice President, New Jersey Blue Cross and Blue Shield, Newark, April 20, 1995)

New York

It is in New York that the influence of ideas on the development and deregulation of rate setting is most evident. While cost pressures in the Medicaid program were prominent in leading to its creation in 1969, the state's strong political culture favoring regulatory solutions to a host of social and economic problems made the establishment of mandatory prospective payment a natural fit—even during the years of Republican political domination by Nelson Rockefeller.

The structure of the policy monopoly was contained within the state

Department of Health, and in particular in the Office of Health Systems Management, but effective control was given to the commissioner and not to an independent commission as occurred in Massachusetts, Maryland, and New Jersey. New York policymakers did not fear the concentration of regulatory authority in one person's hand, and a small succession of commissioners, especially Dr. David Axelrod, used the authority comfortably to bend hospital finances to the will of the state.

In his discussion of regulatory regimes and the politics of hospital reimbursement, Hackey uses the New York NYPHRM model as an illustration of an imposed regime "characterized by the relative strength of the state's regulatory capabilities in relation to the regulated industry; rules, regulations, and prices are dictated by state officials, often amidst cries of protest." Unlike rate setting programs in Massachusetts and New Jersey, the New York system was able to retain a long-term group of experienced and sophisticated program managers and regulators. "From top to bottom, the behavior of public officials in New York's Office of Health Systems Management is guided by a coherent and powerful set of role orientations and ideological beliefs that have solidified over time."[10]

During the 12 years of legislatively created NYPHRMs I–V, all was not peaceful within the policy monopoly that included hospitals, Blue Cross, commercial payers, business, labor, and—most prominently—state government regulators and legislators. The regular involvement of legislators meant that parties had access to means other than the bureaucrats in seeking changes to the system:

> I've also noticed that a lot of the newspaper stories about hospital financial distress will correlate closely in timing with the closeness of the NYPHRM legislative review. (Interview with John Rodat, Consultant, Albany, June 30, 1995)

All New York interviewees were able to articulate a clear sense of the supporting policy idea that sustained rate setting in the state since 1969. The core of the idea included public or social control of health care resources, control of hospital costs and financial security of vulnerable hospitals, payer equity, and preservation of access—all accomplished by a strong centralized bureaucracy.

The critical factors leading to the deregulation process in New York were outlined and explored in chapter 3, including the recent and rapid growth in managed care penetration and the accompanying practice of discounting between hospitals and HMOs, the political change with the election of George Pataki as governor, the growing disillusionment with rate setting's performance, and the changing interest group landscape. But also of significance was the role played by policy ideas in bringing individuals and interests to a different understanding about NYPHRM.

Key in this process was a report published in March 1995 for the State Communities Aid Association and the Life Insurance Council of New York by a former Department of Health and legislative staff person, John Rodat. The report, mentioned previously, was titled "NYPHRM's Paradox: How New York's Attempts to Stabilize Hospital Finances Lead to More Uninsured, Increased Benefit Restrictions, Reduced Hospital Utilization, and Weakened Hospitals." The report reached the following base conclusions: (1) New Yorkers pay more for hospital care than residents of all but one other state (Massachusetts), while hospitals are financially weak; (2) many New Yorkers are losing private health insurance primarily because of rapid premium growth; (3) NYPHRM's statutory price escalator—the "trend factor"—drives up hospital payments leading "directly" to premium increases and tax increases for Medicaid; (4) payers move aggressively into managed care and negotiated rates as well as drop coverage in order to survive; (5) payers' actions lead to reduced hospital utilization, reduced hospital revenues, and increased hospital instability; (6) "New York's regulatory system was designed during the late 1960s for the health care system of that day. *None of the key factors that characterized the health care system for which the regulatory system was designed is still true today.*" The principal conclusion made by Rodat was that New York rate regulation should be abandoned.[11]

Rodat's report had a significant impact on the thinking of some key New York policymakers:

Eliot Shaw from the Business Council described an interesting experience: the Business Council had always advocated more regulation. But a couple of his members kept coming back and saying, "Now explain to me again *why* we're supporting regulation." When John's article came out, one of the members brought it to him and said, "*This is what I have been trying to say.*" (Interview with Gerry Billings, Executive Director, State Communities Aid Association, Albany, June 30, 1995)

We retained John Rodat. We defer to him now to be the institutional knowledge on the system. He has made the case that NYPHRM over the years has changed. What happened has evolved over time, and things are not the same now as when they started. It's now hurting, artificially raising the rates, propping up an overbedded system that causes insurers to raise rates, and causes more people to be uninsured.

It becomes an endless cycle. (Interview with Diane Stuto, Vice President, Life Insurance Council of New York, Albany, July 21, 1995)

Other interviewees agreed that the release of the Rodat report was a turning point in discussions about NYPHRM, and that after publication, parties began to discuss more openly the abandonment of rate regulation. The substitute policy idea is similar to that in evidence in Massachusetts and, to a lesser extent, in New Jersey: the marketplace will be a better force for cost containment and the control of health resources by capital instead of by social forces. There is some degree of irony and even regret on the part of some interviewees who have long been associated with different versions of NYPHRM:

> There has never been a concerted move to eliminate it [NYPHRM]. The alternative was never seriously presented on the table . . . There has not up until now emerged a powerful ideologically driven Republican philosophy of deregulation in New York—up until now . . . The Republican Party in New York is still descended from the legacy of Nelson Rockefeller, and was powerfully involved in creating the system. (Interview with James Tallon, former Assembly Majority Leader, now United Hospital Fund, Portland, OR, August 6, 1995)

> The system originally was thought of as a way to keep a ceiling on costs, which is basically why the business community originally supported it. In recent years, it has in many ways served to keep a floor on costs and to keep up revenues to hospitals which is partly why I have supported it, and why the business community has done an about face on it. (Interview with Richard Gottfried, Chair, Assembly Health Committee, New York City)

> How simple it is to be such a believer in marketplace dynamics! It takes the obligation of ever having to answer a difficult question away. Just trust the marketplace. It will take care of it. (Dan Sisto, President of HANYS, quoted in Council on Health Care Financing proceedings, June 1995)

Some of the structural shifts that accompanied deregulation in Massachusetts and New Jersey also took form in New York even before the actual deregulation had been enacted by the legislature. First, nearly all of the key rate setting regulators who populated the Department of Health for more than a decade left state government during 1995. The continuity in professional managers, a hallmark of the NYPHRM system, quickly became a thing of the past. The Department of Health NYPHRM Task Force outlined the basic thrust of restructuring: "With market forces exerting economic pressure on the health care system, the Task Force no longer considered it necessary for the state to regulate the reimbursement of hospitals. Instead of a large regulatory role for the state, the Task Force envisions a more targeted state role in quality assurance and in areas that the market is unlikely to address."[12]

However, the broad structural changes in evidence in Massachusetts and New Jersey deregulation processes cannot be found in New York. No agencies, bureaucracies, or offices were eliminated or created as part of the process. Indeed, the New York Office of Health Systems Management was retained to continue the function of rate setting for Medicaid fee-for-service rates.

While the philosophy of regulation appears to have changed, some aspects of the New York political culture have not:

> There is still a powerful set of voices not to walk away from graduate medical education and uncompensated care because it is morally and ethically important. This is still a government that sees its responsibility to make the decisions . . . This discussion is policy driven. Those discussing it from the policy view understand that this is a collective bargaining issue among a multitude of interests. (Interview with James Tallon, former Assembly Majority Leader, now United Hospital Fund, Portland, OR, August 6, 1995)

Examination of Punctuated Equilibrium Model Hypotheses

Table 5.2 summarizes findings from each state (and overall) for each of the hypotheses specified in the punctuated equilibrium model of policy change.

Evidence explaining the conclusions for each hypothesis and for each state will be presented in turn.

P1: An identifiable "policy idea" should accompany deregulation.

Massachusetts. Virtually every interviewee could identify a replacement idea to substitute for the policy idea associated with prospective rate setting, whether the individual agreed with that idea or not. The replacement idea had the following two key characteristics: first, while the rate setting system had once been somewhat effective in controlling the growth of hospital costs, it had failed to maintain the ability to control costs over the longer term; because of that change, central economic planning as the vehicle for health sector cost control had fallen out of favor.

Second, market forces had reached the point where they could be more efficient not only in restraining hospital and health sector costs, but also in doing something unthinkable under rate setting, namely, *reducing* the cost of those services. The mechanism for implementing this change was managed care and HMOs using their ability to negotiate rates of payment with hospitals. The best way for payers to reward efficient hospitals and to punish inefficient ones was to stop paying an arbitrary definition of "costs" and instead to pay prices based on the prevailing market.

In addition to comments by interviewees, there is substantial evidence from the legislative process that—at several levels—a serious debate about policy ideas ensued between those arguing for continued rate regulation and those arguing for a system based on market contracting. On the proregulation side were the consumer group Health Care for All, labor

TABLE 5.2.   Punctuated Equilibrium Model Hypotheses and Results

	MD	MA	NJ	NY	Overall
P1. An identifiable "policy idea" should accompany deregulation.	—	YES	YES	YES	YES
P2. In Maryland, we should not observe the emergence of the new policy idea, or else have clear indications of non-acceptance.	YES	—	—	—	YES
P3. In deregulated states, we should observe altered institutional structures to account for the demise of the old idea and the ascension of the new one.	—	YES	YES	MIXED	YES
P4. In Maryland, we should observe no similar institutional change.	YES	—	—	—	YES
P5. In deregulated states, we should observe the emergence of new players who, by broadening the scope of conflict, undermined the rate setting policy monopoly.	—	YES	YES	YES	YES
P6. In Maryland, we should observe either no such new players, or clear indications as to their ineffectiveness.	YES	—	—	—	YES

unions, and supportive academics. On the market competition side were key legislators and administration officials, Blue Cross, and the HMOs; the hospitals and business, while supportive of deregulation, confused their position by taking a number of contrary stances. The evidence for this debate is discussed in chapters 3, 4, and 5 and includes journalistic accounts, reports, and private notes.

The fact that the proregulation side was overwhelmed in votes and support by the procompetition adherents does not at all diminish the assertions that competing policy ideas were a factor in the debate and that the existence of a clear replacement idea was an essential element of the deregulation process. *(YES)*

New Jersey. The replacement policy idea underlying deregulation was less clear and consistent among the New Jersey interviewees than was the case in Massachusetts. Much more prominent to interviewees was the regulatory failure apparent in the workings of the DRG system in its final years. This difference can be attributed to the much smaller rate of HMO penetration evident in New Jersey in the years leading up to deregulation.

Nonetheless, there was also a growing sense that the market was a mechanism that deserved a try and more respect in the New Jersey health care environment:

> We were prepared to let the market work. (Interview with Dana Benbow, Vice President, Prudential Insurance Company, Iselin, New Jersey, April 19, 1995)

> The market will work better and bring down prices. (Interview with William Codey, former Senate Health Chairman, West Orange, NJ, April 19, 1995)

> The market does better at controlling costs and rewarding efficiency. (Interview with Maureen Lopes, Senior VP for Health Affairs, New Jersey Bus. and Ind. Association, Trenton, April 17, 1995)

> Hospitals had grown fat, lazy, inefficient, out of control,—you can't close them—let the chips fall where they may. (Interview with Thomas Terrill, Executive VP, University Health Systems, Princeton, NJ, April 17, 1995)

While not widely shared, an additional replacement idea was put forward by then-Governor James Florio, namely that the focus of government had to shift away from propping up institutions and toward ensuring adequate insurance coverage for individuals. He included this dynamic within his own description of his replacement idea, labeled "structured competition." While his ideas were not broadly shared among interviewees, he was successful in seeing his proposed policies passed and implemented.

There is evidence from interviews as well as from records and news accounts related to the New Jersey Health Care Reform Coalition that policy ideas, new and old, were an important part of their process. Though they stood alone among the key interests, the urban and academic teaching hospitals waged a serious though unsuccessful campaign to preserve the rate setting structure. Competing full-page newspaper advertisements several days before the final legislative votes put the alternative ideas before the broad public. The first, from the Urban Hospital Coalition, stated:

> We can't say no to our patients. We shouldn't have to . . . Urban hospitals need redistribution of the dollars in this bill to our hospitals to achieve the level of funding necessary to continue care for the indigent. (*Newark Star Ledger,* November 29, 1992)

On the other side, an advertisement signed by the New Jersey Business and Industry Association, the New Jersey Hospital Association, the New Jersey HMO Association, and the Medical Society of New Jersey, headlined "End the Gridlock! Enact True Health Care Reform," stated:

> . . . precedent setting reform legislation hammered out by the Democratic Administration and the Republican legislative leadership . . . would eliminate the inefficient DRG system of billing patients at average charges. (*Newark Star Ledger,* November 30, 1992)

Clearly, the debate over replacement funding for the Uncompensated Care Trust Fund dominated legislative concerns and public attention during the review process. However, interviews, journalistic accounts, and other source documents substantiate the claim that a replacement policy idea to the DRG system was present and accepted during the course of legislative review. *(YES)*

New York. Though deregulation with its reliance on the market only recently became legislative fact in New York, it has become well established now as a replacement policy idea for 25 years of hospital rate setting regulation that reached its zenith during the five versions of NYPHRM. Whether complimentary or pejorative, all interviewees were able to characterize the replacement idea:

Deep discounts—negotiating on the basis of cost and quality. (Interview with Ed Reinfurt, Vice President, Business Council of New York State, Albany, June 30, 1995)

The free market—and chaos. (Interview with Debbie Bell, Coordinator of Policy Development, DC37, AFSCME, New York City, July 20, 1995)

The marketplace will be a better force for cost containment. (Interview with Harold Iselin, Counsel, New York HMO Conference, Albany, June 29, 1995)

Control by capital of health care resources—instead of social control. (Interview with Richard Gottfried, Chair, Assembly Health Committee, New York City, July 20, 1995)

As was true in Massachusetts, the rapid growth in managed care and HMO penetration had a profound impact on the attitude of New Yorkers toward rate setting and government sector regulation. The principal evidence that ideas are a part of the New York debate is John Rodat's report for the Life Insurance Council and the State Communities Aid Association that, as described in this chapter, precipitated a sea change in the positions of several key groups including the two sponsors and the Business Council of New York State, all former rate setting supporters.

Central to the punctuated equilibrium model and to this study's conclusions is the assertion that ideas take front and center stage during the periods of instability and systemic disruption, while interests move to the fore during the equilibrium phase. An offhand comment from one key participant affirms this insight:

It hasn't been about ideas in the past. Rate setting debates in New York State always have been about raw political negotiations with the hospitals always winning out. But thanks to John [Rodat] and others raising questions, it may be starting. We haven't talked about ideas since we formulated the original NYPHRM . . . What we were trying to accomplish was to pull the conceptual underpinnings out of NYPHRM. (Interview with Gerry Billings, Executive Director, State Communities Aid Association, Albany, June 30, 1995)

As occurred in New Jersey, the harshest portion of the deregulation debate concerned the source and distribution of replacement financing for uncompensated care, graduate medical education and other uses unique to the New York hospital regulatory environment. During the legislative process in 1996, no single organization or voice stepped forward to promote a continued structure for rate regulation. This suggests more that the replacement idea was long overdue in New York rather than the nonexistence of the new policy idea. *(YES)*

Summary. In all three states that have deregulated, a clear replacement policy idea can be identified. In addition, we can identify clear indications that the ideas were accepted by key players in each state. *(YES)*

> *P2:* In Maryland, we should not observe the emergence of the new policy idea, or else we should have clear indications of nonacceptance.

Health policy leaders in Maryland are aware of the evolution in health policy in other states, including states that deregulated their rate setting systems. The most commonly used description of the replacement policy idea came down to two words: "free market." The second most commonly used term was "marketplace competition." Clearly, the ideas that have been incorporated in the other states have also penetrated here, thus leading to a rejection of the first part of the hypothesis.

The second alternative is clear indications of nonacceptance. In this case, we can observe among interviewees clear signs of nonacceptance—particularly among government officials—or else reluctance to take any steps to promote the alternative policy idea. From some of those rejecting the free market were these comments:

> There's no important political voice that wants deregulation to happen. (Interview with Eugene Feinblatt, Attorney, former Chairman, Maryland Commission on Health Care Financing, Baltimore, June 21, 1995)

> If it ain't broke, don't fix it. (Interview with Sen. Paula Hollinger, Senate Chair, Joint Common on Health Care Delivery and Finance, Annapolis, June 20, 1995)

> I have grave reservations that the delivery of health care lends itself to the free market. (Interview with Casper Taylor, Speaker, Maryland House of Delegates, Annapolis, June 19, 1995)

> If you have deregulation, then it's like road kill. Everyone's in here plucking this piece or that. (Interview with Dr. Martin Wasserman,

Commissioner, Maryland Department of Health and Mental Hygiene, Baltimore, June 23, 1995)

Unlike the other three subject states, there is not a clear record of legislative policy debate that can help to define the nature of a clash in policy ideas. The only recent legislative activity leading to the creation of a special regulatory review panel included preamble language clearly expressing strong and continuing support for continued rate setting. There have been no major newspaper articles that have brought discussions on the future of rate setting to the fore. Almost all of the discussion is beneath the surface and has certainly not affected the public consciousness in any meaningful way:

Rate setting is not a front burner issue in this state. (Interview with Dr. Gerard Anderson, Johns Hopkins School of Public Health, Baltimore, June 22, 1995)

For the time being, the rate setting policy idea retains its hold. While the alternative idea—in the form of the free market—is recognized and understood, we can also discern clear signs of its nonacceptance in the state. *(YES)*

P3: In deregulated states, we should observe altered institutional structures to account for the demise of the old idea and the ascension of the new one.

Massachusetts. Several significant changes in institutional structures accompanied the 1991 rate setting deregulation in Massachusetts. First, the hospital finance division within the Rate Setting Commission lost its authority to regulate hospital changes within one year after enactment. A loose set of hospital-specific limits was established that ultimately affected only one of more than 90 acute care hospitals. The commission has attempted to carve out a new role for itself as the data gatherer and disseminator of information, reports, and analysis on the commonwealth's health system. These reports have included one on preventable hospitalizations and another evaluating trends in HMO premiums. But the overarching role for the hospital finance division within the commission is now substantially diminished.

Equally important has been the rise in structural and independent authority of the Medicaid program. Raised from a division within the Department of Public Welfare to a special division in the Secretariat of Health and Human Services, the program now has complete authority to negotiate rates of payment with acute care hospitals and to avoid oversight from the Rate Setting Commission.

The Hospital Payment Advisory Commission (HOSPAC) was newly established to report to the administration and the legislature on various aspects of the new deregulated system, including fair marketing standards and the treatment of disproportionate share hospitals. HOSPAC was governed by a five-member commission appointed by the governor and run by a professional staff. The organization was never able to establish itself as a strong voice and was formally dissolved in the summer of 1995.

Other changes accompanied the 1991 legislation, including a shift in the administration of the state's free care pool to the Department of Medical Security from Blue Cross and changes in the structure of mental health programs. (In 1996, the DMS was merged into the RSC to create a new Division of Health Care Policy and Finance with administrative control over the Uncompensated Care Pool.) But the first two changes dealing with the powers of the Rate Setting Commission and the Medicaid program are most important in this analysis. The overt hand of state regulation over hospitals was lifted; and the state agency most involved in the expenditure of health dollars for medical services, Medicaid, saw a shift in its statutory definition to move from being a payer to a purchaser of health services. Both of these changes are consistent with the shift in policy ideas reflected in hypothesis P3. *(YES)*

New Jersey. Three key structural changes accompanied New Jersey's rate setting deregulation enacted in 1992. First, as occurred in Massachusetts, the Rate Setting Commission within the Department of Health saw its hospital oversight functions eliminated, and the commission itself is now defunct.

Second, the legislature established a new entity (with considerably more authority than the Massachusetts creation, HOSPAC) called the Essential Health Services Commission. The tasks assigned to the 14-member EHSC included administration and oversight of the newly formed Uncompensated Care Trust Fund, as well as oversight of the new reforms to the small group and individual health insurance markets. Separate advisory boards were also established within the EHSC to regulate the rules within those two distinct insurance markets. Because the compromise funding source for uncompensated care agreed to in 1992—$1.5 billion from the surplus in the state's unemployment insurance trust fund—was only established for three years, a controversy opened up in the state at the end of 1995 over replacement funding for the pool. After lengthy consideration of other alternative funding sources, the governor and legislature agreed to additional use of unemployment insurance trust funds as a financing source for three more years. Controversy has also enveloped the EHSC, which was recommended for disbanding by Governor Whitman, with its duties to be assigned to the Department of Health. Nonetheless, the enacted structure and mission of the EHSC—along with the elimination of Rate Setting—was consistent with the policy direction embodied in the replacement idea, namely, the shift from regulation of providers to support for insurance purchase by individual health consumers.

The other structural change, less prominent than in Massachusetts, was the unshackling of Medicaid's ties to the rate setting structure. Because the state's Medicaid program was not in a position to move aggressively into managed care, the change provided enhanced program flexibility, but not major structural change. *(YES)*

New York. Deregulation in New York brought major changes in the financing arrangements of the health system, but evidence of broad institutional and structural change is not as apparent as in Massachusetts and New Jersey. One strikingly apparent change was the abandonment of the Department of Health and its Office of Health Systems Management by the vast majority of officials who ran the NYPHRM system for many years prior to Governor Pataki's election. These individuals moved to other positions, some finding employment in the hospital community. But this development is more the presage of change rather than structural change itself.

Clearly, the function performed by the Department of Health in establishing approved rates of payment under NYPHRM was eliminated for all private payers, but also was retained for portions of the Medicaid program. The department also continues to administer the various funds for uncompensated care, graduate medical education, and other purposes, even though the legal basis for the collection of funds has been altered to account for the loss of state-approved charges and to address legal issues related to federal preemption under the Employee Retirement Income Security Act (ERISA).

The New York Commissioner of Health, in her Task Force recommendations on the future of New York's financing system, suggested that the system should assume a new, but largely undefined role for the Department of Health in overseeing system quality and access to health plans by consumers. The deregulation legislation establishes a new Task Force with the mandate to address quality improvement issues in a deregulated system. But this Task Force does not hold powers that would suggest any significant structural changes.

In spite of the enormous scope of changes brought on by the deregulation statute, the actual structural changes in the design New York State government are not as substantial as might have been anticipated. The conclusion regarding this hypothesis and New York is less clear. *(MIXED)*

Summary. Altered, created, and abandoned institutional structures are most clearly in evidence in Massachusetts and New Jersey. Additionally, all of the changes in these two states can be tied in a convincing fashion to the shift in the prevailing policy ideas. While major structural changes are not as clearly in evidence in New York, changes in the Medicaid program with the growth in managed care and financing mechanisms provide partial support for this hypothesis. Overall support for this hypothesis is demonstrated by the evidence. *(YES)*

   P4: In Maryland, we should observe no similar institutional change.

   It would be inaccurate to characterize the Maryland rate setting system as static. Throughout its more than 20-year history, the regulations and the central reimbursement formulas have been subjected to significant alteration and change. Indeed, in the current environment, the Health Services Cost Review Commission is now experimenting with its most ambitious form of change in its decades-long history, attempting to permit forms of capitation and alternative payment methods within the rate setting methodology. However, rather than seeing these changes as comparable to the seismic structural transformations evident in the other subject states, the Maryland shifts fit much more comfortably into the punctuated equilibrium model's definition of deliberate incrementalism that characterizes continuing control by the prevailing policy monopoly.
   During the reign of the prevailing policy monopoly, the system is subjected primarily to negative feedback, and initial disturbances become smaller as they work their way through the system over time. The internal and external system managers are able to accommodate and win over critics by making necessary concessions and changes to avoid more serious dissension. Only when a system becomes the object of positive feedback—where disturbances grow in magnitude to become major disruptions over time—does the system itself face potentially fatal threats.
   In 1995, for the first time, serious questions were raised about the future of the Maryland system, from some HMO and business leaders. The legislature responded by establishing the special review committee that has been mentioned previously. In doing so, they included a preamble with a ringing defense of the Maryland rate regulation system that gives no indication of waning support from key political leaders in the state. Thus these disturbances at this time appear to characterize the dynamics of neg-

ative, more than positive feedback. In the past 20 years, there have been no institutional changes affecting the basic hospital finance structure that represent a threat to the role and authority of the HSCRC. As such, we observe sufficient support for the hypothesis. *(YES)*

>   P5. In deregulated states, we should observe the emergence of new players who, by broadening the scope of conflict, undermined the rate setting policy monopoly.

Massachusetts. New players in 1991 in the hospital finance sweepstakes in Massachusetts could be found both inside and outside of state government. Inside government, the new players could be found in both the administration and in the legislature. The key change inside government was the ascension of William Weld as governor, bringing a different approach to governing and a special appreciation for the value of markets in approaching public policy problems. His key advisor, Charles Baker, was recognized by all interviewees as central to the deregulation debate. Though the initial administration bill only called for a three-year phaseout of regulation, his approach emboldened all pro-market forces to advocate aggressively for full deregulation.

Inside the legislature, key changes included the appointment of Thomas Finneran as Chairman of the House Committee on Ways and Means and Carmen Buell as House Chairman of the Joint Committee on Health Care. Both rejected the earlier approaches that favored continued regulation. Finneran, in particular, broke with all prior bills by releasing from his committee legislation to deregulate the finance system within one year. Because both were Democrats, they brought along a party that otherwise easily could have supported continued regulation. While the key leadership positions in the state Senate went unchanged in 1991, the number of Republicans rose from 8 to 16 in the 1990 state elections, giving Governor Weld an important margin that could allow his vetoes to be sustained without Democratic support, another new element that altered the balance of power inside state government.

Outside government, key changes could be found in the insurance community. The Massachusetts Association of HMOs was the only interest group that advocated deregulation consistently for a number of years. Their executive director, Robert Hughes, was well connected with the new administration and pushed deregulation at every opportunity. At Blue Cross of Massachusetts, a new top management team took control during 1990 and 1991, more market- and business-oriented, and willing to part from the standard support provided to rate regulation over many years. Parting from this support also meant parting from their extra charge differential over commercial payers—but this was not an obstacle in the face of fierce and growing pressure from HMOs. Taken together, this combination of new players helped to change the face of health care financing in Massachusetts. *(YES)*

New Jersey. The most important new actors in New Jersey would also be found inside state government. In the administration, Governor Florio and his key policy adviser, Brenda Bacon, would have to be counted among the new players. Throughout the first two years of his governorship, Governor Florio expressed his discontent with the shape of the health care landscape, particularly the high uncompensated care surcharge and the awkwardness and complexity of rate setting. Earlier commissions had recommended changes in health finance that the governor was not able to get through the Democratically controlled legislature. Even before Judge Wolin's ruling in May 1992, Florio had been promoting health system changes to deal with the alarming rise in the number of uninsured residents and to correct problems in the insurance market.

Also important were the new leaders of the New Jersey Assembly and Senate. As a result of voter rebellion in the wake of major tax increases in 1990, the electorate gave control of both branches to the Republicans in the 1991 elections for the first time in more than a generation. The new Republican leaders, especially Speaker Charles Haytaian, saw their elevation as the long-awaited opportunity to eradicate the DRG structure. In the event that Governor Florio wavered in his determination to eliminate rate setting, the legislative leaders would have insisted on deregulation as the price of any other concessions. Noteworthy to recall are the sentiments of Democratic Senator Richard Codey, former Chair of the Senate's Health Committee, who indicated his intention to modify—but not deregulate—the rate setting structure had Democrats held on to control in his chamber in 1991.

In the external environment, the emergence of new players was less apparent. The HMO Conference was clearly a new player, but did not pretend to bring major clout to the table. The only two interests that could potentially be labeled as new would be: first, the building trades unions that began to see their interests as no longer aligned with continued rate setting because of the financial burdens on them through the uncompensated care surcharges; and second, the federal district court—definitely an example of an expanded scope of conflict—that weighed in on behalf of the unions by declaring the surcharge to be a violation of the federal ERISA law. Though Judge Wolin's ruling was thrown out one year later by the Court of Appeals, during the six months after his ruling, he monitored developments in the legislature closely and made clear his intention to hold the state to the November 30, 1992, agreed-upon timetable to find a replacement source of funding for uncompensated care.

The emergence of Governor Florio and the new legislative leadership is the strongest example of new players who helped to change the environment. A new attitude on the part of labor and the emergence of the federal court as a player are additional examples of the emergence of significant new players. *(YES)*

New York. There is only one place where a new set of players shifted the landscape relative to the future of NYPHRM—but it is arguably the most important place, and that is in the governor's office. The departure of Governor Mario Cuomo at the end of 1994 signaled the end of a long era of expansive regulatory control throughout state government. Newly elected Governor George Pataki demonstrated his eagerness to embrace deregulation wherever possible. His new Commissioner of Health, Barbara DeBuono, made public her recommendations for an end to NYPHRM-style rate setting. Their proposals for changes in financing of uncompensated care, graduate medical education, capital funding, and other access programs were significantly altered during the legislative review process, but their basic deregulatory and financing recommendations were adopted.

There was disagreement among interviewees as to whether deregulation would be under consideration in the same way had Governor Cuomo been reelected. Some argue that the changes in the health care landscape would have compelled the same determinations now being made. Others suggest that Department of Health staff were already preparing for only modest revisions for a NYPHRM VI had Governor Cuomo remained. It seems likely that the marketplace changes in the state would have compelled some significant alterations, but whether a scrapping of NYPHRM would have occurred under a fourth Cuomo administration is unknowable. What is clear is that the ascension of Governor Pataki opened the door to a broad and fresh reevaluation of NYPHRM that could easily have not occurred under the other set of circumstances, a change that had considerable effect on the prospects for continued rate setting. No major changes or partisan shifts occurred in the Senate or the Assembly, though the new Senate Health Committee Chair, Kemp Hannon, broke with prior Republican positions by publicly advocating an end to NYPHRM in 1995.

Most of the leaders of the various New York interest groups are the same. The change has not been in new personalities, but rather in individuals and organizations moving away from long and deeply held positions—groups such as Blue Cross, LICONY, the State Communities Aid Association, the Business Council, and others. A change in long-standing policy positions by key groups is also consistent with the hypotheses of the punctuated equilibrium model. While the strength of the observation is not as clear in New York as in the other two states, it is still apparent that the emergence of new actors in the administration and the change in positions by other groups have helped in important ways to shift the dialogue and prospects concerning deregulation in New York. *(YES)*

Summary. The overall evidence strongly suggests that new players inside and outside of government (as well as new positions among old players) emerged in all three states in ways that were vitally important in undermining long-standing support for continued hospital rate regulation. *(YES)*

> P6. In Maryland, we should observe either no new such players, or clear indications as to their ineffectiveness.

There are new players in Maryland, but no partisan shift such as the ones that opened the door for changes in the other subject states. A new administration under Governor Parris Glendening, including a new Commissioner of Health, has led to no significant alteration in views on the Maryland rate setting system. With eyes on the federal dollars associated with the Medicare waiver, administration officials and policymakers on health matters refuse to make any changes that could jeopardize the continued flow of Medicare funds into the state's hospital industry.

The HMO industry, because of its size, is a recognized player that is somewhat new. HMOs have enjoyed huge growth in penetration in Maryland since the late 1980s. Some of the out-of-state–based for-profit HMOs, especially New York Life's Health Plus, have weighed in on the debate, openly suggesting that the state should abandon the rate regulation scheme. However, the HMO Association has explicitly not called for deregulation and will be very careful before making any such move. Public officials are openly disdainful of the calls by Health Plus leaders for a move away from regulation.

Aside from the HMOs, the players in labor, business, Blue Cross, and commercial insurers are essentially the same. While some will raise questions about the ability of the rate setting model to sustain itself in the long run, none has yet broken ranks and advocated explicit deregulation. Thus far, the Health Plus chief, Jeff Emerson, is standing largely alone, without even the support of his state association.

All of this could change. A loss of the federal waiver, a major shift in political control in the legislature or the executive branch, or some other shift in federal policy—any of these or more could lead to a rapid change in consensus. Clearly the loss of the federal waiver would lead to major reconsideration—and quite possibly rapid deregulation. But for now, the judgment is clear: there are few new players calling for deregulation, and no indications that they are being effective. *(YES)*

CHAPTER 6

Conclusions

As someone who views ideas as valuable, and not
someone who thinks that everything happens because of
interest group determinations, I have been sobered over
the past few years about how important it is for ideas to
fit into a framework that fits for certain interested parties.
(Charles Baker, former Massachusetts Undersecretary of
Health and Human Services, Boston, December 27, 1994)

As should be apparent by now, this study is about more than one thing. It
is about mandatory hospital rate setting in four states, and what its continuation or deregulation can tell us about health policy in the 1990s. This
study is also about two theoretical lenses—the theory of economic regulation and the punctuated equilibrium model of policy development—and
what they can tell us about economic, political, and policy phenomena at
work today. Finally, this study is about the broader and deeper interplay
between interests and ideas as engines of policy development and change.
Both have always been with us, in varying degrees, and both always will
be. This chapter summarizes the key findings in each of these three areas
and discusses their significance.

Key Findings: Rate Regulation and Deregulation

Three sets of findings require summarization and discussion at this point.
The first involves the observable pattern associated with deregulation in
Massachusetts, New Jersey, and New York that explains why that policy
option was exercised. The second is the counterpattern observed in Maryland that explains why continued rate setting regulation remains a viable
policy choice there. The third is the overall set of lessons for health policy
that can be learned from the rate setting experience in the states.

Why Rate Setting Deregulation Happened in Three States

While the intensity of each factor varied from state to state, the following
five factors were the critical variables that accounted for or accompanied
the move to deregulation:

The Collision with Managed Care

The original rate setting policy idea was directly related to the belief that the health financing system in the states followed a classic pattern of market failure. The providers, chiefly hospitals, held the advantages and leverage, while the key payers (government, business, insurers, and labor) held few or none. The prevailing reimbursement system of cost-based, retrospective payment was based on inflationary and inefficient incentives. The only entity capable of confronting the power of providers was government, using its legal authority with the political backing of business, insurers, and labor.

The insurgent policy idea that emerged on a national level in the late 1970s, and in the states in the late 1980s, asserted that market failure should be seen as a transitory phenomenon, not a permanent reality. The time lag between national discussion and state implementation can be attributed to the lengthy period required for managed care to reach critical mass in the states, as well as the normal lag time for policymakers to perceive a need for change. During the rate setting epoch, businesses, insurers, and labor used their emerging power to reorganize the framework of the health care financing system. By adopting a paradigm shift that changed their mode of thinking from that of a *payer* of health services to that of an active *purchaser* of services, they could exert market pressures far more effectively than government could to lower prices rather than just to lower the rate of increase in the charges for hospital services. By reorganizing their methods, prudent purchasers could address not just the rise in inpatient hospital costs, but the increase in overall health costs as well.

Whether this shared perception is true is beyond the scope of this investigation. What is germane and clear is that important interests with economic and political leverage in the states embraced this view with enthusiasm in the decade from 1985 to 1995. The key instrument for this transformation was managed care in general, and the HMO in particular. Managed care, in establishing micro-level negotiated rates of payment between purchasers and providers, fundamentally changed the dynamic that had existed previously. Health maintenance organizations were the most visible manifestation of the transition, as well as a political force willing to provide leverage in advancing systemic change.

In our states, the HMO's desire to engage in negotiated rates of payment with hospitals significantly undermined the logic and appeal of governmentally mandated rates. The growth of HMOs, particularly in Massachusetts in the late 1980s and in New York in the early 1990s, created an uneven playing field that threatened the financial and organizational stability of Blue Cross plans in both states. The strong desire of Medicaid programs in both states to begin using their market share to leverage lower rates of payment created further, immense pressures on the regulatory system. While HMO development in New Jersey was not strong enough to destabilize that state's system, interviewees clearly indicated their hope that deregulation would encourage the rapid growth in managed care that was evident in other states—an expectation that has occurred since deregulation, though not to the extent anticipated by deregulation supporters in all regions of the state.

The Link to Political Change
Political change from Democratic to Republican control did not always lead to abandonment of hospital rate setting. In 1981, Republican Governor Thomas Kean's election as New Jersey governor led to a continuation of that state's DRG system implementation. Indeed, had Kean not been elected, it is entirely plausible that a Democratic administration would have lacked sufficient political leverage to convince the Reagan administration to renew its Medicare waiver, a development that would have doomed the system much earlier than 1992.

Nonetheless, each deregulation in the three subject states was accompanied by an immediately prior shift in political control: Republican William Weld's election as Massachusetts governor in 1990, the shift to Republican control of the Assembly and Senate in New Jersey in 1991, and the election of Republican George Pataki as New York governor in 1994. There is evidence to suggest that these deregulations might have occurred anyway—each was accompanied by major health market changes along with some legislative trigger (legislative sunsets in Massachusetts and New York, a federal court mandate in New Jersey). And key Democratic party support was in evidence in Massachusetts (Finneran, Buell, Burke, McGovern), New Jersey (Florio) and New York (Silver, Gottfried) in each state's deregulation initiatives.

However, the shift in political control served as an important "focusing event"[1] for deregulation advocates inside and outside of state government. The change emboldened those seeking to change the system to push beyond what might otherwise have been possible. Continued Democratic dominance could have signaled a call to key parties for only status quo refinements to existing regulatory frameworks. This element of rate setting's fate also confirms a hypothesis from 1963 made by Lowi who found that new departures in policy are more likely at the beginning of a new administration, especially when a former minority party gains control.[2]

The Incomprehensibility Factor and Regulatory Failure
There is strong evidence that the rate setting systems in the subject states were effective in constraining the rate of growth in hospital expenses in the

early years of those systems and up until about the mid-1980s. The empirical research and data described in chapters 2 and 3 demonstrate that mandatory rate setting outperformed nonregulated systems or voluntary systems in other states in holding down the rate of growth of inpatient hospital costs.

This success in cost control also laid the groundwork for later failures. Regulators and legislators responded to intense negative feedback from hospital officials to make concessions in reimbursement policies in a manner that supports in many respects the "capture" predictions of the theory of economic regulation. While New York regulators were able to hold on to long-term and highly professional staff, regulatory agencies in Massachusetts and New Jersey saw rapid turnover and demoralization among those charged with maintaining the day-to-day operations of the system. To respond to the complaints of hospital officials and their legislative allies, regulations and statutes were adjusted, making them even more complex and incomprehensible than before. The administration of the rate setting system became more an insider's game, conducted by a small circle of players that had the only sophisticated understanding of its workings from legal, financial, administrative, or historical perspectives.

In Massachusetts, the statutes were compared with Sanskrit. In New Jersey, the program operated "like a Methadone program." In New York, the complexity provoked "considerable black humor." In each case, both the image of incomprehensibility and the perception of widespread gaming worked to undermine the commitment of the key supporting parties in continuing what appeared to be a bad and worsening regulatory experiment. As the RAND analysis of the New York NYPHRM model concluded, regulatory systems defeat themselves if the incentives are so complicated that even the most conscientious managers can never fully understand them.[3]

The Changing Interest Group Landscape

Rate setting programs did not develop in the states because of any mass citizen mobilization. Rather, they were adopted because of direct self-interest efforts by key power constituencies. In Massachusetts, the key groups were legislative and administration officials looking for effective means to control rising Medicaid expenditures, business officials seeking protection from rising costs, Blue Cross and commercial payers seeking protections against cost shifting, and hospitals at various points seeking to avert federal PPS rules. In New Jersey, the key parties were governmental officials seeking hospital cost containment, along with labor, business, and insurance officials seeking financial protections from the economic power of hospitals. In New York, the key players were the executive and legislative branches, Blue Cross, commercial payers, and business. While disputes and battles marred the overall harmony of key interest groups, none could be observed during early phases advocating deregulation or market solutions—and, in fact, they frequently promoted more aggressive governmental regulation.

The rate setting deregulations in all three states were accompanied by significant alterations in the interest group landscape. Administration officials sought to be free of rate setting constraints so that Medicaid programs could utilize their market leverage to lower public rates of payment. Business leaders saw the ability to engage in competitive discounting as a strategy to lower hospital costs that they felt were artificially high and to force elimination of excess hospital capacity. Blue Cross and commercial payers desired to compete on a level playing field with HMOs who were no longer a tiny, marginal part of the market, but instead the engine reshaping the system. And finally, groups of suburban and community hospitals felt shut out of the "inside circle" of rate setting regulation, run over by their wealthier and more influential academic medical center counterparts.

The new players, associations of HMOs, were supportive of deregulation, primarily because they feared an alternative of tighter regulation that would limit their discounting capabilities. However, in the three states, none was powerful enough to be a major player in behalf of deregulation. More prominently, their mere presence and growing market share were striking symbols of how much markets and political dynamics had changed.

Picking Up the Pieces

A characteristic feature of deregulation in the three subject states was a serious and sometimes controversial effort to preserve some systemic elements that accompanied rate regulation, primarily uncompensated care funding. In Massachusetts, the end of rate setting meant the end of an easily assessed surcharge on hospital charges. With the advent of full and aggressive negotiated contracting, and very few payers remaining who paid full charges, the uncompensated care surcharge on payers became a backdoor assessment on hospitals. The funding for the pool remained capped at the 1988 level of approximately $315 million, but because bad debts were no longer reimbursable, hospitals were able in 1991 to collect all of their allowable charity care charges. The funding for the pool remained capped at about $315 million at least through 1997, with hospitals recouping less than two-thirds of their documented charity care needs. Moreover, in an increasingly competitive contracting environment, the surcharge acted primarily as a hospital revenue tax, leaving those institutions less supportive of its continuation. Most importantly, the critical motivation for policymakers to retain the pool in 1991 was its newfound capacity to generate disproportionate federal share matching funds in the hundreds of millions of dollars. Indeed, the retention of the pool seems to have served state financial interests at least as much as the needs of the uninsured or hospitals. By 1996, hospital officials were terming the funding of uncompensated care in the commonwealth a "crisis," and yet another special commission was formed to come up with an alternative financing arrangement. (The author served as a member of this commission.)

In New Jersey, the battle in 1992 over replacement funding for the Uncompensated Care Trust Fund was waged with full awareness of the substantial federal financial stakes involved. Overall funding for charity care was cut substantially—though the system had become so bloated by 1991 that some trimming seemed reasonable. In addition, the state maintained continued financial support for one year for hospitals with Medicare shortfalls. The clear intention on the part of the Florio administration was to move available public funds from hospital reimbursement needs to insurance subsidies for uninsured persons. Though policymakers agreed in 1992 to use funds from the Unemployment Insurance Trust Fund for no more than three years, in the spring of 1996, facing a policy stalemate on finding alternative funding sources, Governor Whitman and the legislature agreed to use unemployment trust fund monies for an additional two years through the end of 1997.

In New York, the controversy over funding not just for uncompensated care, but also for graduate medical education, hospital capital needs, and the variety of health access and planning functions that have been tied to the NYPHRM regional pools was the reigning concern in the deregulation debate and legislative action. The Health Commissioner's Task Force report to Governor Pataki in December 1995 and the governor's legislative proposals in March 1996 both recommended continued funding for most purposes except hospital capital needs, though at reduced funding levels. The final legislation approved in July 1996 restored a large portion of the funding that had been recommended for reductions to the satisfaction of the major hospital organizations.

We can observe in all three states continuing commitments to fund at least part of the access needs that were met under the rate setting structure. Generally, the funding levels represent a decrease from resources available during the regulatory period and include much tighter expenditure controls. An important part of this commitment has been the continuing ability to use these revenues to leverage federal matching funds. If significant changes in the federal Medicaid system—such as discontinuation of disproportionate share hospital funding—are made, each state's commitment to hospital access for the uninsured once again will be severely tested.

Anticlimax

In none of the three deregulated states could the deregulation process be termed peaceful or serene. In Massachusetts and New Jersey, there were voices advocating continued rate regulation who clamored for and received attention. In New York the debates around the deregulation legislation were strenuous and controversial. But overall, the decision in each of the three states to stop setting rates—as opposed to the other related issues in deregulation legislation—cannot be ranked as legislative controversy of the first order and actually seemed fairly tame. In Massachusetts, consumer groups, labor, and supportive academics were overwhelmed in the House of Representatives by supporters of deregulation; in the Senate, no opposition surfaced at all. In New Jersey, the sharpest fights emerged over the use of Unemployment Insurance Trust funds to finance the Uncompensated Care Trust Fund for three years. While some urban and academic hospitals made a fight for continued regulation, they did so with little or no support from any other quarter. Similarly, in New York the prevailing attitude among interviewees and interest groups was that continuation of NYPHRM was a lost and unworthy cause.

When all was said and done, the rate setting function seemed like the old dead tree in the back yard that someone finally suggested should be taken down. For most interested and semi-interested parties, it was hard to disagree.

Why Rate Setting Continues in Maryland

The same framework used to explain the reasons for rate setting deregulation in Massachusetts, New Jersey, and New York is helpful in explaining why Maryland policymakers have chosen to retain their unique system at least through 1997.

The Collision with Managed Care

Managed care penetration has grown in Maryland since the mid-1980s at a fast rate, with the state having the third highest proportion of residents in HMOs in 1993. This development contradicts a large volume of predictions about the impact of rate setting on the growth of alternative delivery mechanisms such as managed care. Analysts who opposed rate setting as a cost control mechanism in the late 1970s and early 1980 confidently predicted that rate setting would thwart managed care development. There is no evidence to suggest that this occurred in Maryland (or Massachusetts and New York, for that matter)—a state that has successfully maintained tight controls on discounting by all payers, including HMOs.

Despite its growth and stringent rules, the Maryland system has not experienced the collision with managed care that occurred in the other three states. Managed care organizations complain about rate setting's constraints, to be sure, and a few even argue for its elimination. But none can complain that the system has held them back significantly—and the state HMO Association remains cautious in expressing public reservations about the program.

Rather than attempting to retain an outdated model, officials at the Maryland Hospital Cost Review Commission are developing new models of rate setting permitting global and capitated payment mechanisms. During 1995 and 1996, regulators approved nearly all of more than 80 requests from hospitals for various forms of alternative payment. The result of this activity is that regulators and their sponsors can legitimately claim to maintain a system that adapts to changing circumstances. An important reason why regulators can make these adjustments is the considerable latitude provided to them in the original rate setting enabling statute.

In September 1996, HSCRC officials unveiled new changes to the system to provide additional financial support to hospitals that provide disproportionate amounts of uncompensated care to uninsured persons, changes that will primarily benefit urban hospitals. These changes, which include a minor rate adjustment of 0.75 percent for all hospitals, were mandated administratively by the HSCRC, again demonstrating the broad authority granted to the agency. The additional charge will generate more than $33 million, based on 1995 data, that will be distributed to eight urban hospitals that provide disproportionate amounts of uncompensated care. Once again, the ability of the Maryland system to change and to respond to evolving needs is demonstrated.

The Link to Political Change

Political change of the sort that preceded deregulation in Massachusetts, New Jersey, and New York has not occurred in Maryland. Democrats retain control of the executive and legislative branches, and they indicate no desire to change course with regard to their 25-year-old rate setting program. The 1994 gubernatorial election, the closest such race in the nation, had the potential to destabilize the rate setting policy monopoly in the state, though interviewees were not certain how defeated Republican candidate Ellen Sauerbray would have moved on matters relative to rate setting.

Both branches of the legislature remain under Democratic party leadership. The point persons on health policy in both branches have long histories of support for the program and indicate distinctly negative attitudes toward suggestions for deregulation. The leadership in both branches and in the Department of Health express significant "trust" for the regulators who run the HSCRC, even to the point of admitting that they have little sophisticated understanding of the program's workings. That trust is most tangibly expressed in an enabling statute that has had no significant modifications since 1971. It is an enabling statute that provides enormous leeway to the regulators to respond to negative feedback and to modify the system to adapt to changes in the external health system environment.

The Incomprehensibility Factor and Regulatory Failure
To be sure, discussions about hospital rate setting in Maryland are not broad, participatory discussions for mass audiences. The details can be mind-numbingly complex. But HSCRC administrators have been able to hold on to, articulate, and communicate the key set of principles enshrined in the original enabling statute that have guided their work since the 1970s, including access, payer equity, cost control, and institutional stability. The program's statutory and regulatory flexibility has been invaluable to regulators in addressing criticisms and adapting the program to changing developments. While a number of interviewees express dislike for the "policy idea" that underlies rate setting, none would characterize the program as an example of regulatory failure.

The one key regulatory criticism made by some has been the lack of coordination among the three special health commissions, including the HSCRC. The legislature made moves to address this complaint in 1995 by mandating closer cooperation and collaboration among the three entities. While the 1995 call to action was subsequently ignored by all parties, the calls were renewed in 1996 by a gubernatorial appointed panel examining opportunities for regulatory reform in the health sector. Whether this later call will be addressed differently than the first remains to be seen.

The Changing Interest Group Landscape
The glue that holds the coalition of interests together in support of continued rate setting is the Medicare waiver that brings to the state an estimated $200 to $300 million in federal funds that would be lost in the absence of rate setting. Even business leaders and insurance/HMO officials who express distaste for hospital rate regulation are careful in their expressions because of fear for the adverse financial impact that would be associated with the waiver's loss.

The state's hospital leadership remains strongly in support of the program, even as some hospital officials express misgivings. Blue Cross, commercial payers, and the HMO Association all articulate reservations and clearly would not mourn the departure of the system, but they do not want to be associated with the financial consequences that would accompany the waiver's loss. The business community expresses some concerns and supported the "fresh look" endorsed by the legislature in 1995. The labor community remains strongly in support. Despite the misgivings of some, the disintegration of interest group support that preceded deregulations is not evident in Maryland.

The final two themes that described the deregulations in the three subject states—*picking up the pieces* and *anticlimax*—are not relevant to the Maryland situation.

In summary, a unique combination of factors—financial, statutory, political, and cultural—have combined to make continuation of Maryland's unique regulatory model a viable and reasonable option. It also should be equally clear—given this unique and unlikely blend of circumstances—why Maryland stands alone and is likely to do so for the foreseeable future.

Key Lessons from the Rate Setting Experience

Though Maryland continues an all-payer, mandatory rate setting program, it is appropriate to propose summary judgments on the state rate setting experience. Four principal observations, based on the analyses in this study, stand out.

First, the deregulation of state-based rate setting represents more an evolution in prospective payment methodology than an antiregulation revolution or a return to a prior era.

Some interviewees viewed the deregulation experience as an explicit rejection of governmental regulation in general and in the health sector in particular. Given the antiregulatory climate that has prevailed nationally since the late 1970s, as well as the strong distaste expressed by many key interest groups for the way that mandatory rate setting evolved in the subject states, this conclusion seems plausible.

An alternative view is grounded in an analysis of the 30-year evolution in how hospitals get paid for their services. Prior to the enactment of rate setting models in the states, the prevailing payment form was retrospective, cost-based reimbursement for "usual, reasonable, and customary" charges. Broad dissatisfaction was evident in the 1960s and 1970s with that payment form, viewed as inflationary and loaded with inappropriate incentives for hospitals to do more and to charge more for their services. These concerns were heightened by the creation of Medicare and Medicaid.

The alternative policy idea that emerged was prospective payment— determining in advance a rate at which hospitals would be reimbursed, establishing predictability for payers and providers, and removing some of the least efficient incentives associated with the retrospective system. Because costs associated with inpatient hospital services were the largest category in the health care dollar at that time, and because policymakers believed that excessive use of these services triggered the expenditure of many more dollars into the system, this area of spending became the focus for cost control. Because government was the only part of society at the time believed to hold sufficient leverage over the hospital community, other key interests—business, labor, insurers—supported the use of government power to enforce the new regulations.

The first prospective payment methodology used was per diem reimbursement, establishing a set level of payment for each day of hospitalization. While the imposition of this control is credited with reducing the rate of growth in hospital expenditures, its own set of inappropriate incentives—including ones that led to increased lengths of stay—was soon apparent and triggered the search for more effective mechanisms. The New Jersey SHARE program as well as the first two versions of NYPHRM were prominent examples of this form of payment control.

The replacement cost control mechanism was per case or per diagnosis, or, more specifically, diagnosis-related groups that eliminated incentives to extend artificially hospital lengths of stay. DRGs also provided incentives to reduce the intensity of services provided to patients once the diagnosis was apparent. Pioneered in New Jersey, the method spread to the national Medicare system and to other rate setting states such as Maryland, Massachusetts, and New York (albeit not until 1989). The Medicare Resource Based Relative Value Scale (RBRVS) is the extension of per case prospective payment methods to physician services reimbursement.

But the limitations of the per case cost control method also became apparent. Chief among them was the focus of regulation on inpatient hospital costs even though the locus of service had begun to shift rapidly out of the hospital inpatient category. Also, while governmentally sponsored regulation was able to reduce the rate of growth in charges, it proved unable to force price reductions that some observers began to see as necessary and possible. Further, the complexity required to administer these systems led to substantial gaming and political maneuvering by hospitals that often negated successful cost control influences.

The next stage of prospective payment regulation, capitation, differed from the prior two approaches in two important ways. Capitation—or prepayment for covered lives instead of for days or diagnoses—allowed for financial control of all health spending, not just inpatient costs. Also, the more effective regulatory control mechanism was thought to be in the hands of private and public sector purchasers of services instead of by independent government regulators.

Thus the advent of government rate setting deregulation does not signal a return to an earlier era when payment control mechanisms were nonexistent or primitive. Rather, it reflects a transition from per diem and per case prospective payment to capitated prospective payment, and the shift in regulatory control from government rate setters to purchasers. Ironically, in some respects the new structure resembles the way that Maryland hospitals were treated by Maryland Blue Cross before state rate setting was established in 1971. Once again, hospitals face severe treatment at the hands of private sector payers. Increasingly, across the nation, they (along with all other health providers) chafe at the new form of constraints as bitterly as they complained about rate setting regulators. This time, the controls involve more payers, the treatment is rougher, and there are few other places left to which they can shift costs.

Second, the near-end of the rate setting experience signals a different and more limited role for state government in health sector regulation.

While the evolutionary aspect of deregulation should be recognized, it is also clear that this change represents both a rejection of the role of government as a price setter and an explicit move toward more market-based mechanisms. This is entirely consistent with larger trends observable in government in the 1990s at the federal, state, and local levels.

The architects of rate setting systems were most often passionate believers in the role of government as the driver of health policy. Frequently, they envisioned hospital rate setting as an evolutionary stage leading to stronger and more expansive state controls, including forms of single-payer systems. Indeed, DoH officials in New York during the late 1980s and early 1990s spent considerable time developing a proposal known as UNY*CARE that would have made state government the single collector of all payments to hospitals from public and private sources, and also the sole payer of bills to hospitals. UNY*CARE now joins the expansive pantheon of untried and untested health system reform ideas.

A clear casualty in the rate setting deregulation is the public utility model of hospital regulation. The all-encompassing role for states in directing health system financing and delivery is no longer discussed in the current environment. Some suggest that, in the future, a new utility form of regulation will be demanded to control the new mega–health plans. But for now, public utility regulation of hospitals has been largely abandoned.

The abandonment of rate setting does not suggest a cessation of state health system intervention or regulation. Massachusetts and New Jersey deregulations, for example, were accompanied by an expanded role for state government in regulating their small group insurance markets. New Jersey added to that a new program for those in need of the individual insurance market as well as a commitment to provide substantial public subsidies to assist uninsured individuals and families in entering that market.

We can observe in the new environment that the regulatory focus is shifting—from a model that placed hospitals at the center of the health system universe to one that focuses on insurance markets, the needs of individual consumers, and accountability of managed care health plans. As the health system moves away from a preoccupation with the hospital, so has the intensity of interest by state governments as well.

Third, the history of state hospital rate setting illustrates the substantial capacity of regulatory targets to game and manipulate reimbursement rules and financing incentives.

Under per diem and per case prospective payment, the gamers were the hospitals. Under capitation, the gamers are the managed care entities, especially the HMOs. The players are different; the rules are not quite the same; the environment is significantly altered. But the games go on.

Under state rate setting, the hospital community demonstrated an ability to learn the rules of the regulatory system better than any other affected interests, and to use their knowledge and political skills to win substantial concessions from regulators, legislators, or both. At many turns, the situation closely resembled Stigler's "capture" model.[4] The principal example of this occurred in New Jersey where regulators and legislators in 1991 simply threw up their hands and handed hospitals about $1 billion in extra charge increases rather than attempt to resolve the thousands of outstanding appeals and retrospective settlement cases. Members of the Rate Setting Commission admitted an inability to comprehend the dealings between DoH staff and hospital finance officials, but perceived that gaming was out of control.

In Massachusetts, the hospital industry circumvented regulators and won huge financial concessions from legislators through the new finance rules in the 1988 Universal Health Care law, chapter 23. More than 10,000 hospital workers rallying on the Boston Common, bused in at hospital expense, made the knees of legislators buckle under constituent pressure.

Even after the 1988 concessions, hospitals continued to form subgroups to file bills seeking special treatment, often provided in legislation to groups of hospitals as small as one. In addition, Massachusetts regulators saw the same problems of retrospective settlements that plagued the New Jersey system.

New York's NYPHRM system had a track record that was far tougher on the hospital industry, leading to serious and periodic financial crises for vulnerable institutions. However, the trends evident in Massachusetts and New Jersey were also apparent in New York in the inside dealings between hospitals and the DoH rate setting staff. The rules of NYPHRM became so extraordinarily complicated that only a very small cadre of inside players in hospitals and DoH understood the real workings, much less the actual incentives provided to institutions.

So what lessons does this experience hold for today?

As the nation's health system moves into new capitated forms of payment regulation, particularly in the Medicare program, we can expect the behavior of the new regulatory targets to mimic that of hospitals in important respects. One interviewee, in particular, made this important connection:

> We have millions from HCFA to study capitation. But in many ways it's the same methodology as rate setting. The problems are exactly the same. We're concerned about gaming, predictive accuracy, and administrative feasibility. When we set rates for capitation, how do we identify the people so that they are paid for the same level of illness. Because of the experience with rate setting and hospitals, we are forewarned that the HMO industry will play with the risk adjustment methods. We are aware that we can do something administratively quite elaborate to address it; but we are also aware of the system problems in terms of data limitations.
>
> What we have learned is how they're going to game. Sometimes you're right with the predictions and sometimes you're not. In 1978 and 1983, I helped to design the Carter hospital cost control bill and PPS. There were things we knew they would do and they did; but there were others that we never thought of that they did. But you find that you're right more often than you're wrong. (Professor Gerard Anderson, Johns Hopkins School of Public Health)

The rate setting experience should provide us with renewed caution and humility regarding the ability of states to implement and maintain complex and contentious systems. While the four states have been able to perform impressive regulatory feats in establishing and running complex systems, their limitations are also important to remember. The example of the New Jersey system, where policy entrepreneurs who designed and set up the DRG system quickly left state service and the system itself collapsed under the weight of its complexity, is matched by bureaucratic problems encountered in Massachusetts and New York, where the system's complexity became a recurring source of black humor. It is also important to remember that most state governments do not begin to compare with our subject states in terms of administrative capacity and depth, either legislatively or administratively. This further limits the applicability of the rate setting model to other locales.

Fourth, the long experience with state prospective rate setting demonstrates the ability of states to meet some important policy objectives. (In other words, it wasn't a total failure.)

This final observation will strike some readers as being in conflict with judgments two and three. Yet it is important to recognize that for lengthy periods within its 25-year history—with widely varying ranges—the four states were able to achieve multiple goals of reduced cost growth, improved access, and other important health policy objectives.

We often view regulatory schemes and other public programs according to standards and expectations developed after such initiatives were created. With the advantage of hindsight and revised expectations, it is often too easy to conclude that the initiative missed the mark. In the case of rate setting, we should view these programs at least partially according to their ability to meet the purposes for which they were created: to reduce the growth in hospital costs relative to the performance of retrospective, cost-based reimbursement systems, to reduce cost shifting among different payers, to stabilize threatened hospitals, and to improve access by uninsured persons.

In Maryland's case, policymakers have been able to achieve substantial changes in the cost performance of the hospital sector, significantly reducing the rate of growth on a per admission and per capita basis. That system has dramatically lowered the cost shifting among various payers. It has provided stability to hospitals and maintained open access to hospital services for the state's uninsured. It has done all of this with a regulatory structure that has continuously evolved over 25 years. It is and will remain an important point of comparison with states that have adopted aggressive competitive and market-based health system strategies.

In Massachusetts, the rate setting system was able to reduce that state's rate of growth in hospital costs, the highest in the nation, significantly between 1975 and 1987. It developed a viable and controlled mechanism to assist hospitals in meeting their charity care obligations. It provided the means to keep vulnerable institutions such as Boston City Hospital viable in an era when other public hospitals began rapidly to disappear from the scene. The deterioration of the system after 1988 can be attributed to many factors, some within the control of policymakers and some that were not. But the mistakes that led to its collapse should not lead to dismissal of the system's accomplishments during the first two-thirds of its existence.

It is perhaps hardest to find the silver lining in New Jersey, given the substantial deterioration that happened in the late 1980s and early 1990s. Perhaps it would be useful for public policy practitioners and students to study the New Jersey system to learn how to avoid its mistakes. But New Jersey should also be remembered for the pioneering role it played in the development of diagnosis-related groups, an experience that directly informed rate setting developments in other states as well as prospective payment evolution for physicians and hospitals in the Medicare program. And it should also be noted that during the SHARE years and the early DRG years, the system was able to restrain the rate of growth below that experienced in most other states.

And finally, there is New York, the regulatory equivalent of a roller coaster, a system that was created to keep hospitals from the brink of financial catastrophe and moved them back and forth from the edge over 20 years. The uncompensated care pools provided a level of access that did not and still does not exist in most other states, even though funds were spent in a hugely inefficient manner. The system allowed the creation of a host of innovative and significant access and health reform programs that would not have found their way into the state's annual appropriations budget. The system provided a mechanism for all interests to work together to plan for and meet important state health objectives. While we can judge NYPHRM by its failures, of which there were many, we may also do the same in the not-too-distant future when we evaluate our own current romance with the free market and unrestrained competition.

But when NYPHRM is viewed through the lens of the era in which it was created, recognizing its strengths and flaws, the final judgment may be different:

> If you go back to the mid 1970s or to the late 1970s . . . hospitals were frantic over a growing problem in urban hospitals in dealing with uncompensated care. If I look at the 1978 chaos, and the fact that New York's health system has survived and that New York has still maintained the values of trying to provide care for the medically indigent population with all of its imperfections, and has continued to keep the system available, in that sense, I'm not sure that there was a

better way to get from 1978 to 1995. (James Tallon, former Assembly Majority Leader, current President, United Hospital Fund, Portland, OR, August 6, 1995)

Conclusions: Theory of Economic Regulation and Punctuated Equilibrium

We now turn to the theoretical models that form the core of this investigation. The basic research questions of this study, presented in chapter 1, were:

What factors help to explain the demise of mandatory hospital rate setting in Massachusetts, New Jersey, and New York between 1991 and 1996, and the continuation of rate setting in Maryland? To what extent can these outcomes be explained by the theory of economic regulation and the punctuated equilibrium model of policy change?

This section summarizes the conclusions relative to the second question. The theory of economic regulation provides some help in understanding the dynamics of the regulatory process and the role of interest groups. First, the theory directs us to ask the question, "who gets what?" with respect to the creation, maintenance, and destruction of rate setting. In particular, by compelling us to question the motives of both system designers and the regulated industry, we can see the dynamics of the regulatory process in a way that a pure public interest model would disguise. In particular, we are required in this model to examine the "capture" hypothesis, whether relevant or not, in a way that forces significant scrutiny and "truth-telling" onto the process. Using the theory of economic regulation leads us to ask useful and important evaluative questions, even if the final judgment is to reject the overall relevance of the model.

But reject the model we must. The evidence that rate setting systems benefited hospitals more than consumers is weak. In Maryland, the evidence is nonexistent, and in Massachusetts and New York, it is sparse. Only in New Jersey could the capture thesis be validated, and then only in the period between 1987 and 1992. The notion that elected and public officials play second fiddle to the agendas of the interest groups is flatly rejected by the evidence; and the hypothesis that shifts in campaign donations led to support for deregulation is rejected because of the lack of any confirmatory evidence. The only hypothesis that is supported addresses shifts in the configuration of interest group support prior to deregulation. It should be noted, however, that those shifts were consistently less pronounced than the shifts in support by key policymakers.

Ultimately, the theory of economic regulation is rejected because it represents too deterministic a model, too formulaic a construct, in the face of the volatile and fluid political context in each state. The ground of interest group influence and conflict is rich in the world of state health regulation. But the rigid formulations of the theory of economic regulation seem to freeze more than loosen the soil for helpful examination. The search for the elusive and powerful "cartel" that directs the activities of legislators, executives, and regulators is not successful because there are too many contestants in this field for any one player to be able to determine all of the outcomes. It is too rigid to suggest that the producers must always win out over the consumers: sometimes consumers do win, even if by accident! It is not realistic to suggest that public officials are simply ciphers in search of favors and campaign dollars from the wealthiest interests. We come back to Wilson's comments in relation to Niskanen's rigid bureaucratic formulations: "The truth is more complicated."[5]

By contrast, the hypotheses of the punctuated equilibrium model of policy development are strongly supported by the evidence. We can discern clearly that a "policy idea" undergirded the rate setting structures developed in the subject states in the 1960s, 1970s, and 1980s. We can also observe the development over the course of the 1980s of a replacement "policy idea" that toppled rate setting's hegemony. Recognition of and

TABLE 6.1.   Theory of Economic Regulation Hypotheses and Results

	MD	MA	NJ	NY	Overall
E1. Rate setting should benefit hospitals more than consumers.	NO	MIXED	YES	MIXED	MIXED
E2. Shifts in the configuration of interest groups supporting rate setting should accompany deregulation.	—	YES	YES	YES	YES
E3. Shifts in interest group support should not be observable in Maryland.	MIXED	—	—	—	MIXED
E4. Elected officials should play only a secondary role, with interest groups leading the agenda.	NO	NO	NO	NO	NO
E5. Identifiable shifts in overt political support from interest groups to key legislative leaders should be identifiable.	NO	NO	NO	NO	NO

support for the new idea developed slowly, gained momentum (often at a rapid rate, as in New Jersey in the summer of 1992), and definitively replaced what had come before. Except in Maryland, policymakers in the other three states found themselves periodically evaluating and reshaping the contours of their regulatory model, most especially in Massachusetts and New York where regular sunsets were built into each new rate setting model. There were plenty of opportunities between the late 1970s and the 1990s to get rid of rate setting. Policymakers weren't willing or able to do that until a replacement idea reached maturation. When it did, they moved.

As the punctuated equilibrium model suggests, we can clearly identify policy monopolies in each state, differing in shape and effectiveness, that maintained and defended the rate setting idea throughout its history and evolution. As the replacement policy idea gained momentum, we can observe in the subject states alterations in the makeup of the policy

TABLE 6.2.   Punctuated Equilibrium Model Hypotheses and Results

	MD	MA	NJ	NY	Overall
P1. An identifiable "policy idea" should accompany deregulation.	—	YES	YES	YES	YES
P2. In Maryland, we should not observe the emergence of the new policy idea, or else have clear indications of nonacceptance.	YES	—	—	—	YES
P3. In deregulated states, we should observe altered institutional structures to account for the demise of the old idea and the ascension of the new one.	—	YES	YES	MIXED	YES
P4. In Maryland, we should observe no similar institutional change.	YES	—	—	—	YES
P5. In deregulated states, we should observe the emergence of new players who, by broadening the scope of conflict, undermined the rate setting policy monopoly.	—	YES	YES	YES	YES
P6. In Maryland, we should observe either no such new players, or clear indications as to their ineffectiveness.	YES	—	—	—	YES

monopoly—both through the addition of new participants and through changed positions of some central players. What is most clear, however, is that policy ideas support and legitimize the policy monopolies, and replacement ideas lead to the monopoly's destruction.

Finally, we can also observe the alteration of the institutional landscape as a result of deregulation and the ascendance of the new policy monopoly. In two of the three deregulated states, some institutions and structures disappear and others form to reflect the passing of one regulatory form for another. Consistently, each new structure reflects an aspect of the new prevailing policy idea.

Overall, the punctuated equilibrium model presents a flexible but definable pattern of behavior in regulatory systems: regulatory schemes are born out of explosive crises when old ideas no longer work and the status quo no longer meets current needs; after a period of seeming stability and equilibrium as the new idea evolves, the new system inevitably confronts a new crisis leading to a new replacement policy idea and structure. At both the broad and minute levels, this model fits well the development and disposition of rate setting in the subject states. It is a model well worth investigation and testing on other regulatory and policy structures.

Conclusions: Interests and Ideas in Health Policy

While not consistently true, it was generally the case among the more than 60 interviewees that interest group subjects viewed interests as a more powerful influence on policy than ideas, while policymakers viewed ideas as the more important dynamic. (Because this study was developed, undertaken, and written by a policymaker, readers should beware.) This finding should not be surprising. Leaders of interest groups represent distinct and compelling sets of requirements that demand constant attention. Interest group representatives must satisfy their own boards and constituencies or face speedy dismissal. At one level, the groups speak for the ideals and the worldviews of their respective industries, but at another level, they simply represent trades seeking their optimal place in and share of a given market. Dollars-and-cents considerations play very powerfully in their operations and agenda setting. Ideas and other abstractions seem too often a desired luxury rather than a daily imperative.

Public policymakers must listen to interest group concerns carefully or face their own potential dismissals. But policymakers' constituencies are more diverse and dispersed; the fine details of regulatory subsystems miss the attention spans of most voters, and like it or not, the interest groups always have to come back for more. Even with rate setting deregulation, all of the interest groups in the states that were former members of the policy monopolies are still at work in their respective state capitals, pushing agendas, making deals, and looking for favored treatment in whatever the health system issue of the day happens to be.

Though it would surely be considered a heretical notion by Stigler, Feldstein, or any of the other economic regulation theorists, there is a higher purpose than interest group agendas that attracts and holds many, though not all, policymakers and interest group leaders to the policy process. Ideas matter and cannot be dismissed. They have a distinct life of their own, and they force both interest groups and policy makers to follow along, frequently against their wills. Like it or not, policymakers and interest groups at the state and federal levels must react to the marketplace of ideas that have developed overwhelming momentum in the current culture. Just as clearly, however, these prevailing ideas will change and will be replaced by other notions and ideas that will force an entirely different set of reactions and responses by the same and future policymakers and interest group leaders.

Consistent with the punctuated equilibrium model, we can observe that ideas are more in play at some times than others. When policy monopolies are in the seeming "equilibrium" stage, and the prevailing policy idea is not under challenge, the battle of ideas takes a back seat and interest group politics prevail—who gets what, when, and why, in Laswell's formulation.[6] But the time inevitably arises when interest groups take a back seat to the battle of ideas, when the fate of the current policy idea is very much at question, and when the shape of the replacement policy idea is still not fully formed. It is the political process itself that gives the new idea its most recognizable shape and appearance. That process is extraordinarily tough, often merciless, and leaves many potential and promising ideas stranded by the wayside. The process does not guarantee that the "best" ideas survive, only the most durable, and only the ones that have the best "fit" with the culture and climate of the times.

Implicit in the rejection of the theory of economic regulation is a parallel rejection of rational choice theory as the universal explainer of human behavior. Morality, solidarity, patriotism, love, hate, jealousy, and a wide array of irrational behaviors have a share in shaping what happens in all of our lives, not the least in our public lives. Self-interest is not rejected by this critique. Oftentimes it is dominant. It is foolish to leave self-interest unexamined when any political behavior comes into question. But it is equally implausible to suggest, as too many rational choice theorists attempt, that nearly every aspect of life and public policy can be explained through analysis of self-interest.

This conclusion fits with the findings and research of other writers who have sought and found a new basis for a normative politics that does not retreat from a discussion of values. Shapiro writes in *The New Politics of Public Policy,* "No statement of the public good may be absolutely true even for one time and place, let alone for all times and places, but some statements of the good are truer than others, and there are ways through which we can know which moral statements are truer than others, at least for a particular set of circumstances. It is this revived faith in moral knowledge, that man *can know* the good, or at least the better, which is the soul of the new politics."[7] Contrary to the views of the rational choice school, there is something that can be termed "the public good" or at least "the public better." It may often be difficult to find, subject to manipulation, or distorted—but that should not excuse us from continuing the search.

We conclude by affirming the importance of dual motivation in the analysis of public policy and public affairs. Rational choice and public interest can both be found in most politicized situations in different measures. Interests count, and so do ideas in the construction and deconstruction of policy.

CHAPTER 7

Aftermath

When the tide is receding from the beach, it is easy to
have the illusion that one can empty the ocean by
removing water with a pail. (Rene Dubos, *The Mirage of
Health*, 1959)

Though this study is limited to an examination of the conclusion or continuation of hospital rate setting in four states, it is appropriate to address
developments that have occurred in the aftermath of deregulation in Massachusetts, New Jersey, and New York. Though deregulation represents the
end of a major epoch in these three states, life and health policy went on
after the demise of rate setting; and for providers, payers, consumers, insurers, and public officials, life has not been dull. As with the rest of the nation,
the three health systems are undergoing rapid change, some related to
deregulation and some not. While Massachusetts and New Jersey have
lived with deregulation for approximately five years, New York is immersed
in the transition as this final chapter is written. The following discussion
highlights significant events and developments in the three states.

Two limitations must be mentioned. First, even five years is
insufficient to evaluate the full impact of deregulation. The consequences
of changes in the market and government will take much longer to be fully
evaluated and understood. Second, there is a tendency in much public discussion and rhetoric to create causal relationships where none or not much
of one exists. Some of the developments mentioned in this chapter would
not have happened absent deregulation, and some would have occurred
even with continued regulation. It is beyond the scope of this chapter to
establish clear linkages. I leave it to readers and analysts to make their own
judgments in this regard. While the following discussion is, thus, hardly
conclusive or exhaustive, it is meant to provide a beginning portrait of the
postregulatory environment.

The discussion is presented in two parts, health system changes and
public policy changes. Developments from each state will be discussed in
turn. Some summary—and tentative—conclusions also will be presented.

Health System Changes

Massachusetts

The most visible changes in the Massachusetts health market since the enactment of the 1991 deregulation statute have been a series of well-publicized mergers, affiliations, and restructurings in the hospital and insurer communities. The hospital organizational activity has been statewide and has involved nearly every one of the more than 90 acute care institutions that existed in the commonwealth in 1991.

A 1995 report on the acute hospital industry identified three patterns of organizational activity among hospitals: (1) *Within-market activity* involving the merger or affiliation of institutions in the same geographic market, including well-publicized affiliations such as Brigham and Women's and Massachusetts General Hospitals into the Partners Health Care System, and mergers such as that of Boston City Hospital and University Hospital into the new, quasi-public Boston Medical Center. (2) *Hub-and-spoke activity* involving large academic medical centers acquiring or affiliating with smaller community hospitals in surrounding areas; examples of this include the University of Massachusetts Medical Center affiliating with institutions in smaller communities such as Athol, Harrington, Milford, and Leominster and Deaconess Hospital's formation of the Pathway Health System through an affiliation with four smaller community hospitals in the Greater Boston area; the Deaconess system has since been taken over by Boston's Beth Israel Hospital. 3) *Partnering with physicians* and other types of community-based health care providers to provide a steady stream of referral sources; examples of this activity include Partners Health Care System and Lahey Clinic, both of which have purchased primary care physician practices throughout metropolitan Boston.[1]

More recently, the Massachusetts market has seen national, for-profit hospital chains entering the region for the first time. In 1995, Columbia/HCA, based in Tennessee, announced plans to purchase the Metrowest Medical Center in Framingham, itself the product of a within-market merger of Framingham Union and Leonard Morse Hospitals. The move by Columbia generated both support and opposition from numerous quarters. The agreement was approved by Massachusetts Attorney General Scott Harshbarger in early 1996. Also in 1996, another national for-profit hospital chain, OrNda HealthCorp, announced its intention to purchase and rebuild St. Vincent's Hospital in Worcester as part of that city's major downtown redevelopment plan. OrNda has since been purchased by the Tenet hospital system, though the St. Vincent's project still continues. In early 1997, Columbia/HCA was rebuffed in its attempts to purchase New England Medical Center, a major Boston academic institution, but has moved forward with other initiatives in the Greater Boston market. While these moves represent the first for-profit acute care hospital acquisitions in any of the four states, few expect them to be the last.[2]

The insurer community has also seen significant change. Two of the state's largest HMOs, Harvard Community Health Plan and Pilgrim Health Care, merged in 1995 to form Harvard Pilgrim Health Care, the largest HMO in New England. Blue Cross has moved to transform itself into a managed care organization and has made a series of moves to expand its base of operations throughout New England, though serious financial problems in 1996 and 1997 have once again created doubts about the company's long-term ability to remain independent. Also, national for-profit managed care companies have shown interest in the Massachusetts market. HealthSource, a national HMO, received approval in late 1995 to acquire a small, central Massachusetts nonprofit HMO as their starting base of operations in the commonwealth. While the other major national chains, US Healthcare and United Healthcare, have been unable to develop substantial penetration in the state, their activities are eyed warily by the homegrown HMO community.

Finally, public and private purchasers, the third leg of the health care triangle, have been active in new ways. In 1992, large employers and public purchasers formed the Massachusetts Healthcare Purchaser Group, which by 1996 included nearly 50 public and private purchasers representing more than one million covered lives. Included in its ranks are large employers such as Raytheon, Polaroid, Hewlett-Packard, universities such as Harvard and Brandeis, large municipalities, and state agencies such as Medicaid and the purchaser for state employees. Since 1994, the group has set annual targets for HMO premium increases that have been largely met: 6.4 percent in 1994, 0 percent in 1995, and –3 percent in 1996. Development of a group purchasing approach as well as Health Plan "report cards" for employers and employees are two of the Group's future plans as its size and sophistication increase.

While limited in their scope, a series of reports and analyses released between 1994 and 1996 provide an emerging portrait of the state's health care system during the early deregulation years. The first, released in 1994 by the state's Rate Setting Commission, examined premium trends for the six largest HMOs in the state between 1990 and 1994. After a decade of rapid HMO growth, enrollment increases began to level off in 1993 at about 35 percent of the state's population. Consistent with national trends during this period, a slowing of the rate of growth in HMO premiums to single digits was apparent by 1993 and 1994. The targets established by the

Massachusetts Healthcare Purchaser Group since 1994 indicate that pressure on premium growth has accelerated.[3]

An early evaluation of the financial status of the state's acute care hospital industry during the deregulation years, performed by the Rate Setting Commission in 1995, suggests that moderating hospital cost increases were accompanied by improved institutional financial health. Data for hospital fiscal years 1992 and 1993 indicate that case-mix–adjusted discharge costs for inpatient activity were increasing at rates slower than general inflation, while net income for hospitals increased during the FY90 to FY93 period. "The financial health of the industry seems generally to be good. The small number of financially ailing institutions do not exhibit a pattern in terms of geography or other characteristics related to access."[4]

A more recent financial analysis of the performance of acute hospitals since deregulation in Worcester County suggests that hospital financial health is not as strong as the earlier analysis indicated. Hospitals in that region were grouped into three categories. Four hospitals (termed "Advantaged"), chiefly larger teaching institutions, did well financially, and better than during the pre-deregulation period. Four more (termed "Improving") that experienced serious financial distress before deregulation saw substantial improvements in their finances. Three more institutions (termed "Deteriorating") exhibited serious financial distress.[5]

The study found that improved financial performance during the 1992 through 1994 period had little to do with the new competitive environment: "The primary reasons for the observed improvement in financial health appear to be related to Medicare payment policies and to the drawing down of revenue reserves built up during the regulatory period, rather than to significant improvements in hospital efficiency." The "advantaged" hospitals realized their net revenues because of financial support from Medicare's Indirect Medical Education subsidies to their teaching programs, and they appear to have lost money on revenues paid from private payers operating under the competitive framework. In other words, the relative financial stability enjoyed during the first several years of deregulation could be short-lived even for the healthiest institutions, especially if major changes are adopted by the federal government that would limit medical education subsidies.[6]

Another analysis is consistent with the Worcester findings and suggests that harder days are coming for the Massachusetts health care market. A national consulting group's 1995 report on "Boston's $3 Billion Health Care Opportunity" characterizes the regional market as "relatively immature, with little evidence of the restructuring or the aggressive competitive behavior that characterizes more advanced local markets." In

1994, Boston's HMO monthly premiums were pegged at $175 to $185 per member, 25 percent higher than the national average and nearly 40 percent higher than more mature HMO markets such as Minneapolis. Two factors that inhibited competition in the past—a heavy regulatory environment and a passive health purchasing community—have both changed, and the market is now poised for dramatic restructuring.[7]

"For-profit organizations (such as Columbia/HCA) will initially drive restructuring by introducing lower-cost pricing to gain a foothold in the market . . . For-profit health plans are similarly on the verge of establishing a greater market presence . . . Boston's newly active health care purchasing community is unlikely to allow health plans to keep monthly prices in the $175 to $185 range and pocket the surplus extracted from the system . . . Raytheon Company gained a 25 percent reduction in costs for 1996 by negotiating aggressively and reducing the benefits offered to its 18,000 Massachusetts-based workers. This level of discounting demonstrates that health plans believe there is room to significantly lower medical expenses."[8]

While some observers believe that this analysis is overstated, it is possible that the first five years post-deregulation may only be a prelude for dramatic changes yet to come. Anticipating and responding to these imminent changes is part of the responsibility of state government. As we will observe in the next section of this chapter, government has not been inactive.

New Jersey

A principal difference between New Jersey and the other three subject states was its significantly lower rate of HMO penetration during the rate setting years. While Massachusetts was poised for a more rapid response to the deregulatory environment because of its huge HMO enrollment figures in 1992, New Jersey was still climbing that first hill several years after the enactment of deregulation in December 1992. By the end of 1994, the state's HMO penetration of 17.0 percent was still below the national average of 19.5 percent.[9] While observers report that enrollment is growing at a much faster rate in the past several years, the industry still does not have the depth that is evident in other states.

New Jersey hospitals have engaged in the same type of integration and merger activity that has characterized hospitals in other states. Some especially large integrations have characterized this phase in the state's hospital sector. St. Barnabus Hospital, for example, has formed a new system consisting of eight hospitals with nearly 3,000 beds and a revenue base of approximately $8 billion. Northwest Covenant Hospital has developed a network with six participating hospitals. The Robert Wood Johnson Hospital is another institution in the midst of affiliation and merger activity. Cross-state activity is beginning to influence the hospital sector as well as the insurance sector, with plans pending for alliances between several New Jersey and New York hospitals. As of mid-1996, no national for-profit hospital chains had attempted to enter the New Jersey market, though health industry observers would not be surprised by an entry in the near future.

The hospital industry's financial health has improved since the advent of deregulation, with net profit margins up from 2.44 percent in 1991 to 3.24 percent in 1995, and days of operating cash rising from 38.4 to 78.7 during the same time period. The number of facilities dropped from 83 in 1991 to 80 in 1995 (interview with Stephen Fillebrown, New Jersey Health Care Facilities Finance Authority, September 26, 1996). The New Jersey Hospital Association, which splintered during the deregulation debate, losing about one-third of its member hospitals from the urban and teaching segments of the industry, has been able to bring several of those institutions back into its fold. However, other urban and teaching institutions have remained in their own distinct organizations.

Organizational change has also affected the insurance industry, with Pennsylvania-based US Healthcare, New Jersey's largest HMO, being acquired by Aetna in 1996. Blue Cross is engaged in its own activities, proposing to merge first with Delaware Blue Cross and Blue Shield and then announcing an acquisition by Anthem Inc., the Blue Cross plan of Indiana and Kentucky that is establishing a multistate market from Washington, DC, to Maine. Both plans face regulatory obstacles as this study goes to press. Regional insurance penetration beyond state borders is a trend that can be observed in all three states, but especially in New Jersey.

The health purchasing community had organized the New Jersey Payers Coalition in 1992 before the enactment of deregulation. Unlike their Massachusetts counterpart, this organization has included substantial representation from labor, including unions such as the Carpenters who were instrumental in triggering deregulation through their suit against the Uncompensated Care Pool. While the Massachusetts purchasers organization has developed a public profile by creating premium growth targets for state HMOs, the New Jersey counterpart has pursued the establishment of a purchasing cooperative to bypass health plans, dealing directly with physicians, hospitals and other providers. While the main organization includes 60 member groups representing some 700,000 covered lives, the purchasing cooperative negotiated on behalf of about 10 percent of that number during 1996. The coalition also intervened in the controversy concerning the future of the Uncompensated Care Pool (described in the next section), breaking with business and labor to support diversions from the Unemployment Insurance Trust Fund to finance hospital indigent care for two more years.

New York

The 1996 deregulation statute, approved by the legislature in July, signed by the governor in September, and effective in January 1997, is too recent to permit broad perspective on the aftermath of NYPHRM's demise. Even at this stage, however, some developments are apparent.

Most striking has been a wave of mergers and affiliations in anticipation of negotiated rates and market competition, similar to the restructuring wave that occurred in Massachusetts, but in a more compressed time frame. One such move, announced in July 1996, has resulted in the creation of the New York and Presbyterian Hospitals Health Care System, including more than 20 hospitals with combined annual revenues of $2.5 billion. At the same time, Columbia and Cornell University Hospitals also announced plans to merge, establishing a 2,800-physician alliance among their faculty doctors to negotiate patient care contracts with HMOs. Other announced alliances in the wake of deregulation include one between New York University Medical Center and Mount Sinai Medical Center and another involving Long Island Jewish Medical Center and Beth Israel Medical Center (*American Medical News,* August 12, 1996, 3).

The intensity of the merger trend among hospitals led New York's Health Commissioner, Dr. Barbara DeBuono, to warn hospitals against hasty and poorly considered arrangements: "All the hospitals are in this mating game. They're just desperately trying to find a partner . . . They need to be careful about being a little bit more visionary . . . They all do their little mating dance, and they call me up and say, 'By the way, we want you to know we're dating'" (*American Medical News,* August 19, 1996, 27). In spite of the fast-paced merger frenzy, Dr. DeBuono and other observers still expect that the new outlines of the system will take three to five years to take clear form:

> We're going to see half a dozen systems develop in the New York City area, and a lot in the rest of the state—two systems in Rochester, two to three in Albany, etc. But it will be much more vertically integrated. First, we see the hospitals come together, but then we will see verticalization. (Barbara DeBuono, Commissioner of Health, New York City, September 12, 1996)

Regarding the insurance and HMO industry, the major structural move in 1996 was the announcement by Empire Blue Cross of their intention to convert to for-profit status, a move that will be scrutinized closely by many different public and private interests. The other major movement has been the rapid growth in HMO penetration in the New York City metropolitan area, traditionally a bastion of fee-for-service medicine hostile to managed care. That resistance is breaking down, particularly with the growth of managed care in the City's huge Medicaid program.

The organization that has taken shape in Massachusetts and New Jersey among health purchaser groups is not apparent in New York. Because of the state's enormous size and varying markets, regional purchaser coalitions are considered more viable than a statewide group. The two most active regions are Albany and Rochester, though neither has moved yet to influence price, focusing instead on educating employers on quality measures related to health plans. Another coalition on Long Island is focused on pooling employer purchasing power. Like the rest of the health care scene in New York, it is too early to assess the direction or impact of purchaser influence at this time.

Political System Responses

Massachusetts

The predictions of some deregulation proponents that market competition would lead to decreased levels of uninsurance because of lowered prices did not come to pass. Instead, two studies found that the numbers of Massachusetts residents without insurance coverage increased dramatically in the early 1990s. A Harvard School of Public Health study pegged the increase in uninsured from 455,000 in 1989 to 683,000 in 1995.[10] A Boston University School of Public Health study, based on Current Population Survey data, estimated an increase from about 480,000 in 1988 to 750,000 in 1994.[11] These data are consistent with findings from other states documenting an increase in numbers of uninsured residents; however, the Massachusetts data indicate that the commonwealth experienced a faster rate of growth in uninsurance than the rest of the nation during the early 1990s.

The Weld administration in 1994 applied for a Section 1115 waiver from the federal Medicaid program to accomplish two objectives: first, to restructure the Medicaid program to permit all families with incomes below 133 percent of the federal poverty level to be eligible for enrollment; and second, to create a program of subsidies and tax credits for low-wage workers and their employers to encourage the purchase of private insurance. Principal funding for the second part was proposed to come from a diversion of monies from the state's uncompensated care hospital pool. Approved by the federal government in 1995, but subject to legislative approval, the waiver was the object of substantial controversy and was paired with Governor Weld's proposal to repeal the health insurance employer mandate that had been part of the Chapter 23 hospital finance and universal health care law of 1988.

In 1996, the legislature approved a new health access law over Governor Weld's veto. The new law included most of the governor's recommendations regarding Medicaid, provided further coverage expansions for uninsured children, and repealed the 1988 employer mandate that had been repeatedly delayed by the legislature. The legislature failed to approve the subsidy and tax credit proposal or any diversion of funds from the Uncompensated Care Pool, substituting instead a 25 cent increase in the state's cigarette excise tax as a principal funding source. (The author was involved intimately in this and other Massachusetts health policy processes between 1995 and 1997 as House Chairman of the Legislature's Joint Committee on Health Care.)

The future of the Uncompensated Care Pool had become especially problematic for the hospital industry during 1996. Prior to deregulation, all private purchasers of hospital services (except HMOs) were required to pay an explicit surcharge that was used to fund $315 million in pool assessments, a surcharge that varied at different times between 6 and 13 percent of charges. With deregulation and negotiated rates, hospitals found that payer demands for lower prices eroded their ability to finance the pool. In the spring of 1996, Blue Cross pushed hospitals to agree to a new three-year contract commencing in October 1996 that significantly cut back on that large insurer's payments. A coalition of community hospitals severely affected by the Blue Cross contract aggressively promoted legislation to compel insurers and HMOs to finance directly $200 million of the pool's funding. Instead, the legislature established a special commission to develop recommendations for consideration in the 1997 session. In early 1997, the commission recommended changes to the pool, including a new $100 million assessment on purchasers and health plans and new funding from the commonwealth. The commission also recommended implementation of a more limited tax credit/subsidy plan that was included in the original 1115 waiver. The Commission's recommendations became law in the spring of 1997.

In other matters, state lawmakers joined a national trend to restrict the practices of HMOs by requiring minimum 48-hour hospital stays for most maternity patients, by prohibiting so-called gag clauses in HMO contracts that would prevent physicians from giving information to patients, and by requiring insurers to open their plans to participation by all willing pharmacies. After several years of trying, the market for individual insurance (or "nongroup") was restructured in 1996 to enable individuals and families who are shut out of the group market to obtain coverage; this reform was a companion to the "small-group" insurance reforms that were part of the 1991 deregulation statute, and it mirrors in many respects the reforms that were part of New Jersey deregulation in 1992.

New Jersey

As mentioned earlier, New Jersey Governor James Florio's success in working with the legislature to resolve the multiple health sector crises of 1992 did not guarantee his reelection the following year. In a hotly contested race, Republican Christine Todd Whitman defeated Florio on a platform that emphasized major tax cuts. While substantial changes have resulted because of that political shift, the fundamental orientation of the three 1992 statutes has continued—with one significant exception—and health policy matters have not taken sharp turns under this administration.

The major health controversy in recent years involved the fate of the state's Uncompensated Care Pool. In 1992, the legislature and Governor Florio agreed to use approximately $1.6 billion in funding from the Unemployment Insurance Trust Fund to finance uncompensated care costs in decreasing amounts for three years until the end of 1995. By the end of that period, policymakers in the Assembly, Senate, and Governor's Office were unable to agree on a replacement funding source, though business and labor groups strongly opposed any additional use of Unemployment Insurance Trust Funds. In December 1995, Governor Whitman proposed an increase in the state's cigarette excise tax by 25 cents as a replacement funding package, a proposal rejected by the legislature. The funding stalemate dragged into the spring of 1996 with increasing pressure and threats from hospitals that were receiving no reimbursements for indigent care costs.

In the spring of 1996, the legislature and governor agreed to an additional two more years of funding from the Unemployment Insurance Trust Fund, in amounts of $300 million per year, with the state making its own contribution for the first time, $10 million in 1996 and $25 million in 1997. While business groups opposed the diversion, labor and their Democratic allies were mollified by unemployment eligibility and benefit expansions for workers. No provisions have been made for funding beyond the end of 1997, a gubernatorial election year in New Jersey. The new legislation directed the administration to develop a plan to reduce uncompensated care costs by introducing managed care principles to the use of funds—a mandate that state policymakers are struggling to implement. State officials are also examining the potential of using Medicaid 1115 waivers to expand coverage.

As occurred in Massachusetts, New Jersey has seen a sharp increase in numbers of uninsured residents during the early 1990s, from 600,000 in 1987 to more than one million in 1994. A slight decrease in the numbers of uninsured was reported between 1993 and 1994, the first year of the small employer and individual market programs' operation.[12] The small group and nongroup insurance reforms, enacted during the deregulation process in 1992, were intended to address the needs of this population. In particular, increasing amounts of funding were to be moved from hospital uncompensated care reimbursements to subsidies for individual insurance purchase, from $50 million in 1993, and $100 million in 1994, to $150 million in 1995. The source of the funds was the same as the source for uncompensated care—the unemployment insurance trust fund. The individual program, however, was not launched until April 1995, and enrollment was capped at 20,000 individuals and expenditures of $25 million. In the 1996 legislative compromise on uncompensated care funding, the legislature and governor agreed to cap enrollment and subsidies for individual coverage at current levels. Thus, a major policy commitment made during the 1992 process to increase insurance subsidies to the state's uninsured—former Governor Florio's major priority—has been abandoned. Interviewees indicated that no interest groups or legislators voiced objections to the policy shift.

On other fronts, the state is moving quickly to place Medicaid recipients into HMOs, a move that is generating concerns among hospitals, particularly teaching institutions that receive medical education subsidies through their Medicaid rates. New Jersey has also joined the march of states in placing restrictions on the practices of HMOs. Following Maryland's lead, New Jersey became the second state to enact maternity discharge standards, a measure publicly embraced by Governor Whitman. Her health commissioner, Dr. Leonard Fishman, produced in late 1995 a major overhaul of managed care regulations, measures currently in the implementation stage that are among the most far-reaching in the nation in establishing new public standards for HMOs and similar entities. Among other requirements, the new regulations establish a public grievance process for citizens who are dissatisfied with treatment decisions by their health plans. The state also plans to produce HMO report cards for the public.

New York

Once again, the policy responses to the aftermath of deregulation are less easy to track in New York because of the recent enactment of the deregulation law. However, the trends that have been observable in Massachusetts and New Jersey are also apparent in New York.

Of particular concern to the hospital industry and others is the fate of the new structure for uncompensated care and graduate medical education funding. Hospital industry leaders were eager in their negotiations to avoid the fate of Massachusetts hospitals who increasingly negotiate away any payer contributions to uncompensated care. A further concern was that any replacement funding mechanism had to conform to federal law requirements, particularly the Employee Retirement Income Security Act of 1974. Any funding mechanism that forced payers to contribute directly to a state pool would likely fail an ERISA test and thus face federal preemption.

The solution developed by policymakers requires all purchasers of hospital services to contribute an additional 32 percent to charges that will be used to finance the new pools; alternatively, purchasers may pay an eight percent surcharge directly to the state. The purchaser "option" is designed to survive an ERISA test while exempting hospitals from having to collect the surcharge directly. Because the insurance community in New York state was supportive of the new structure, including Blue Cross, HMOs, and the commercial insurance industry, the plan is considered to have a strong chance of survival. By early 1997, at least one ERISA challenge to the new system had been filed by the cement makers union, though the prospects for the suit were not clear in early 1997.

The new structure for uncompensated care and graduate medical education has a three-year life span, with no guarantees beyond 1998. Hospital and state officials are in agreement that changes in the structure of New York's graduate medical education system must be high on the agenda during the coming three years, though hospital officials hope that such changes can be negotiated in tandem with looming federal changes. The signing ceremony for the NYPHRM deregulation statute, held at Mount Sinai Hospital in Manhattan on September 12, 1996, was an upbeat event, with hospital, insurer, labor, HMO, legislative, and other officials expressing satisfaction with compromises made and prospects for successful implementation. Behind the smiles rest concerns about the shape of the new system and worries about who will be forced out of the picture in the near future.

Regarding insurance reforms, New York policymakers did not wait for deregulation to address the problems of consumers in need of individual insurance. In 1993, the state adopted the most far-reaching market reforms in the nation, approving statewide community rating for individual insurance products without age, geographic, or other restrictions. These reforms were nationally controversial, and debate about their impact became part of the larger debate around national health care reform in 1993 and 1994. While the impact of the changes remains the object of controversy, the actual market impacts have long since been absorbed, and no efforts have been made in recent years to undo community rating.

Managed care regulation has also been a policy matter addressed by lawmakers. In 1996, during the same session that NYPHRM deregulation was approved, the legislature approved omnibus managed care legislation that had been brokered by Governor Pataki's representatives with insurer, provider, consumer, and business organizations. The legislation addressed public concerns about so-called physician gag rules, access to emergency services, provider protections, and other matters. Left out were sections desired by the Democratic-controlled Assembly to establish a public grievance process for HMO members and access to specialty care. Earlier in the 1996 session, the legislature also approved the 48-hour maternity discharge proposal. In a short period of time, New York has moved to establish one of the more extensive sets of HMO regulations of any state. The regulation of HMOs also comes as the state moves to push all Medicaid recipients into HMOs, a process that will accelerate during 1997.

Summary: Laying the Groundwork for the Next Policy Revolution

Developments in the three states show strong consistency between 1992 and 1997. In the market, intense hospital reorganization has been a dominant theme, as the sector prepares itself to negotiate more effectively with payers and purchasers, and as it struggles with downsizing. While no hospital in any of the three states closed its doors outright, many have done reorganization activity, and many more have reduced their licensed capacities. While only Massachusetts has seen the entry of for-profit hospitals, officials in New Jersey expect their entry in the future, and New York officials assume that pressures will mount to challenge their law that prohibits for-profit ownership of acute care hospitals. Hospitals finding themselves on the losing end of competition will be drawn to the financial strength of the national for-profit chains.

Insurers have not experienced the same pace of corporate reorganization as hospitals, but major changes have occurred, and all feel the intense demand of purchasers to decrease their price. Massachusetts currently leads the three regarding plan reorganization and organized pressure from the health purchasing community, but similar pressures are evident in New Jersey and New York and are mounting.

On the governmental side, public officials in New York and Massachusetts have made expansion of coverage for uninsured individuals a policy focus, with a particular emphasis on expanded coverage for children. New Jersey's efforts to subsidize individual insurance purchase have stalled far below levels promised in 1992. All three states have had difficulty in sustaining their uncompensated care pools in the new environment—New York has been able to learn from the mistakes of the other two states and may be the best positioned to sustain their structure for some time. All have moved aggressively to enroll Medicaid recipients into managed care plans. All have approved substantial measures to regulate the practices of managed care organizations, especially HMOs. Increasingly, the policy approaches of these formerly rate-regulated states are more consistent with the regulatory profile of most other states, particularly large, industrial states. After decades of exceptionalism because of their high degree of regulatory activity, Massachusetts, New Jersey, and New York increasingly resemble the rest of the pack.

Because the punctuated equilibrium model of policy change has been demonstrated in this study to be a helpful explainer of the fate of rate setting in these states, it seems appropriate to conclude with a brief (and admittedly inconclusive) discussion of the aftermath of deregulation in the context of the model. Specifically, if the punctuated equilibrium model holds relevance for state health policy beyond the example of rate setting policy, we should expect to find some version of the following: (1) a powerful supporting policy idea that undergirds the new managed care structure (this has already been identified and quantified in chapter 5); (2) a new policy monopoly that seeks to sustain the idea, to structure public participation, and to recommend modifications in response to negative feedback; and potentially (3) the beginning outlines of a replacement policy idea and monopoly that could eventually challenge the market/managed care model and gain hegemony.

The new policy idea in the three deregulated states, as has been outlined, is that marketplace competition is a more efficient and appropriate organizer of health care services than state price setting or regulation; the operational vehicle for the new idea is managed care. The new policy monopoly consists of some or all of the following groups: those hospitals positioned (or believing themselves to be so) to prosper in the competitive market; HMOs and insurers who are able to provide value to customers through aggressive managed care; employers and other large purchasers who are organized to influence the new market and to obtain the best possible value for their respective constituencies; and public officials, legislative and executive, who accept and promote the logic of the new structure. The players in the new policy monopoly do not always have to cooperate or agree with each other—the rate setting policy monopoly participants often engaged in bitter quarrels—but they must unite to address threats to the system.

Principal challenges to the system have come in the form of proposals to restrict the practices and operations of HMOs. Indeed, imposing new requirements and obligations on HMOs was the most significant source of health policy legislation in the mid-1990s, with hundreds of bills being proposed to control various aspects of managed care.[13] In these legislative and regulatory battles, a realignment of interest group activity can be observed. Increasingly, providers and consumer groups join together to promote restrictions, while insurers/HMOs link with business/purchaser interests to fight or limit new requirements. A key shift has been the physician community, which increasingly has aligned itself with consumer organizations. During the years of the rate setting policy monopoly, physicians were silent or junior partners in the prevailing structure, most frequently united with hospitals in the pursuit of regulatory largesse. Physicians typically find themselves now outside of the new prevailing policy monopoly, united with other providers and consumer organizations to loosen the restrictions and controls exerted by HMOs.

The responsibility of a policy monopoly is to respond effectively to negative feedback so that such criticism does not evolve into positive feedback that could topple the new system. Thus, it is not surprising to find some managed care groups agreeing to various legislative and regulatory restrictions—for example, the 1996 New York Managed Care Reform Act was enacted, albeit reluctantly, with the support of the state's HMO Conference. Similarly, managed care organizations in many states have either endorsed or not opposed various proposals involving 48-hour maternity discharge protections and prohibition of so-called gag rules in physician contracts. Failure by the new policy monopoly to agree to changes could lead to the creation of coalitions that could incite more revolutionary changes.

Rate setting systems, however, were not replaced until a mature replacement policy idea could be identified that could attract a viable supporting coalition. Opponents to the new market/managed care paradigm are held back in the mid- to late 1990s by the lack of a viable replacement model. Two candidates currently can be identified.

The first is the so-called single-payer public financing model, most readily exemplified by the Canadian health care system. While considerable interest and support for this plan was generated during the financing and access crises between 1988 and 1993, the proposal has not been able to generate sufficient support to pass any federal or state legislative chamber since 1991. In 1994, single-payer proponents placed their plan on the state ballot in California where it received a nearly three-to-one defeat. While prospects for adoption appear dim, single payer is one coherent replacement framework that could generate increased support if dissatisfaction with the managed care framework continues to grow.[14]

The second candidate is the market-oriented approach exemplified by proposals to establish so-called Medical Savings Accounts that permit individuals to use tax deferred savings accounts to finance their own medical expenses. The plan has been most aggressively promoted by the Golden Rule Insurance Company from Indiana, a company noted for its unwillingness to join the industry march away from indemnity-based coverage and toward managed care. The approach has won significant adherents, especially among Republican members of Congress; by mid-1996, 15 state governments had established their own forms of MSAs. In August 1996, President Bill Clinton signed national insurance portability legislation (known as "Kennedy-Kassebaum" for its two principal sponsors) that included a national demonstration of the MSA concept for no more than 750,000 qualified individuals who work in firms with fewer than 50 employees. The national demonstration will provide the first substantial national test of the concept as applied to a larger population base.

Interestingly, physicians have been outspoken advocates of *both* single-payer and MSA structures as replacement policy ideas for the current managed care framework. Aside from these two models, no coherent replacement policy idea is apparent on the horizon. But as we observed with the rate setting policy monopoly, structures can remain in place for many years or decades without substantive or coherent challenge.

A third possibility is that increasing statutory and regulatory restrictions will diminish the effectiveness of managed care in controlling costs over time and that society will learn again to accommodate a higher level of health care inflation than has been experienced during the middle part of the 1990s decade. Such a trend would be accompanied by an acceleration of the trend where employers either stop providing health insurance coverage for workers or else significantly limit benefits and increase employee cost sharing. This trend would lead to new pressures on public officials to find ways to control increases in health costs, triggering the chain that brought on both the rate setting and managed care structures in the first place in the 1960s and 1970s. One possible outcome could be the imposition of a new form of public utility–style regulation on the managed care giants.

Life, indeed, goes on, and so does evolution in health policy. There is no ultimate end, only new challenges, threats, and opportunities. In evaluating them, a sophisticated understanding of the dynamics of policy change—one that focuses on ideas and on the formation of policy monopolies that challenge existing structures and reshape society—can help us to approach these changes in responsible and helpful ways.

Appendixes

APPENDIX A

Interview Subjects

Maryland

(Positions listed are current as of June, 1995)

Dr. Gerard Anderson, Professor, Johns Hopkins School of Public Health

Livio Broccolino, Chief Legal Officer, Blue Cross and Blue Shield of Maryland

Miles Cole, Director of Business Affairs, Maryland Chamber of Commerce

Ernie Crofoot, former member of Health Services Cost Review Commission; AFL-CIO

Geni Dunnells, Executive Director, Maryland Association of HMOs

Eugene Feinblatt, Attorney, Chairman of Maryland Commission on Health Care Financing

Thomas Goddard, Director of Legislative and Regulatory Affairs, New York Life Health Plus

Paula Hollinger, State Senator, Chair, Joint Committee on Health Care Delivery and Finance

Robert Kowal, Chief Executive Officer, Greater Baltimore Medical Center

Larry Lawrence, Executive Vice President, Maryland Hospital Association

Robert Murray, Executive Director, Maryland Health Services Cost Review Commission

Deborah Rivkin, Executive Director, League of Life and Health Insurers of Maryland

Jerry Schmith, Deputy Director, Maryland Health Services Cost Review Commission

Casper Taylor, Speaker, Maryland House of Delegates

Dr. Martin Wasserman, Commissioner, Maryland Department of Health and Mental Hygiene

Massachusetts

(Positions identified are those held during 1991)

Charles Baker, Massachusetts Undersecretary of Health and Human Services

Bruce Bullen, Commissioner, Massachusetts Division of Medical Assistance

Carmen Buell, Representative, Chair, Joint Committee on Health Care

Edward Burke, Senator, Chair, Joint Committee on Health Care

William Carroll, President, Life Insurance Association of Massachusetts

Thomas Finneran, Representative, Chair, House Committee on Ways and Means

Paula Griswold, Chairperson, Massachusetts Rate Setting Commission

Stephen Hegarty, President, Massachusetts Hospital Association

Robert Hughes, Executive Director, Massachusetts Association of HMOs

Richard Knox, Medical Editor, *The Boston Globe*

Judith Kurland, Chief Executive Officer, Boston City Hospital

Richard Lord, Director of Research, Associated Industries of Massachusetts

Robert Restuccia, Executive Director, Health Care for All

Elizabeth Rothberg, Director of Issues Management, Life Insurance Association of Massachusetts

Steven Tringale, Vice President for External Affairs, Blue Cross of Massachusetts

Celia Wcislo, President, Service Employees Local Union 285

New Jersey

(Positions identified are those held during 1992)

Dana Benbow, Vice President, Prudential Insurance Company

Murray Bevan, Vice President for Government Relations, New Jersey Hospital Association

Joel Cantor, Director of Evaluation Research, Robert Wood Johnson Foundation

Richard Codey, Senator, former Health Committee Chairman

Pamela Dickson, Assistant Commissioner, New Jersey Department of Health

Al Evanoff, New Jersey United Senior Alliance

Dale Florio, Legislative and Regulatory Counsel, New Jersey HMO Association

James Florio, Governor
Charles Haytaian, Speaker, New Jersey Assembly
George Laufenberg, Administrator, New Jersey Carpenters Fund; Rate
    Setting member
Maureen Lopes, Senior Vice President for Health Affairs, New Jersey
    Business and Industry Council
Charles Marciante, President, New Jersey AFL-CIO
Dennis Marco, Vice President, Blue Cross and Blue Shield of New Jersey
Thomas Terrill, Executive Vice President, University Health Systems of
    New Jersey
Victoria Wicks, Chief Executive Officer, Health Insurance Plan of New
    Jersey

New York

(Positions listed are current as of July, 1995)

Debbie Bell, Coordinator of Policy Development, District Council 37,
    AFSCME
Gerry Billings, Executive Director, State Communities Aid Association
Barbara DeBuono, Commissioner, Department of Health
Robin Frank, Senior Program Advisor for Health, Governor's Office
Richard Gottfried, Assemblyman, Chairman, Health Committee
Kemp Hannon, Senator, Chairman, Health Committee
Harold Iselin, Counsel, New York HMO Conference
Richard Kirsch, Executive Director, New York Citizen Action
David Oakley, Counsel, New York State Conference of Blue Cross and
    Blue Shield Plans
Kenneth Raske, President, Greater New York Health Care Association
Ed Reinfurt, Vice President, Business Council of New York State
John Rodat, Consultant
Dr. John Rossman, Vice President for Economics and Policy
    Development, Hospital Association of New York State
Diane Stuto, Vice President, Life Insurance Council of New York State
Ray Sweeney, Executive Vice President, Healthcare Association of New
    York State; former Director of New York Office of Health Systems
    Management
James Tallon, President, United Hospital Fund of New York, former
    State Assembly Majority Leader
Mark Van Guysling, Assistant Deputy Director of Health Care
    Financing, New York Department of Health

Interview Instrument

Maryland

A. Current Support for Hospital Rate Setting
    1. Why do policymakers in your state continue the hospital rate set-
ting system?
    2. What have been the key events in the evolution of rate setting in
recent years?
    3. What are the key governmental institutions involved in the contin-
uance of the rate setting system?
    4. What is your perception of how well or poorly the rate setting law
works today? Key indicators of success or failure?
B. The Role of Interests
    1. Are the following groups—in general—winners or losers because
of the existence of hospital rate setting in your state?
        —hospitals
        —commercial insurers
        —Blue Cross
        —managed care interests/HMOs
        —consumers
        —business
        —labor
    2. Who are the key individuals in the state who are most identified
with support for the continuation of rate setting?
    3. Is there pressure in your state to deregulate the rate setting system?
If yes, how strong is the pressure, and do you see any changes in
support for this position?
    4. Are there any key individuals or groups whom you can identify as
key advocates for deregulation? If so, are these new or long-standing positions in support of deregulation?
    5. Are government officials active movers in decisions about the hos-
pital rate setting law or more passive responders to the agendas and
needs of various stakeholders/interests?
    6. Of the groups interested in health policy, which are the key in pro-

viding political support to legislative and statewide candidates for office? Have there been changes in degrees of support in recent years?

C. The Role of Ideas
1. Can you identify the policy "idea" behind hospital rate setting in your state?
2. Is there an alternative policy idea current today that could replace it?
3. Are discussions about hospital rate setting more about interest group agendas or policy ideas?

Massachusetts, New Jersey, and New York

A. The Deregulation Decision
1. Why did policymakers in your state decide to deregulate the hospital rate setting system?
2. What were the key events that led to the deregulation process?
3. Did any government institutions disintegrate, form, or significantly change because of the deregulation decision?
4. What was your perception of the operation of the rate setting law? How well did it work?

B. The Role of Interests
1. Was implementation of the rate setting law favorable or hostile to the following interests:
   —hospitals
   —commercial insurance
   —Blue Cross
   —managed care/HMOs
   —consumers
   —business
   —labor
2. Which groups or individuals were most prominent in advocating deregulation? Did this represent a change in their historic position?
3. Which groups or individuals were most prominent in opposing deregulation? Did this represent a change or a continuation in their historic position?
4. Were government officials active movers in the deregulation decision, or were they more passive responders to the demands of the affected interests?
5. Of the above mentioned interest groups, which are most prominent in providing political support to legislators and statewide candi-

dates? Have there been identifiable changes in the levels of support among these groups in the years leading up to deregulation?

C. The Role of Ideas

    1. What was the policy "idea" behind hospital rate setting in your state? Who was most associated with the idea?

    2. What is the prevailing "idea" behind hospital regulation in the deregulated system?

    3. Was the discussion of a new "idea" a prominent feature of the deregulation debate? If so, how can it be demonstrated?

Notes

Chapter 1

1. G. F. Anderson, "All-Payer Rate Setting: Down But Not Out," *Health Care Financing Review* (1991 Annual Supplement): 35–41.

2. B. J. Biles, C. J. Schramm, and J. G. Atkinson, "Hospital Cost Inflation Under State Rate-Setting Programs," *New England Journal of Medicine* 305 (September 1980): 664–68.

3. N. Kraus, M. Porter, and P. Ball, *Managed Care: A Decade in Review: 1980–1990,* The Interstudy Edge, ed. InterStudy (Excelsior, MN: Interstudy, 1991), 500.

4. L. Brown, *Politics and Health Care Organization: HMOs as Federal Policy* (Washington, DC: Brookings Institution, 1983), 500.

5. GHAA, *1995 National Directory of HMOs,* Group Health Associations of America (Washington, DC: GHAA, 1995), 26.

6. Anderson, "All-Payer Rate Setting."

7. C. J. Schramm, S. R. Renn, and B. Biles, "Controlling Hospital Cost Inflation: New Perspectives on State Rate Setting," *Health Affairs* 5, no. 3 (1986): 22–33.

8. G. Allison, "Conceptual Models and the Cuban Missile Crisis," *American Political Science Review* 63 (September 1969): 689–718.

9. G. Stigler, "The Theory of Economic Regulation," in *Chicago Studies in Political Economy,* ed. G. Stigler (Chicago: University of Chicago Press, 1988), 209–33. Feldstein, P., *The Politics of Health Legislation: An Economic Perspective* (Ann Arbor: Health Administration Press, 1988), chap. 2.

10. P. Feldstein, *Health Care Economics,* 3d ed. (New York: John Wiley and Sons, 1988), 279–91.

11. Feldstein, *Health Care Economics,* 305–8.

12. F. R. Baumgartner and B. D. Jones, *Agendas and Instability in American Politics* (Chicago: University of Chicago Press, 1993).

13. H. S. Luft, "Competition and Regulation," *Medical Care* 23, no. 5 (1985): 383–400.

14. R. K. Yin, *Case Study Research: Design and Methods,* 3d ed. Applied Social Research Methods Series, vol. 5 (Newbury Park, CA: SAGE Publication, 1994).

15. Yin, *Case Study Research.* R. K. Yin, *Applications of Case Study*

Research. Applied Social Research Methods Series, vol. 34. (Newbury Park, CA: SAGE Publications, 1993).

Chapter 2

1. F. Sloan, "Rate Regulation for Hospital Cost Control: Evidence From the Last Decade," *Milbank Memorial Fund Quarterly* 1983 (61): 195–217.

2. G. F. Anderson, "All-Payer Rate Setting: Down But Not Out," *Health Care Financing Review* 1991 Annual Supplement: 35–41.

3. C. J. Schramm, S. R. Renn, and B. Biles, "Controlling Hospital Cost Inflation: New Perspectives on State Rate Setting," *Health Affairs* 5, no. 3 (1986): 22–33.

4. Sloan, "Rate Regulation."

5. M. A. Morrissey et al., "Hospital Rate Review: A Theory and an Empirical Review," *Journal of Health Economics* 3, no. 1 (1984): 25–47.

6. K. R. Cone and D. Dranove, "Why Did States Enact Hospital Rate-Setting Laws?," *Journal of Law and Economics* 29, no. 2 (1986): 287–302.

7. D. Crozier, "State Rate Setting: A Status Report," *Health Affairs* 1, no. 3, (summer 1982): 66–83.

8. B. J. Biles, C. J. Schramm, and J. G. Atkinson, "Hospital Cost Inflation Under State Rate-Setting Programs," *New England Journal of Medicine* 305 (September 1980): 664–68.

9. Anderson, "All-Payer Rate Setting." J. Goldsmith, "Death of a Paradigm: The Challenge of Competition," *Health Affairs* 3, no. 3 (1984): 5–19.

10. Crozier, "State Rate Setting."

11. Crozier, "State Rate Setting."

12. Sloan, "Rate Regulation."

13. J. L. Ashby, "The Impact of Hospital Regulatory Programs on Per Capita Costs, Utilization, and Capital Investment," *Inquiry* 21 (1984): 45–59.

14. Schramm, "Controlling Hospital Cost Inflation."

15. C. Coelen and D. Sullivan, "An Analysis of the Effects of Prospective Reimbursement Programs on Hospital Expenditures," *Health Care Financing Review* 2, no. 3 (1981): 1–40.

16. D. Zuckerman, "Rate Setting and Hospital Cost Containment: All-Payer versus Partial-Payer Approaches," *Health Services Research* 22, no. 3 (1987): 307–26.

17. S. Zuckerman et al., *Alternative Approaches to All-Payer Rate Setting* (The Urban Institute, 1993).

18. Biles, "Hospital Cost Inflation."

19. C. Coelen, S. Mennemeyer, and D. Kidder, *Effects of Prospective Reimbursement Programs on Hospital Revenue, Expense and Financial Status* (Cambridge, MA: Abt Associates, 1986).

20. Schramm, "Controlling Hospital Cost Inflation."

21. J. C. Robinson and J. S. Luft, "Competition, Regulation, and Hospital Costs, 1982 to 1986," *Journal of the American Medical Association* 260, no. 18 (1988): 2676–81.

22. C. G. McLaughlin, "HMO Growth and Hospital Expenses and Use: A Simultaneous Equation Approach," *Health Services Research* 22, no. 2 (1987): 183–206.

23. M. A. Morrisey, F. A. Sloan, and S. A. Mitchell, "State Rate Setting: An Analysis of Some Unresolved Issues," *Health Affairs* 3, no. 2 (1983): 36–47.

24. Schramm, "Controlling Hospital Cost Inflation."

25. M. D. Finkler, "State Rate Setting Revisited," *Health Affairs* 6, no. 4 (1987): 82–89.

26. C. Coelen and R. Yaffe, "The National Hospital Rate-Setting Study: Summary of Current Findings on the Effects of Hospital Prospective Payment Systems," in *Labor Management Health Care Cost Containment Conference* (Atlantic City, NJ, 1983.

27. J. A. Lanning, M. A. Morrisey, and R. L. Ohsfeldt, "Endogenous Hospital Regulation and Its Effects on Hospital and Non-hospital Expenditures," *Journal of Regulatory Economics* 1991, no. 3: 137–54.

28. W. C. Hsiao et al., "Lessons of the New Jersey DRG Payment System," *Health Affairs* 5, no. 2 (1986): 32–43.

29. K. E. Thorpe, "Does All-Payer Rate Setting Work? The Case of the New York Prospective Hospital Reimbursement Methodology," *Journal of Health Politics, Policy and Law* 12, no. 3 (1987): 391–409.

30. Thorpe, "Does All-Payer Rate Setting Work?" S. Zuckerman and J. Holahan, "PPS Waivers: Implications for Medicare, Medicaid, and Commercial Insurers," *Journal of Health Politics, Policy and Law* 13, no. 4 (1988): 663–81. M. D. Rosko, "A Comparison of Hospital Performance Under the Partial-Payer Medicare PPS and State All-Payer Rate Setting Systems," *Inquiry* 26 (spring 1989): 48–61.

31. D. Kidder and D. Sullivan, "Hospital Payroll Costs, Productivity, and Employment under Prospective Reimbursement," *Health Care Financing Review* 4, no. 2 (1982): 89–100.

32. J. Hadley and K. Swartz, "The Impacts on Hospital Costs Between 1980 and 1984 of Hospital Rate Regulation, Competition, and Changes in Health Insurance Coverage," *Inquiry* 26 (spring 1989): 35–47.

33. G. F. Anderson and J. R. Lave, "State Rate-Setting Programs: Do They Reward Efficiency in Hospitals?," *Medical Care* 22, no. 5 (1984): 494–98.

34. N. L. Worthington and P. A. Piro, "The Effects of Hospital Rate-Setting Programs on Volumes of Hospital Services: A Preliminary Analysis," *Health Care Financing Review* 4, no. 2 (1982): 47–66.

35. Ashby, "Impact of Hospital Regulatory Programs."

36. F. A. Sloan, "Hospital Rate Review: A Theory and an Empirical Review," *Journal of Health Economics* 3, no. 1 (1984): 83–86.

37. Morrissey, "Hospital Rate Review."

38. S. M. Shortell and E. F. X. Hughes, "The Effects of Regulation, Compe-

tition, and Ownership on Mortality Rates among Hospital Inpatients," *New England Journal of Medicine* 318, no. 17 (1988): 1100–1107.

39. G. L. Gaumer, E. Poggio, and C. Sennett, "Effects of State Prospective Reimbursement Programs on Hospital Mortality," *Medical Care* 27, no. 7 (1989): 724–36.

40. Anderson, "All-Payer Rate Setting."

41. J. Cromwell and J. R. Kanak, "The Effects of Prospective Reimbursement Programs on Hospital Adoption and Service Sharing," *Health Care Financing Review* 4, no. 2 (1982): 67–88.

42. Coelen, "Effects of Prospective Reimbursement Programs."

43. P. L. Joskow, *Controlling Hospital Costs: The Role of Government Regulation* (Cambridge: MIT Press, 1981), 142–55.

44. McLaughlin, "HMO Growth."

45. Zuckerman 1987, "Rate Setting."

46. Anderson, "All-Payer Rate Setting."

47. P. B. Ginsburg and F. A. Sloan, "Hospital Cost Shifting," *New England Journal of Medicine* 310, no. 14 (1984): 893–98.

48. C. L. Eby and D. R. Cohodes, "What Do We Know about Rate Setting?," *Journal of Health Politics, Policy and Law* 10, no. 2 (1985): 299–327.

49. A. Enthoven, *Health Plan: The Only Practical Solution to the Soaring Costs of Medical Care* (Reading, PA: Addison-Wesley, 1980).

50. Sloan 1983, "Rate Regulation."

51. Ginsburg, "Hospital Cost Shifting."

52. Finkler, "State Rate Setting Revisited."

53. D. R. Wholey, J. B. Christianson, and S. Sanchez, "The Effect of State Regulation on Development of HMO Markets," in *Advances in the Study of Entrepreneurship and Economic Growth* (JAI Press, Inc., 1990)

54. L. G. Goldberg and W. Greenberg, "The Determinants of HMO Enrollment and Growth," *Health Services Research* 16, no. 4 (1981): 421–38.

55. A. Over, J. M. Watt, and D. Roenigh, *Private Sector Health Care Initiatives: Market Area Characteristics. Analysis and User Documentation* (US Department of Health and Human Services, 1983).

56. Anderson, "All-Payer Rate Setting."

57. McLaughlin, "HMO Growth."

58. M. A. Morrissey and C. A. Ashby, "An Empirical Analysis of HMO Market Share," *Inquiry* 19 (summer 1982): 136–49.

59. Schramm, "Controlling Hospital Cost Inflation."

60. P. B. Ginsburg and K. E. Thorpe, "Can All-Payer Rate Setting and the Competitive Strategy Coexist?," *Health Affairs* 11, no. 3 (1992): 73–86.

61. T. Rice, "Including an All-Payer Reimbursement System in a Universal Health Insurance Program," *Inquiry* 29 (summer 1992): 203–12.

62. Anderson, "All-Payer Rate Setting."

63. D. J. Boorstin, *The Creators* (New York City: Random House, 1992), 62.

64. A. Hamilton, J. Madison, and J. Jay, *The Federalist Papers* (New York: New American Library, 1961), 77–84.

65. C. Beard, *An Economic Interpretation of the Constitution of the United States* (New York: Macmillan, 1935), 324–25.

66. J. Schumpeter, *Capitalism, Socialism, and Democracy* (New York: Harper and Row, 1962), 256–64.

67. A. Downs, *An Economic Theory of Democracy* (New York: Harper and Row, 1957), 3–35.

68. J. Buchanan and G. Tullock, "The Calculus of Consent" (1962), in *The Power of Public Ideas,* ed. R. Reich (Cambridge, MA: Ballinger, 1988), 32.

69. S. Huntington, "The Marasmus of the ICC," *Yale Law Journal* 61 (April 1952): 467–509.

70. G. Stigler, "The Theory of Economic Regulation," in *Chicago Studies in Political Economy,* ed. G. Stigler (Chicago: University of Chicago Press, 1988), 209–33.

71. D. B. Truman, *The Governmental Process: Political Interests and Public Opinion* (New York: Knopf, 1951).

72. Stigler, 209–33.

73. Stigler, 209–33.

74. G. Hilton, "The Basic Behavior of Regulatory Commissions," *American Economic Review* 62, no. 2 (1972): 47–54.

75. S. Peltzman, "Toward a More General Theory of Regulation," in *Chicago Studies in Political Economy,* ed. G. Stigler (Chicago: University of Chicago Press, 1988), 234–66.

76. E. Latham, *The Group Basis of Politics* (Ithaca: Cornell University Press, 1952), 35.

77. M. P. Fiorina, *Congress: Keystone of the Washington Establishment,* 2d ed. (New Haven: Yale University Press, 1989), 37–52. W. Niskanen, *Bureaucracy and Representative Government* (New York: Aldine-Atherton, 1971), chaps. 2–4.

78. J. Q. Wilson, "The Rise of the Bureaucratic State," in *The American Commonwealth, 1976,* ed. N. Glazer and I. Kristol (New York: Basic Books, 1976).

79. P. Feldstein and G. McInick, "Congressional Voting Behavior on Hospital Legislation: An Exploratory Study," *Journal of Health Politics, Policy and Law* 8, no. 4 (winter 1984): 686–701.

80. P. J. Feldstein, *The Politics of Health Legislation: An Economic Perspective* (Ann Arbor: Health Administration Press, 1988), chap. 2.

81. P. Feldstein, *Health Care Economics,* 3d ed. (New York: John Wiley and Sons, 1988), 305–9.

82. G. Becker, "Public Policies, Pressure Groups and Dead Weight Costs," in *Chicago Studies in Political Economy,* ed. G. Stigler (Chicago: University of Chicago Press, 1988), 85–105.

83. P. MacAvoy, *The Regulated Industries and the Economy* (New York: Norton, 1979).

84. J. J. Mansbridge, "On the Relation of Altruism and Self-Interest," in *Beyond Self-Interest,* ed. J. J. Mansbridge (Chicago: University of Chicago Press, 1990), 140–41.

85. K. J. Meier, *Regulation: Politics, Bureaucracy and Economics* (New York: St. Martin's Press, 1985), 19.

86. S. Kelman, "Congress and the Public Spirit: A Commentary," in *Beyond Self-Interest,* ed. J. J. Mansbridge (Chicago: University of Chicago Press, 1990), 206.

87. Cone, "Why Did States Enact Hospital Rate-Setting Laws?"

88. M. Derthick and P. Quirk, *The Politics of Deregulation* (Washington, DC: Brookings, 1985), 27, 238–45.

89. R. Noll, "Government Regulatory Behavior: A Multidisciplinary Survey and Synthesis," in *Regulatory Policy and the Social Sciences,* ed. R. Noll (Berkeley: University of California Press,. 1985), 6.

90. J. M. Buchanan, "Then and Now, 1961–1986: From Delusion to Dystopia," in *Institute for Human Studies,* quoted in *Beyond Self-Interest,* ed. J. J. Mansbridge (Chicago: University of Chicago Press, 1990), 314.

91. D. Green and I. Shapiro, *Pathologies of Rational Choice Theory: A Critique of Applications in Political Science* (New Haven: Yale University Press, 1994), 202–4.

92. T. Kuhn, *The Structure of Scientific Revolutions,* 2d ed. (Chicago: University of Chicago Press, 1970).

93. N. Eldredge and S. J. Gould, "Punctuated Equilibria: An Alternative to Phyletic Gradualism," in *Models in Paleobiology,* ed. T. J. Scoph (San Francisco: Freeman Cooper, 1972).

94. M. Tushman and E. Romanelli, "Organizational Evolution: A Metamorphosis Model of Convergence and Reorientation," in *Research in Organizational Behavior,* ed. L. Cummings and B. Staw (Greenwich, CT: JAI Press, 1985).

95. F. R. Baumgartner and B. D. Jones, *Agendas and Instability in American Politics* (Chicago: University of Chicago Press, 1993), chap. 1.

96. M. Schneider and P. Teske, *Public Entrepreneurs: Agents for Change in American Government* (Princeton: Princeton University Press, 1995), 4.

97. E. E. Schattschneider, *The Semi-Sovereign People* (New York: Holt, Rinehart and Winston, 1975).

98. E. E. Schattschneider, "The Scope and Bias of the Pressure System," in *Classic Readings in American Politics,* ed. P. Nivola (New York: St. Martin's Press, 1986), 247–58.

99. M. Olson, "Collective Action: The Logic," in *Classic Readings in American Politics,* ed. P. Nivola (New York: St. Martin's Press, 1986), 213–23.

100. Meier, 10–14.

101. W. T. Gormley, "Regulatory Issue Networks in a Federal System," *Polity* 18, no. 4 (1986): 595–620.

102. Schattschneider, 247–58.

103. D. Stone, *Policy Paradox and Political Reason* (HarperCollins, 1988), 13–26.

104. C. E. Van Horn, D. C. Baumer, and W. T. Gormley, *Politics and Public Policy* (Washington, DC: CQ Press, 1992), 25.

105. Baumgartner, chap. 1.

106. Kuhn, 77.

107. Derthick, 238.

108. M. A. Eisner, *Regulatory Politics in Transition* (Baltimore: Johns Hopkins University Press, 1993).

109. H. Heclo, "Issue Networks and the Executive Establishment," in *The New American Political System,* ed. A. King (Washington, DC: American Enterprise Institute, 1978), 87–124.

110. E. S. Redford, *Democracy in the Administrative State* (New York: Oxford University Press, 1969), 107–31.

111. Goldsmith, "Death of a Paradigm."

112. Goldsmith, "Death of a Paradigm."

113. Van Horn, 293.

114. C. E. Lindblom, "The Science of Muddling Through," *Public Administration Review* 19 (1959): 79–88.

115. A. Wildavsky, *The Politics of the Budgetary Process* (Boston: Little Brown, 1984), chap 2.

116. W. Riker, *Liberalism Against Populism: A Confrontation Between the Theory of Democracy and the Theory of Social Choice* (San Francisco: WH Freeman and Co., 1982), 188–89.

117. G. Allison, "Conceptual Models and the Cuban Missile Crisis," American Political Science Review 63 (September 1969): 689–718.

Chapter 3

1. C. Coelen, S. Mennemeyer, and D. Kidder, *Effects of Prospective Reimbursement Programs on Hospital Revenue, Expense and Financial Status* (Cambridge, MA: Abt Associates, 1986), chap. 1.

2. F. A. Sloan, "Rate Regulation as a Strategy for Hospital Cost Control: Evidence from the Last Decade," *Milbank Memorial Fund Quarterly* 61, no. 2 (1983): 195–217.

3. P. Fanara and W. Greenberg, "Factors Affecting the Adoption of Prospective Reimbursement by State Governments," in *Incentives vs. Controls in Health Policy,* ed. J. A. Meyer (Washington, DC: American Enterprise Institute, 1985), 144–56.

4. K. R. Cone and D. Dranove, "Why Did States Enact Hospital Rate-Setting Laws?," *Journal of Law and Economics* 29, no. 2 (1986): 287–302.

5. Cone and Dranove, "Why Did States Enact Hospital Rate-Setting Laws?"

6. F. A. Sloan, "Hospital Rate Review: A Theory and an Empirical Review," *Journal of Health Economics* 3, no. 1 (1984): 83–86.

7. C. L. Eby and D. R. Cohodes, "What Do We Know about Rate Setting?," *Journal of Health Politics, Policy and Law* 10, no. 2 (1985): 299–327.

8. US GAO, *Health Care Spending: Nonpolicy Factors Account for Most State Differences* (Washington, DC: US GAO, 1992).

9. K. O. Morgan, S. Morgan, and N. Quitno, *Health Care State Rankings, 1995,* 3d ed. (Lawrence, KS: Morgan Quitno Press, 1995).

10. P. Jacobsen, R. Merritt, L. Bartlett, M. Marquis, S. Long, H. Leeds, I. Fraser, and G. Kominski, *State Health Care Reform Initiatives: Progress and Promise* (RAND, 1994), chap. 4.

11. J. Rodat, *NYPHRM's Paradox: How New York's Attempts to Stabilize Hospital Finances Lead to More Uninsured, Increased Health Benefit Restrictions, Reduced Hospital Utilization, and Weakened Hospitals* (Albany, NY: Signalhealth, 1995).

12. B. C. Vladeck, ed., *Health Care Financing in New York State: A Blueprint for Change* (New York: United Hospital Fund, 1993), chap. 1.

13. D. G. Safran and J. P. Ruger, *The Massachusetts Health Care Industry: Pathways to the Future* (Boston: Governor's Council on Economic Growth and Technology, 1994).

14. D. J. Elazar, *The American Mosaic: The Impact of Space, Time and Culture on American Politics* (Boulder: Westview Press, 1994), 330, chap. 8.

15. J. L. Walker, "The Diffusion of Innovations Among the American States," *American Political Science Review* 63, no. 3 (1969): 880–95.

16. V. Gray, "Innovation in the States: A Diffusion Study," *American Political Science Review* 67, no. 4 (1973): 1174–85.

17. D. Miller and P. H. Friesen, "A. Longitudinal Study of the Corporate Life Cycle," *Management Science* 30 (1984): 1161–83.

18. J. Ashby, *Achievement, Access, and Accountability: An Overview of Maryland's Twenty-Two Years of Hospital Rate Regulation 1971–1993* (Maryland Hospital Association, 1994), 7–21.

19. J. S. Jacobs, *Maryland Legislation on Hospital Rate Regulation: A Historical Perspective of Policy Development* (College Park: University of Maryland, 1974), 21.

20. Jacobs, *Maryland Legislation,* 21–22.

21. Jacobs, *Maryland Legislation,* 25.

22. Jacobs, *Maryland Legislation,* 27.

23. R. Kronick, "The Slippery Slope of Health Care Finance: Business Interests and Hospital Reimbursement in Massachusetts," *Journal of Health Politics, Policy and Law* 15, no. 4 (1990): 887–913.

24. A. Dunham and J. Morone, "The Politics of Innovation: The Evolution of DRG Rate Regulation in New Jersey," in *DRG Evaluation Volume IV-A* (Princeton: Health Research and Educational Trust, 1983).

25. C. Devine-Perez, "Comparative State Hospital Financing Politics: New Jersey and New York," in *Wagner School of Public Service* (New York: New York University, 1995), 122–23.

26. F. Hellinger, "Prospective Reimbursement Through Budget Review: New Jersey, Rhode Island, and Western Pennsylvania," *Inquiry* 1976: 312.

27. Devine-Perez, 128–30

28. R. S. Powell, *Bureaucratic Malpractice: Hospital Regulation in New Jersey* (Princeton, NJ: Center for the Analysis of Public Issues, 1974).

29. Devine-Perez, 134–35.

30. A. Dunham and J. Morone, "Slouching Toward National Health Insur-

ance: The Unanticipated Politics of DRGs," *Bulletin of the New York Academy of Medicine* 1986.

31. Devine-Perez, 136–38.

32. Devine-Perez, 139.

33. Devine-Perez, 244–46.

34. Jacobsen, chap. 4.

35. Jacobsen, chap. 4.

36. Devine-Perez, 247.

37. Ashby, 8.

38. Kronick, "Slippery Slope."

39. L. A. Bergthold, "Purchasing Power: Business and Health Policy Changes in Massachusetts," *Journal of Health Politics, Policy and Law* 13, no. 3 (1988): 425–51.

40. Bergthold, "Purchasing Power."

41. Devine-Perez, 282.

42. Kronick, "Slippery Slope."

43. M. Rosko, "The Impact of Prospective Payment: A Multi-dimensional Analysis of the New Jersey SHARE Program," *Journal of Health Politics, Policy and Law* 9, no. 1 (1984): 81–101.

44. M. Rosko and R. Broyles, "Short-Term Responses of Hospitals to the DRG Prospective Pricing Mechanism in New Jersey," *Medical Care* 25, no. 2 (1987): 88–99.

45. W. C. Hsiao et al., "Lessons of the New Jersey DRG Payment System," *Health Affairs* 5, no. 2 (1986): 32–43.

46. K. Volpp, G. Siegel, and B. Siegel, "Long-Term Experience With All-Payer State Rate Setting," *Health Affairs* (summer 1993): 59–65.

47. H. M. Sapolsky, J. Aisenberg, and J. Morone, "The Call to Rome and Other Obstacles to State-Level Innovation," *Public Administration Review* 1987 (March/April): 135–42.

48. S. L. Weiner and H. M. Sapolsky, *Hospital Payment Reform: The Case of New Jersey 1980–1994* (Cambridge: Massachusetts Institute of Technology, 1994).

49. K. E. Thorpe, "Does All-Payer Rate Setting Work? The Case of the New York Prospective Hospital Reimbursement Methodology," *Journal of Health Politics, Policy and Law* 12, no. 3 (1987): 391–409.

50. Jacobsen, chap. 4.

51. Jacobsen, chap. 4.

52. Thorpe 1987, "Does All-Payer Rate Setting Work?"

53. Ashby, 8–21.

54. Kronick, "Slippery Slope."

55. Hsiao, "Lessons of the New Jersey DRG Payment System."

56. J. C. Cantor, "Health Care Unreform: The New Jersey Approach," *Journal of the American Medical Association* 270, no. 24 (1993): 2968–70.

57. Weiner, *Hospital Payment Reform.*

58. Weiner, *Hospital Payment Reform.*

59. H. S. Berliner and S. Delgado, "The Rise and Fall of New Jersey's

Uncompensated Care Fund," *Journal of American Health Policy* 1, no. 2 (1991): 47–50.

60. Volpp 1993, "Long-Term Experience With All-Payer State Rate Setting."

61. R. Kronick, *Health Insurance for the Uninsured in New Jersey* (Trenton: NJ Department of Health, 1990).

62. Weiner, *Hospital Payment Reform.*

63. Jacobsen, chap. 4.

64. Vladeck 1993, *Health Care Financing in New York State.*

65. Vladeck 1993, *Health Care Financing in New York State.*

66. Vladeck 1993, *Health Care Financing in New York State.*

67. Jacobsen, chap. 4.

68. Vladeck 1993, *Health Care Financing in New York State.*

69. Jacobsen, chap. 4.

70. Vladeck 1993, *Health Care Financing in New York State.*

71. K. E. Thorpe, "Uncompensated Care Pools and Care to the Uninsured: Lessons from the New York Prospective Hospital Reimbursement Methodology," *Inquiry* 25 (1988): 90–99.

72. Vladeck 1993, *Health Care Financing in New York State.*

73. Cresap-Tillinghast, *Blue Cross Blue Shield of Massachusetts: Corporate Review* (New York: Cresap-Tillinghast, 1990).

74. J. E. McDonough, "Mass. Retreat: The Demise of Massachusetts Hospital Rate Regulation," *Journal of American Health Policy* 2, no. 2 (1992): 40–44.

75. Volpp 1993, "Long-Term Experience With All-Payer State Rate Setting."

76. Weiner, *Hospital Payment Reform.*

77. Devine-Perez, 326–27.

78. J. E. McDonough, *The Decline of State-Based Hospital Rate Setting: Findings and Implications* (Portland, ME: National Academy for State Health Policy, United Hospital Fund of New York, 1995).

79. B. A. DeBuono, *New Directions for a Healthier New York: Reform of the Health Care Financing System* (Albany: New York Department of Health, 1995).

80. DeBuono, *New Directions.*

81. Jacobsen, chap. 4.

Chapter 4

1. S. M. Tully and A. A. Grannis. "Health and Health Care Financing in Transition: Proceedings of the Meeting of the Council on Health Care Financing," in *Council on Health Care Financing* (Albany, NY: 1995).

2. R. Kronick, "The Slippery Slope of Health Care Finance: Business Interests and Hospital Reimbursement in Massachusetts," *Journal of Health Politics, Policy and Law* 15, no. 4 (1990): 887–913.

3. Cresap-Tillinghast, *Blue Cross Blue Shield of Massachusetts: Corporate Review* (New York: Cresap-Tillinghast, 1990).

4. B. J. Biles, C. J. Schramm, and J. G. Atkinson, "Hospital Cost Inflation Under State Rate-Setting Programs," *New England Journal of Medicine* 305 (September 1980): 664–68.

C. J. Schramm, S. R. Renn, and B. Biles, "Controlling Hospital Cost Inflation: New Perspectives on State Rate Setting," *Health Affairs* 5, no. 3 (1986): 22–33.

5. S. L. Weiner and H. M. Sapolsky, *Hospital Payment Reform: The Case of New Jersey 1980–1994* (Cambridge: Massachusetts Institute of Technology, 1994).

6. L. Brown, *Politics and Health Care Organization: HMOs as Federal Policy* (Washington, DC: Brookings Institution, 1983), 16.

7. J. B. Christianson et al., "The HMO Industry: Evolution in Population Demographics and Market Structures," *Medical Care* 48, no. 1 (1991): 3–46.

8. Kronick, "Slippery Slope."

9. A. Downs, *An Economic Theory of Democracy* (New York: Harper and Row, 1957), 254–55.

10. M. Olson, "Collective Action: The Logic," in *Classic Readings in American Politics,* ed. Nivola (1965), 211–26.

11. W. T. Gormley, *The Politics of Public Utility Regulation* (Pittsburgh: University of Pittsburgh Press, 1983), 152–77.

12. P. J. Feldstein, *The Politics of Health Legislation: An Economic Perspective* (Ann Arbor: Health Administration Press, 1988), chap. 2.

13. B. C. Vladeck, "Interest-Group Representation and the HSAs: Health Planning and Political Theory," *American Journal of Public Health* 67, no. 1 (1977): 23–29.

14. J. T. Tierney, "Organized Interests in Health Politics and Policy-Making," *Medical Care Review* 44, no. 1 (1987): 89–118.

15. W. A. Niskanen, *Bureaucracy and Representative Government* (Chicago: Aldine-Atherton, 1971), chaps. 2–4.

16. J. Q. Wilson, *Bureaucracy: What Government Agencies Do and Why They Do It* (New York: Basic Books, 1989), 118–19.

17. R. Noll, "Government Regulatory Behavior: A Multidisciplinary Survey and Synthesis," in *Regulatory Policy and the Social Sciences,* ed. R. Noll (Berkeley: University of California Press, 1985), 38.

18. Gormley, 6–35.

19. Wilson, 199.

20. Weiner and Sapolsky, *Hospital Payment Reform.*

21. Tierney, "Organized Interests."

Chapter 5

1. J. C. Robinson and J. S. Luft, "Competition, Regulation, and Hospital Costs, 1982 to 1986," *Journal of the American Medical Association* 260, no. 18 (1988): 2676–81.

2. J. Goldsmith, "Death of a Paradigm: The Challenge of Competition," *Health Affairs* 3, no. 3 (1984): 5–19.

3. B. Mitnick, *The Political Economy of Regulation: Creating, Designing and Removing Regulatory Form* (New York: Columbia University Press, 1980), 431.

4. F. R. Baumgartner and B. D. Jones, *Agendas and Instability in American Politics* (Chicago: University of Chicago Press, 1993), chap. 1.

5. A.A.A.M. Project, *Which Hospitals Are Vulnerable? Characteristics that Might Endanger Massachusetts Hospitals under a Competitive Payment Plan* (Boston: Boston University School of Public Health, 1991).

6. S. Weiner et al., "Economic Incentives and Organizational Realities: Managing Hospitals under DRGs," *Milbank Quarterly* 65, no. 4 (1987): 463–87.

7. W. C. Hsiao et al., "Lessons of the New Jersey DRG Payment System," *Health Affairs* 5, no. 2 (1986): 32–43.

8. H. M. Sapolsky, J. Aisenberg, and J. Morone, "The Call to Rome and Other Obstacles to State-Level Innovation," *Public Administration Review* (March/April 1987): 135–42.

9. C. Devine-Perez, "Comparative State Hospital Financing Politics: New Jersey and New York," in *Wagner School of Public Service* (New York: New York University, 1995), 165–66.

10. R. Hackey, "Trapped between State and Market: Regulating Hospital Reimbursement in the Northeastern States," *Medical Care Review* 49, no. 3 (1992): 355–88.

11. J. Rodat, *NYPHRM's Paradox: How New York's Attempts to Stabilize Hospital Finances Lead to More Uninsured, Increased Health Benefit Restrictions, Reduced Hospital Utilization, and Weakened Hospitals* (Albany, NY: Signalhealth, 1995).

12. B. A. DeBuono, *New Directions for a Healthier New York: Reform of the Health Care Financing System* (Albany: New York Department of Health, 1995).

Chapter 6

1. J. W. Kingdon, *Agendas, Alternatives, and Public Policies* (Harper-Collins, 1984), 99–105.

2. T. Lowi, "Toward Functionalism in Political Science: The Case of Innovation in Party Systems," *American Political Science Review* 57, no. 2 (1963): 570–83.

3. P. Jacobsen, R. Merritt, L. Bartlett, M. Marquis, S. Long, H. Leeds, I. Fraser, and G. Kominski, *State Health Care Reform Initiatives: Progress and Promise* (RAND, 1994), chap. 4.

4. G. Stigler, "The Theory of Economic Regulation," in *Chicago Studies in Political Economy,* ed. G. Stigler (Chicago: University of Chicago Press, 1988), 209–33.

5. J. P. Wilson, *Bureaucracy: What Governments Do and Why They Do It* (New York: Basic Books, 1989), 118.

6. H. Laswell, *Politics: Who Gets What, When and How* (New York: World, 1936).

7. M. Shapiro, "Of Interests and Values: The New Politics and the New Political Science," in *The New Politics of Public Policy,* ed. M. Landy and M. Levin (Baltimore: The Johns Hopkins University Press, 1995), 10.

Chapter 7

1. D. McKenzie, *Monitoring the Acute Hospital Industry* (Boston: Massachusetts Rate Setting Commission, 1995).

2. R. Kuttner, "Columbia/HCA and the Resurgence of the For-Profit Hospital Business," *New England Journal of Medicine* 335, no. 5 (1996): 362–67.

3. A. Simms et al., *Premium Trends for Six HMOs in Massachusetts* (Boston: Massachusetts Rate Setting Commission, 1994).

4. McKenzie, *Monitoring the Acute Hospital Industry.*

5. N. Kane, *Report on Findings: Hospital Behavior in Worcester County, Pre and Post Passage of Chapter 495* (Boston: Harvard School of Public Health, 1996).

6. Kane, *Report on Findings.*

7. J. Mora, "Boston's $3 Billion Health Care Opportunity," in *1995 Health Care Annual: Issues and Comparative Payor Performance Data,* ed. J. R. Mehn V, and C. Gorman Wanfried (New York: McKinsey and Company, 1995), 65–80.

8. Mora, "Boston's $3 Billion Health Care Opportunity."

9. GHAA, *National Directory of HMOs* (Washington, DC: Group Health Association of America, 1995).

10. R. Blendon, K. Swartz, and K. Donelan, *Massachusetts Residents Without Health Insurance, 1995* (Boston: Harvard School of Public Health, Lou Harris and Associates, 1995).

11. A. Sager, D. Socolar, and P. Hiam, *Three Quarters of a Million Citizens of the Commonwealth—One Person in Eight—Now Lack Health Insurance: The Problem Must Be Acknowledged and New Remedies Are Needed* (Boston: Boston University School of Public Health, 1995).

12. K. O'Leary, *Progress Report: Reform of New Jersey's Individual and Small Employer Health Coverage Markets, April 1993—April 1996* (Trenton: New Jersey Individual Health Coverage Program Board, 1996).

13. Families, USA, *HMO Consumers at Risk: States to the Rescue* (Washington, DC: Families, USA, 1996).

14. J. Shikles, *Canadian Health Insurance: Lessons for the United States* (Washington, DC: General Accounting Office, 1991).

Bibliography

Allison, G. "Conceptual Models and the Cuban Missile Crisis." *American Political Science Review* 63 (September 1969): 689–718.

Anderson, G. F. "All-Payer Rate Setting: Down But Not Out." *Health Care Financing Review* (1991 Annual Supplement): 35–41.

Anderson, G. F., and J. R. Lave. "State Rate-Setting Programs: Do They Reward Efficiency in Hospitals?" *Medical Care* 22, no. 5 (1984): 494–98.

Ashby, J. L. "The Impact of Hospital Regulatory Programs on Per Capita Costs, Utilization, and Capital Investment." *Inquiry* 21 (1984): 45–59.

Ashby, J. L. *Achievement, Access and Accountability: An Overview of Maryland's Sixteen Years of Hospital Rate Regulation.* Maryland Hospital Association, 1988.

Ashby, J. L. *Achievement, Access, and Accountability: An Overview of Maryland's Twenty-Two Years of Hospital Rate Regulation 1971–1993.* Maryland Hospital Association, 1994.

Baumgartner, F. R., and B. D. Jones. *Agendas and Instability in American Politics.* Chicago: University of Chicago Press, 1993.

Beard, C. *An Economic Interpretation of the Constitution of the United States.* New York: Macmillan Publishing, 1935.

Becker, G. "Public Policies, Pressure Groups and Dead Weight Costs." In *Chicago Studies in Political Economy,* ed. G. Stigler, 85–105. Chicago: University of Chicago Press, 1988.

Bergthold, L. A. " Purchasing Power: Business and Health Policy Changes in Massachusetts." *Journal of Health Politics, Policy and Law* 13, no. 3 (1988): 425–51.

Berliner, H. S., and S. Delgado. "The Rise and Fall of New Jersey's Uncompensated Care Fund." *Journal of American Health Policy* 1, no. 2 (1991): 47–50.

Berliner, H. S., and S. Delgado. "From DRGs to Deregulation: New Jersey Takes the Road Less Traveled." *Journal of American Health Policy* 3, no. 4 (1993): 44–48.

Biles, B. J., C. J. Schramm, and J. G. Atkinson. "Hospital Cost Inflation Under State Rate-Setting Programs." *New England Journal of Medicine* 305 (September 1980): 664–68.

Billings, W. G. "Testimony on New York's Health Care Financing System in Transition." In *Testimony before the New York Senate Health Committee, Council on Health Care Financing, and Senate Insurance Committee,* 10. Albany, NY, 1995.

Blendon, R., K. Swartz, and K. Donelan. *Massachusetts Residents Without Health Insurance, 1995.* Boston: Harvard School of Public Health, Lou Harris and Associates, 1995.

Boorstin, D. J. *The Creators.* New York: Random House, 1992.

Brown, L. *Politics and Health Care Organization: HMOs as Federal Policy.* Washington, DC: Brookings Institution, 1983.

Buchanan, J., and G. Tullock. *The Calculus of Consent.* Ann Arbor: University of Michigan Press, 1962.

Buchanan, J. M. "Then and Now, 1961–1986: From Delusion to Dystopia." In *Institute for Human Studies,* 1986. Quoted in *Beyond Self-Interest,* ed. J. J. Mansbridge. Chicago: University of Chicago Press, 1990.

Caligiuri, L., ed. *Health Care Financing in New York State: A Blueprint for Change.* New York: United Hospital Fund, 1993.

Cantor, J. C. "Health Care Unreform: The New Jersey Approach." *Journal of the American Medical Association* 270, no. 24 (1993): 2968–70.

Christianson, J. B., et al. "The HMO Industry: Evolution in Population Demographics and Market Structures." *Medical Care* 48, no. 1 (1991): 3–46.

Cobb, R. W., and C. D. Elder. *Participation in American Politics: The Dynamics of Agenda-Building.* Baltimore: Johns Hopkins University Press, 1983.

Coelen, C., S. Mennemeyer, and D. Kidder. *Effects of Prospective Reimbursement Programs on Hospital Revenue, Expense and Financial Status.* Cambridge, MA: Abt Associates, 1986.

Coelen, C., and D. Sullivan. "An Analysis of the Effects of Prospective Reimbursement Programs on Hospital Expenditures." *Health Care Financing Review* 2, no. 3 (1981): 1–40.

Coelen, C., and R. Yaffe. "The National Hospital Rate-Setting Study: Summary of Current Findings on the Effects of Hospital Prospective Payment Systems." In *Labor Management Health Care Cost Containment Conference.* Atlantic City, NJ, 1983.

Commission, H.S.C.R. *Report on the Financial Condition of Maryland Hospitals.* Health Services Cost Review Commission, 1991.

Commission, M.H.S.C.R. *Report to the Governor: Fiscal Year 1994.* Baltimore: HSCRC, 1994.

Cone, K. R., and D. Dranove. "Why Did States Enact Hospital Rate-Setting Laws?" *Journal of Law and Economics* 29, no. 2 (1986): 287–302.

Cramton, R. "The Why, Where and How of Broadened Public Participation in the Administrative Process." *Georgetown Law Journal,* 1972 (February): 525–46.

Cresap-Tillinghast. *Blue Cross Blue Shield of Massachusetts: Corporate Review.* New York: Cresap-Tillinghast, 1990.

Cromwell, J., and J. R. Kanak. "The Effects of Prospective Reimbursement Programs on Hospital Adoption and Service Sharing." *Health Care Financing Review* 4, no. 2 (1982): 67–88.

Crozier, D. "State Rate Setting: A Status Report." *Health Affairs* 1, no. 3 (summer 1982): 66–83.

Davis, K., et al. *Health Care Cost Containment.* Baltimore: The Johns Hopkins University Press, 1990.

DeBuono, B. A. *New Directions for a Healthier New York: Reform of the Health Care Financing System.* Albany: New York Department of Health, 1995.

Derthick, M., and P. Quirk. *The Politics of Deregulation.* Washington, DC: Brookings, 1985.

Devine-Perez, C. "Comparative State Hospital Financing Politics: New Jersey and New York." In *Wagner School of Public Service.* New York: New York University, 1995.

Dowling, W. L. "Prospective Reimbursement of Hospitals." *Inquiry* 11, no. 3 (1974): 163–80.

Downs, A. *An Economic Theory of Democracy.* New York: Harper and Row, 1985.

Dranove, D., and K. Cone. "Do State Rate Setting Regulations Really Lower Hospital Expenses." *Journal of Health Economics* 4, no. 2 (1985): 159–65.

Dunham, A., and J. Morone. "The Politics of Innovation: The Evolution of DRG Rate Regulation in New Jersey." In *DRG Evaluation.* Princeton, NJ: Health Research and Educational Trust, 1983.

Dunham, A., and J. Morone. "Slouching Toward National Health Insurance: The Unanticipated Politics of DRGs." *Bulletin of the New York Academy of Medicine,* 1986, 146–61.

Dunn, D. L., and M. Chen. "Uncompensated Hospital Care Payment and Access for the Uninsured: Evidence from New Jersey." *Health Services Research* 29, no. 1 (1994): 113–30.

Eby, C. L., and D. R. Cohodes. "What Do We Know about Rate Setting?" *Journal of Health Politics, Policy and Law* 10, no. 2 (1985): 299–327.

Eisner, M. A. *Regulatory Politics in Transition.* Baltimore: Johns Hopkins University Press, 1993.

Elazar, D. J. *American Federalism: A View from the States.* New York: Thomas Crowell Company, 1966.

Elazar, D. J. *The American Mosaic: The Impact of Space, Time and Culture on American Politics.* Boulder: Westview Press, 1994.

Eldredge, N., and S. J. Gould. "Punctuated Equilibria: An Alternative to Phyletic Gradualism." In *Models in Paleobiology,* ed. T. J. Scoph. San Francisco: Freeman Cooper, 1972.

Enthoven, A. *Health Plan: The Only Practical Solution to the Soaring Costs of Medical Care.* Reading, PA: Addison-Wesley, 1980.

Esposito, A., et al. "Abstracts of State Legislated Hospital Cost Containment Programs." *Health Care Financing Review* 4 (December 1982): 129–58.

Families, USA. *HMO Consumers at Risk: States to the Rescue.* Washington, DC: Families, USA, 1996.

Fanara, P., and W. Greenberg. "Factors Affecting the Adoption of Prospective Reimbursement by State Governments." In *Incentives vs. Controls in Health Policy,* ed. J. A. Meyer, 144–56. Washington, DC: American Enterprise Institute, 1985.

Feldstein, P. *Health Care Economics.* 3d ed. New York: John Wiley and Sons, 1988.

Feldstein, P. J. *The Politics of Health Legislation: An Economic Perspective.* Ann Arbor: Health Administration Press, 1988.

Feldstein, P., and McInick, G. "Congressional Voting Behavior on Hospital Legislation: An Exploratory Study." *Journal of Health Policy, Politics and Law* 8,
no. 4 (winter 1977): 686–701.

Finkler, M. D. "State Rate Setting Revisited." *Health Affairs* 6, no. 4 (1987):
82–89.

Fiorina, M. P. *Congress: Keystone of the Washington Establishment.* 2d ed. New
Haven: Yale University Press, 1989.

Furst, R. W. "The 'Success' of State Rate Review: View with Caution." *Health
Care Management Review* 15, no. 4 (1982): 53–57.

Gaumer, G., E. Poggio, and C. Sennett. "Elective Surgery Outcomes and State
Prospective Reimbursement Programs." *Health Care Financing Review.* 1987
Annual Supplement (Pub. No. 03258).

Gaumer, G. L., E. Poggio, and C. Sennett. "Effects of State Prospective Reimbursement Programs on Hospital Mortality." *Medical Care* 27, no. 7 (1989):
724–36.

Gaumer, G., M. Sumner, and J. Boland. *National Hospital Rate-Setting Study.
Volume II. Case Study of Prospective Reimbursement in Connecticut.* Cambridge, MA: Abt Associates, 1979.

Gaumer, G., M. Sumner, and J. Boland. "Prospective Reimbursement in Connecticut." *Topics in Health Care Financing* 6, no. 1 (1979): 51–57.

Gaumer, G., et al. *Case Study of Prospective Reimbursement in Connecticut.* U.S.
Dept. of Health and Human Services, 1980.

GHAA. *Patterns in HMO Enrollment.* 3d ed., 54. G.H.A. of America. Washington, DC: GHAA, 1993.

GHAA. *National Directory of HMOs.* Washington, DC: Group Health Association of America, 1995.

Ginsburg, P. B., and F. A. Sloan. "Hospital Cost Shifting." *New England Journal
of Medicine* 310, no. 14 (1984): 893–98.

Ginsburg, P. B., and K. E. Thorpe. "Can All-Payer Rate Setting and the Competitive Strategy Coexist?" *Health Affairs* 11, no. 3 (1992): 73–86.

Goldberg, L. G., and W. Greenberg. "The Competitive Response of Blue Cross to
the Health Maintenance Organization." *Economic Inquiry,* 1980 (January).

Goldberg, L. G., and W. Greenberg. "The Determinants of HMO Enrollment and
Growth." *Health Services Research* 16, no. 4 (1981): 421–38.

Goldsmith, J. "Death of a Paradigm: The Challenge of Competition." *Health
Affairs* 3, no. 3 (1984): 5–19.

Gormley, W. T. *The Politics of Public Utility Regulation.* Pittsburgh: University of
Pittsburgh Press, 1983.

Gormley, W. T. "Regulatory Issue Networks in a Federal System." *Polity* 18, no.
4 (1986): 595–620.

Gray, V. "Innovation in the States: A Diffusion Study." *American Political Science
Review* 67, no. 4 (1973): 1174–85.

Green, D., and I. Shapiro. *Pathologies of Rational Choice Theory: A Critique of
Applications in Political Science.* New Haven: Yale University Press, 1994.

Gruber, R., M. Shadle, and C. L. Polich. "From Movement to Industry." *Health
Affairs* 7 (1988): 197–208.

Hackey, R. "Trapped between State and Market: Regulating Hospital Reimbursement in the Northeastern States." *Medical Care Review* 49, no. 3 (1992): 355–88.

Hadley, J., and K. Swartz. "The Impacts on Hospital Costs Between 1980 and 1984 of Hospital Rate Regulation, Competition, and Changes in Health Insurance Coverage." *Inquiry* 26 (spring 1989): 35–47.

Hamilton, A., J. Madison, and J. Jay. *The Federalist Papers.* New York: New American Library, 1961.

Hamilton, D., et al. *Case Study of Prospective Reimbursement in Washington.* US DHHS, 1980.

Hamilton, D., and G. Kamers. *Case Study of Prospective Reimbursement in New York, Vol. VII of "National Hospital Rate Setting Study."* US DHHS, 1980.

Hamilton, D., et al. *Comparative Review of Nine Prospective Rate-Setting Programs.* US DHHS, 1980.

Hannon, S. K., S. M. Tully, and S. G. Velella. *New York's Health Care Financing System in Transition.* Albany: New York State Legislature, 1995.

Heclo, H. "Issue Networks and the Executive Establishment." In *The New American Political System,* ed. A. King. Washington, DC: American Enterprise Institute, 1978.

Hellinger, F. "Prospective Reimbursement Through Budget Review: New Jersey, Rhode Island, and Western Pennsylvania." *Inquiry,* 1976.

Hellinger, F. J. "Recent Evidence on Case Based Systems for Setting Hospital Rates." *Inquiry* 22, no. 1 (1985): 78–91.

Hilton, G. "The Basic Behavior of Regulatory Commissions." *American Economic Review* 62, no. 2 (1972): 47–54.

Hospitals. "Rate Review: A Look at State Programs." In *Hospitals* 1980: 99–101.

Hsiao, W. C., et al. "Lessons of the New Jersey DRG Payment System." *Health Affairs* 5, no. 2 (1986): 32–43.

Huntington, S. "The Marasmus of the ICC." *Yale Law Journal* 61 (April 1952): 467–509.

Institute, M.H.E. *Guide to Rate Review in Maryland Hospitals.* Lutherville: Maryland Hospital Education Institute, 1989.

Jacobs, J. S. *Maryland Legislation on Hospital Rate Regulation: A Historical Perspective of Policy Development,* 41. College Park: University of Maryland, 1974.

Jacobsen, P., R. Merritt, L. Bartlett, M. Marquis, S. Long, H. Leeds, I. Fraser, and G. Kominski. *State Health Care Reform Initiatives: Progress and Promise.* RAND, 1994.

Joskow, P. L. *Controlling Hospital Costs: The Role of Government Regulation.* Cambridge: MIT Press, 1981.

Kane, N. *Report on Findings: Hospital Behavior in Worcester County Pre and Post Passage of Chapter 495.* Boston: Harvard School of Public Health, 1996.

Kelman, S. "Congress and the Public Spirit: A Commentary." In *Beyond Self-Interest,* ed. J. Mansbridge. Chicago: University of Chicago Press, 1990.

Kidder, D., and D. Sullivan. "Hospital Payroll Costs, Productivity, and Employment under Prospective Reimbursement." *Health Care Financing Review* 4, no. 2 (1982): 89–100.

Kingdon, J. W. *Agendas, Alternatives, and Public Policies.* HarperCollins, 1984.

Kraus, N., M. Porter, and P. Ball. *Managed Care: A Decade in Review: 1980–1990,* 131. The Interstudy Edge. Excelsior, MN: Interstudy, 1991.

Kronick, R. *Health Insurance for the Uninsured in New Jersey.* Trenton: New Jersey Department of Health, 1990.

Kronick, R. "The Slippery Slope of Health Care Finance: Business Interests and Hospital Reimbursement in Massachusetts." *Journal of Health Politics, Policy and Law* 15, no. 4 (1990): 887–913.

Kuttner, R. "Columbia/HCA and the Resurgence of the For-Profit Hospital Business." *New England Journal of Medicine* 335, no. 5 (1996): 362–67.

Lanning, J. A. *The Impact of Hospital Rate Setting on Health Expenditures.* University of Alabama, 1988.

Lanning, J. A., M. A. Morrisey, and R. L. Ohsfeldt. "Endogenous Hospital Regulation and Its Effects on Hospital and Non-hospital Expenditures." *Journal of Regulatory Economics* 3 (1991): 137–54.

Latham, E. *The Group Basis of Politics.* Ithaca: Cornell University Press, 1952.

Lindblom, C. E. "The Science of Muddling Through." *Public Administration Review* 19 (1959): 79–88.

Lopes, M. E. "New Jersey's Health Care System Reforms." *Benefits Quarterly.* 3d Quarter, 1993: 26–31.

Lowi, T. "Toward Functionalism in Political Science: The Case of Innovation in Party Systems." *American Political Science Review* 57, no. 2 (1963): 570–83.

Luft, H. S. "Competition and Regulation." *Medical Care* 23, no. 5 (1985): 383–400.

MacAvoy, P. *The Regulated Industries and the Economy.* New York: Norton, 1979.

Mansbridge, J. J. "On the Relation of Altruism and Self-Interest." In *Beyond Self-Interest,* ed. J. J. Mansbridge. Chicago: University of Chicago Press, 1990.

Mansbridge, J. J. "The Rise and Fall of Self-Interests in the Explanation of Political Life." In *Beyond Self-Interest,* ed. J. J. Mansbridge, 3–24. Chicago: University of Chicago Press, 1990.

McDonough, J. E. "Mass. Retreat: The Demise of Massachusetts Hospital Rate Regulation." *Journal of American Health Policy* 2, no. 2 (1992): 40–44.

McDonough, J. E. *The Decline of State-Based Hospital Rate Setting: Findings and Implications.* Portland, ME: National Academy for State Health Policy, United Hospital Fund of New York, 1995.

McKenzie, D. *Monitoring the Acute Hospital Industry.* Boston: Massachusetts Rate Setting Commission, 1995.

McLaughlin, C. G. "HMO Growth and Hospital Expenses and Use: A Simultaneous Equation Approach." *Health Services Research* 22, no. 2 (1987).

McNeil, R., and R. E. Schlenker. "HMOs, Competition, and Government." *Health and Society* (spring 1975): 195–224.

Meier, K. J. *Regulation: Politics, Bureaucracy and Economics.* New York: St. Martin's Press, 1985.

Melnick, G. A., J. R. C. Wheeler, and P. J. Feldstein. "Effects of Rate Regulation on Selected Components of Hospital Expenses." *Inquiry* 1981 (8): 240–46.

Miller, D., and P. H. Friesen. "A Longitudinal Study of the Corporate Life Cycle." *Management Science* 30 (1984): 1161–83.

Mitchell, S. A. "Issues, Evidence, and the Policymaker's Dilemma." *Health Affairs* 1, no. 3 (1982): 84–98.

Mitnick, B. *The Political Economy of Regulation: Creating, Designing and Removing Regulatory Forms.* New York: Columbia University Press, 1980.

Mora, J. "Boston's $3 Billion Health Care Opportunity." In *1995 Health Care Annual: Issues and Comparative Payor Performance Data,* ed. J. R. Mehn, V.; Gorman Wanfried, C., 65–80. New York: McKinsey and Company, 1995.

Morrissey, M. A., and C. A. Ashby. "An Empirical Analysis of HMO Market Share." *Inquiry* 19 (summer 1982): 136–49.

Morgan, K. O., S. Morgan, and N. Quitno. *Health Care State Rankings, 1995.* 3d ed., 472. Lawrence, Kansas: Morgan Quitno Press, 1995.

Morrisey, M. A., F. A. Sloan, and S. A. Mitchell. "State Rate Setting: An Analysis of Some Unresolved Issues." *Health Affairs* 3, no. 2 (1983): 36–47.

Morrissey, M. A., D. Conrad, S. Shortell, and K. Cook. "Hospital Rate Review: A Theory and an Empirical Review." *Journal of Health Economics* 3, no. 1 (1984): 25–47.

Niskanen, W. *Bureaucracy and Representative Government.* New York: Aldine-Atherton, 1971.

Noll, R. "Government Regulatory Behavior: A Multidisciplinary Survey and Synthesis." In *Regulatory Policy and the Social Sciences,* ed. R. Noll. Berkeley: University of California Press, 1985.

Noll, R., and B. Owen. *The Political Economy of Deregulation: Interest Groups in the Regulatory Process.* Washington, DC: American Enterprise Institute, 1983.

Office, U.S. General Accounting. *Health Care Spending: Nonpolicy Factors Account for Most State Differences.* Washington, DC: US, GAO, 1992.

O'Leary, K. *Progress Report: Reform of New Jersey's Individual and Small Employer Health Coverage Markets, April 1993–April 1996.* Trenton: New Jersey Individual Health Coverage Program Board, 1996.

Olson, M. "Collective Action: The Logic." In *Classic Readings in American Politics,* ed. Nivola, 1965, 211–26.

Olson, M. *The Logic of Collective Action: Public Goods and the Theory of Groups.* Cambridge: Harvard University Press, 1965.

Over, A., J. M. Watt, and D. Roenigh. *Private Sector Health Care Initiatives: Market Area Characteristics. Analysis and User Documentation.* U.S. Department of Health and Human Services, 1983.

Peltzman, S. "Toward a More General Theory of Regulation." In *Chicago Studies in Political Economy,* ed. G. Stigler. Chicago: University of Chicago Press, 1988.

Powell, R. S. *Bureaucratic Malpractice: Hospital Regulation in New Jersey.* Princeton: Center for the Analysis of Public Issues, 1974.

Prestianni, F. *Benchmarks I: A National Comparison: A Report on the Costs and Financial Performance of New Jersey Hospitals.* Trenton: New Jersey Department of Health, Division of Health Care Planning, 1994.

Redford, E. S. *Democracy in the Administrative State.* New York: Oxford University Press, 1969.

Rice, T. "Including an All-Payer Reimbursement System in a Universal Health Insurance Program." *Inquiry* 29 (summer 1992): 203–12.

Riker, W. *Liberalism Against Populism: A Confrontation Between the Theory of Democracy and the Theory of Social Choice.* San Francisco: WH Freeman and Co., 1982.

Robinson, J. C., and J. S. Luft. "Competition, Regulation, and Hospital Costs, 1982 to 1986." *Journal of the American Medical Association* 260, no. 18 (1988): 2676–81.

Rodat, J. "Hospital Reimbursement Revisited." In *Empire State Report* 1994: 47–52.

Rodat, J. "Killing Hospitals With Kindness." In *Empire State Report* 1995: 58.

Rodat, J. *NYPHRM's Paradox: How New York's Attempts to Stabilize Hospital Finances Lead to More Uninsured, Increased Health Benefit Restrictions, Reduced Hospital Utilization, and Weakened Hospitals.* Albany, NY: Signalhealth, 1995.

Rosko, M. "The Impact of Prospective Payment: A Multi-dimensional Analysis of the New Jersey SHARE Program." *Journal of Health Politics, Policy and Law* 9, no. 1 (1984): 81–101.

Rosko, M. D. "A Comparison of Hospital Performance Under the Partial-Payer Medicare PPS and State All-Payer Rate Setting Systems." *Inquiry* 26 (spring 1989): 48–61.

Rosko, M. "The Impact of the New Jersey All-Payer Rate Setting System: An Analysis of Financial Ratios." *Hospital and Health Services Administration* 34, no. 1 (1989): 53–69.

Rosko, M. D., and R. W. Broyles. "The Impact of the New Jersey All-Payer DRG System." *Inquiry* 23 (spring 1986): 67–75.

Rosko, M., and R. Broyles. "Short-Term Responses of Hospitals to the DRG Prospective Pricing Mechanism in New Jersey." *Medical Care* 25, no. 2 (1987): 88–99.

Safran, D. G., and J. P. Ruger. *The Massachusetts Health Care Industry: Pathways to the Future.* Boston: Governor's Council on Economic Growth and Technology, 1994.

Sager, A., D. Socolar, and P. Hiam. *Three Quarters of a Million Citizens of the Commonwealth—One Person in Eight—Now Lack Health Insurance: The Problem Must Be Acknowledged and New Remedies Are Needed.* Boston: Boston University School of Public Health, 1995.

———. *Which Hospitals Are Vulnerable? Characteristics that Might Endanger Massachusetts Hospitals under a Competitive Payment Plan.* Project A.A.A.M. Boston: Boston University School of Public Health, 1991.

Salamon, L. M. *Beyond Privatization: The Tools of Government Action.* Washington, DC: Urban Institute Press, 1989.

Salkever, D. S., D. M. Steinwachs, and A. Rupp. "Hospital Cost and Efficiency under Per Service and Per Case Payment in Maryland: A Tale of the Carrot and the Stick." *Inquiry* 23, no. 1 (1986): 56–66.

Sapolsky, H. M. "Prospective Payment in Perspective." *Journal of Health Politics, Policy and Law* 11, no. 4 (1986): 633–45.

Sapolsky, H. M., J. Aisenberg, and J. Morone. "The Call to Rome and Other Obstacles to State-Level Innovation." *Public Administration Review* 1987 (March/April 1987): 135–42.

Schattschneider, E. E. *The Semi-Sovereign People.* New York: Holt, Rinehart and Winston, 1975.

Schattschneider, E. E. "The Scope and Bias of the Pressure System." In *Classic Readings in American Politics,* ed. P. Nivola. New York: St. Martin's Press, 1986.

Schneider, M., and P. Teske. *Public Entrepreneurs: Agents for Change in American Government.* Princeton: Princeton University Press, 1995.

Schramm, C. J., S. R. Renn, and B. Biles. "Controlling Hospital Cost Inflation: New Perspectives on State Rate Setting." *Health Affairs* 5, no. 3 (1986): 22–33.

Schumpeter, J. A. *The Theory of Economic Democracy.* Cambridge: Harvard University Press, 1934.

Schumpeter, J. *Capitalism, Socialism, and Democracy.* New York: Harper and Row, 1962.

Shapiro, M. "Of Interests and Values: The New Politics and the New Political Science." In *The New Politics of Public Policy,* ed. M. Landy and M. Levin, 10. Baltimore: The Johns Hopkins University Press, 1995.

Shikles, J. *Canadian Health Insurance: Lessons for the United States.* Washington, DC: General Accounting Office, 1991.

Shortell, S. M., and E. F. X. Hughes. "The Effects of Regulation, Competition, and Ownership on Mortality Rates among Hospital Inpatients." *New England Journal of Medicine* 318, no. 17 (1988): 1100–1107.

Siegel, B. *A National Comparison: A Report on the Costs and Financial Performance of New Jersey Hospitals.* New Jersey Department of Health, 1994.

Siegel, B., A. Weiss, and D. Lynch. "Setting New Jersey Hospital Rates: A Regulatory System Under Stress." *University of Puget Sound Law Review* 14 (spring 1991).

Simms, A., T. Abu-Jaber, R. Fitzmaurice, and A. Kao. *Premium Trends for Six HMOs in Massachusetts.* Boston: Massachusetts Rate Setting Commission, 1994.

Sloan, F. A. "Regulation and the Rising Cost of Hospital Care." *Review of Economics and Statistics* 63 , no. 4 (1981): 479–87.

Sloan, F. "ReViews: An Economist." *Health Affairs* 1, no. 3 (1982): 113–18.

Sloan, F. A. "Rate Regulation as a Strategy for Hospital Cost Control: Evidence from the Last Decade." *Milbank Memorial Fund Quarterly* 61, no. 2 (1983): 195–217.

Sloan, F. A. "Hospital Rate Review: A Theory and an Empirical Review." *Journal of Health Economics* 3, no. 1 (1984): 83–86.

Sloan, F., and B. Steinwald. *Insurance, Regulation and Hospital Costs.* Lexington, MA: Lexington Books, 1980.

Steinwald, V., and F. A. Sloan. "Regulatory Approaches to Hospital Cost Containment: A Synthesis of the Empirical Evidence." In *A New Approach to the Economics of Health Care,* ed. M. Olson, 273–317. Washington, DC: American Enterprise Institute, 1981.

Stigler, G. "The Theory of Economic Regulation." In *Chicago Studies in Political Economy,* ed. G. Stigler, 209–33. Chicago: University of Chicago Press, 1988.

Stone, D. *Policy Paradox and Political Reason.* HarperCollins, 1988.

Thorpe, K. E. "Does All-Payer Rate Setting Work? The Case of the New York Prospective Hospital Reimbursement Methodology." *Journal of Health Politics, Policy and Law* 12, no. 3 (1987): 391–409.

Thorpe, K. E. "Uncompensated Care Pools and Care to the Uninsured: Lessons from the New York Prospective Hospital Reimbursement Methodology." *Inquiry* 25 (1988): 90–99.

Thorpe, K. E., and C. E. Phelps. "Regulatory Intensity and Hospital Cost Growth." *Journal of Health Economics* 9, no. 2 (1990): 143–66.

Tierney, J. T. "Organized Interests in Health Politics and Policy-Making." *Medical Care Review* 44, no. 1 (1987): 89–118.

Truman, D. B. *The Governmental Process: Political Interests and Public Opinion.* New York: Knopf, 1951.

Tully, S. M. *The Development of Health Care Networks in New York State.* Albany: New York State Council on Health Care Financing, 1994.

Tully, S. M., and A. A. Grannis. "Health and Health Care Financing in Transition: Proceedings of the Meeting of the Council on Health Care Financing." In *Council on Health Care Financing.* Albany, NY, 1995.

Tushman, M., and E. Romanelli. "Organizational Evolution: A Metamorphosis Model of Convergence and Reorientation." In *Research in Organizational Behavior,* ed. L. Cummings and B. Staw. Greenwich, CT: JAI Press, 1985.

Urban, N., and T. W. Bice. *Measuring Regulation and Its Effects on Hospital Behavior.* Department of Health Services, University of Washington, 1981.

Van Horn, C. E., D. C. Baumer, and W. T. Gormley. *Politics and Public Policy.* Washington, DC: CQ Press, 1992.

Vladeck, B. C. "Interest-Group Representation and the HSAs: Health Planning and Political Theory." *American Journal of Public Health* 67, no. 1 (1977): 23–29.

Vladeck, B. C., ed. *Health Care Financing in New York State: A Blueprint for Change,* 60. New York: United Hospital Fund, 1993.

Volpp, K. G., and B. Siegel. "Long-Term Experience with All-Payer State Rate Setting." *Health Affairs,* summer 1993: 59–65.

Walker, J. L. "The Diffusion of Innovations Among the American States." *American Political Science Review* 63, no. 3 (1969): 880–95.

Walter, R. W., and J. DeMarco. *National Hospital Rate-Setting Study. Volume IV. Case Study of Prospective Reimbursement in Massachusetts.* Cambridge, MA: Abt Associates, Inc., 1979.

Walter, R., and J. DeMarco. *Case Study of Prospective Reimbursement in Massachusetts.* US DHHS, 1980.

Weiner, S., J. Maxwell, H. Sapolsky, D. Dunn, and W. Hsiao. "Economic Incentives and Organizational Realities: Managing Hospitals under DRGs." *Milbank Quarterly* 65, no. 4 (1987): 463–87.

Weiner, S. L., and H. M. Sapolsky. *Hospital Payment Reform: The Case of New Jersey 1980–1994.* Cambridge: Massachusetts Institute of Technology, 1994.

Weinstein, R., and J. DeMarco. "Prospective Rate Setting in Massachusetts." *Topics in Health Care Financing* 6, no. 1 (1979): 69–80.

Weiss, A. F. "Role of the Essential Health Services Commission in Health Care Reform." *New Jersey Medicine* 1993: 478–79.

Welch, W. P. "HMO Enrollment: A Study of Market Forces and Regulation." *Journal of Health Politics, Policy and Law* 8, no. 4 (1984): 743–58.

Welch, W. P., and R. G. Frank. "The Predictors of HMO Enrollee Populations: Results from a National Sample." *Inquiry* 23 (spring 1986): 16–22.

Wholey, D. R. *State Regulation and The Development of Local HMO Markets.* Carnegie Mellon University, 1991.

Wholey, D. R., J. B. Christianson, and S. Sanchez. "The Effect of State Regulation on Development of HMO Markets." In *Advances in the Study of Entrepreneurship and Economic Growth.* JAI Press, Inc., 1990.

Wholey, D. R., and S. Sanchez. *The Effect of Regulatory Tools on Organizational Populations.* University of Arizona, 1989.

Wildavsky, A. *The Politics of the Budgetary Process.* Boston: Little Brown, 1984.

Wilson, J. Q. "The Rise of the Bureaucratic State." In *The American Commonwealth, 1976,* ed. N. Glazer and I. Kristol. New York: Basic Books, 1976.

Wilson, J. Q. *The Politics of Regulation.* New York: Basic Books, 1980.

Wilson, J. Q. *Bureaucracy: What Government Agencies Do and Why They Do It,* 432. New York: Basic Books, 1989.

Worthington, N. L., J. Cromwell, and G. Kamens. "Prospective Reimbursement in New Jersey." *Topics in Health Care Financing* 6, no. 1 (1979): 87–96.

Worthington, N. L., K. Tyson, and M. Chin. "Prospective Reimbursement in Maryland." *Topics in Health Care Financing* 6, no. 1 (1979): 59–68.

Worthington, N., J. Cromwell, G. Kamens, and J. Kanak. *National Hospital Rate Setting Study. Volume VI. Case Study of Prospective Reimbursement in New Jersey.* Cambridge, MA: Abt. Associates, Inc., 1979.

Worthington, N., K. Tyson, and M. Chin. *National Hospital Rate-Setting Study. Volume III. Case Study of Prospective Reimbursement in Maryland.* Cambridge, MA: Abt Associates, Inc., 1979.

Worthington, N., J. Cromwell, and G. Kamens. *National Hospital Rate-Setting Study. Volume VI. Case Study of Prospective Reimbursement in New Jersey.* DHEW, 1979.

Worthington, N., K. Tyson, and M. Chin. *Case Study of Prospective Reimbursement in Maryland, Vol. III of "National Hospital Rate Setting Study."* US DHHS, 1980.

Worthington, N., J. Cromwell, and G. Kamens. *Case Study of Prospective Reim-*

bursement in New Jersey, Vol. VI of "National Hospital Rate-Setting Study." US DHHS, 1980.

Worthington, N. L., and P. A. Piro. "The Effects of Hospital Rate-Setting Programs on Volumes of Hospital Services: A Preliminary Analysis." *Health Care Financing Review* 4, no. 2 (1982): 47–66.

Yin, R. K. *Applications of Case Study Research.* Vol. 34, 130. Newbury Park, CA: SAGE Publications, 1993.

Yin, R. K. *Case Study Research: Design and Methods.* 3d ed. Applied Social Research Methods Series, vol. 5, 160. Newbury Park, CA: SAGE Publications, 1994.

Zuckerman, D. "Rate Setting and Hospital Cost Containment: All-Payer versus Partial-Payer Approaches." *Health Services Research* 22, no. 3 (1987): 307–26.

Zuckerman, S., and J. Holahan. "PPS Waivers: Implications for Medicare, Medicaid, and Commercial Insurers." *Journal of Health Politics, Policy and Law* 13, no. 4 (1988): 663–81.

Zuckerman, S., J. Holahan, C. Coelen, M. Sulvetta, M. Miller, and J. Hadley. *Alternative Approaches to All-Payer Rate Setting.* The Urban Institute, 1993.

Index

ment of Medicaid recipents in, 230; for-profit, 129–30; influence in Maryland, 129–30; New York Managed Care Reform Act (1996), 231; regulations in New Jersey, 227; regulations in New York, 229. *See also* Health maintenance organizations (HMOs)

Managed Care Reform Act (1996), New York, 231

Mandel, Marvin, 164

Marciante, Charles, 81–82, 139

Marco, Dennis, 80, 124, 174, 176

Maryland: all-payer system, 105–6, 167; controls on hospital price discounting, 76–77; Guaranteed Inpatient Revenue and Total Patient Revenue systems, 105; Health Care Cost and Access Commission, 75, 145; health insurance coverage, 53; Health Services Cost Review Commission (HSCRC), 60, 67, 75–76, 105–6, 145, 164, 189; HMO discounting, 104; HMO penetration in, 54, 77, 104, 129; hospital reimbursement policy, 66–67; hospitals' market strategies, 107; hospitals' role in rate setting, 115–22; idea of deregulation in, 185–86; Medicaid and Medicare waivers, 14, 67–68, 75–76, 107, 165, 193–94; Medicaid program, 46, 145, 148; per capita health care and hospital spending, 41–45; political culture category, 55–56, 105; political innovation score, 56; rate-setting system, 32, 58–61, 164, 189; uncompensated care policy, 68, 107, 108, 110

Massachusetts: all-payer rate setting, 69–70, 77–78, 157; deregulation process and statute (1991), 157, 169–72, 226; Division of Health Care Policy and Finance, 187; health access law (1996), 225; Health Care Coalition, 77–78, 134, 168; health insurance coverage, 52–53, 224;

HMO discounting for hospital services, 4, 87; HMO growth and influence, 53–55, 69–70, 79, 87, 130–31; hospital costs, 169; Hospital Payment Advisory Commission (HOSPAC), 172, 187; hospitals' role in rate setting, 115–22; institutional changes with deregulation, 186–87; insurance reform, 226; Medicaid spending, rates, cost control, and authority, 46, 62–63, 78, 153, 167, 169, 186–87; Medicaid waiver, 224–25; Medicare waiver, 69, 77, 153; per capita health care and hospital spending, 41–45; political culture category, 55–56; political innovation score, 56; post-1991 changes in health market, 218; Rate Setting Commission, 61–62, 69, 145–46, 168, 187, 219–20; rate-setting development in, 58–60; three-payer wraparound, 78; Uncompensated Care Pool, 78, 79, 187, 225; Universal Health Care Law (1988), 78, 89, 130, 134, 168

Massachusetts Healthcare Purchaser Group, 219

Medicaid program: with deregulation in Massachusetts, 88–89, 186–87; Maryland, 145, 148; Massachusetts, 62, 146, 148–49, 172, 196–97, 224–25; New Jersey, 146–47, 149, 188; New York, 71–72, 149–50, 188–89, 196–97; rate setting relation to, 36; role in mandatory rate setting, 66; spending at state level, 45–46; state-level financing and costs of, 147–48

Medicaid recipients: enrollment in managed care plans in New York, New Jersey, and Massachusetts, 88–89, 230; moving to HMOs in New York, 99, 229; in New Jersey HMOs, 227

medical education, graduate, in New York, 84, 228

in, 58–60; uncompensated care pool, 16–17, 102; UNY*CARE proposal, 206

Niskanen, W., 144, 147, 151

Noll, R., 26, 144

Oakley, Dave, 125

Olson, M., 29, 141

Over, A., 20

Pataki, George, 100, 147, 177, 192, 197

payers' coalition, New Jersey, 222–23

Peltzman, S., 24

physicians: alliances in New York, 223; physician payment system, 1, 205; physician-to-population ratios, 50–52; position on single-payer and MSAs, 232

policy, or public, entrepreneurs, 28

policy monopoly: based on all-payer mandatory rate setting, 74; conditions creating change in, 30–31; effect on ideas, 111; interest groups in deregulated environment, 231; Maryland, 165–67, 189; Massachusetts, 168; New Jersey, 174; New York, 176–77; in punctuated equilibrium model, 30; rate-setting interest groups, 231; strategy to upset, 29

political culture, state-level, 55–56

political systems: changes in, 31–32; control in states with institutional change, 197

politics, idea of conflict in, 28–30

Powers, Alvin, 67

prospective payment concept: evolution in methodology of, 204–6; for hospital reimbursement, 205; New Jersey, 172–73; as replacement policy idea, 161–62

Prospective Payment System (PPS): New York, 83; Social Security Act amendments (1983), 1

punctuated equilibrium model of policy change: to explain disposition of

state-level rate setting, 2–3, 230; explained, 4–6; hypotheses related to, 33–34, 163–64, 212–14. *See also* economic regulation theory

Quirk, D., 26, 30

RAND report, New York, 85, 100–101

Raske, Ken, 121–22, 140

rate setting: AHA classification system for, 13–14; Carter proposal, 1; characteristics of mandatory-regulatory systems, 14–19; characteristics of states in study, 3–4, 11, 14; continued interest in, 21; defined, 3, 13; demise of state-level (1990s), 2; deregulation in relation to shift in political control, 197; deregulation of state-based, 204–5; development of mandatory hospital, 35–38; with HMO discounting, 4; marginalized, 13; of Medicare Resource Based Relative Value Scale, 1; Medicare under all-payer, 14; role of hospitals in state-level, 114–22; Social Security Act amendments (1982, 1983), 1; state-level, 1–3, 13, 15–19

Rate Setting Commission, New Jersey, 174

rate-setting studies: based on per admission/per discharge, 15; based on per capita spending, 15–16; based on total health costs, 16

rate-setting systems: conditions for replacement of, 231; deregulation at state level (1986–97), 12–13; Maryland's all-payer mandatory, 204; reimbursement for uncompensated care, 16–17

rational choice theory, 23–27

Reagan administration: ending federal grants to HMOs, 2, 129; position on rate setting, 1; rejection of rate-setting policy, 12; state-level Medicare waivers, 197